Realizing Business Model Innovation

Martin Trapp

Realizing Business Model Innovation

A Strategic Approach for Business Unit Managers

Springer Gabler

Martin Trapp
Nürnberg, Germany

Dissertation Friedrich-Alexander-Universität Erlangen-Nürnberg 2013

ISBN 978-3-658-05093-1 ISBN 978-3-658-05094-8 (eBook)
DOI 10.1007/978-3-658-05094-8

The Deutsche Nationalbibliothek lists this publication in the Deutsche Nationalbibliografie; detailed bibliographic data are available in the Internet at http://dnb.d-nb.de.

Library of Congress Control Number: 2014931846

Springer Gabler

Printed on acid-free paper

Springer Gabler is a brand of Springer DE.
Springer DE is part of Springer Science+Business Media.
www.springer-gabler.de

Foreword

To Kelly

Despite my presumption of the topic's importance, my initial search for literature on business model innovation revealed a dearth of relevant information. In the same manner, my well-educated colleagues had never been exposed to this subject. Nevertheless, the little information I found during my preliminary research already energized me as I understood this concept's huge potential to help firms remain relevant and survive. My determination was triggered; I would devote my doctoral research on extending the knowledge of business model innovation.

The dissertation at hand grew out of a two-and-a-half-year period as an external doctoral candidate at the Chair of Industrial Management at the University of Erlangen-Nuremberg. To accomplish it would have been impossible without the help of so many others.

To begin with, although their identities remain confidential, I express my gratitude to each professional, from business unit to senior project manager, who has allowed me access to his or her accumulated knowledge and experience. This study could not have occurred without their willingness to participate and their direct personal time sacrifices made to support these efforts. I will always be indebted to each of them.

From an academic perspective, I am greatly obliged to my advisor, Prof. Dr. Kai-Ingo Voigt, for providing me with the chance to develop under his guidance, for introducing to me the exciting research field of business model innovation, for challenging my mindset and for setting a rigorous standard that will benefit me throughout my career to come. I am further much obliged to Prof. Dr. Alexander Brem for his valuable advice and for co-refereeing this dissertation. Additionally, I would like to thank Dr. Lothar Czaja for helping me through this journey by being available at all times and by providing clear suggestions and reassurance. Furthermore, I appreciate the important insights of Dr. Christian Scheiner.

Outside of the University of Erlangen-Nuremberg, I wish to thank Prof. Dr. Juergen Mihm from INSEAD for a very fruitful conversation. Moreover, I am grateful to the financial support and flexibility granted by my employer. Dr. Klaus Probst promoted my aspiration of pursuing doctoral studies. Christian Spies constantly helped and encouraged me, even during the most difficult phases of this research; I am tremendously indebted to him. I also thank my colleagues for their continuous optimistic support.

To my parents, Norbert and Christina Trapp, I owe my desire to learn and to strive forward. They always will be inspiring examples. Above all, I express my deepest gratitude to Kelly Trapp, my wife and closest soul mate. Your precious input on the semantics, structure and logic made this work yours as much as mine. Thank you for your faith and patience. I dedicate this work to you with all my love and respect.

Martin Trapp (Nuremberg, January 2014)

Table of Contents

List of Figures

List of Tables

List of Abbreviations

BM	Business Model
BMI	Business Model Innovation
bn	billion(s)
BU	Business Unit
CE	Corporate Entrepreneurship
CS	Case Study
€	Euro(s)
e.g.	exemplum gratia: for example
et al.	et alii: and others
EU	European Union
EURAM	European Academy of Management
etc.	et cetera
FC	Forecast
FTTx	Fiber-to-the-x (x: h-house, b-building, n-node etc.)
G&A	General & Administrative
i.e.	id est: that is, in other words
IRR	Internal Rate of Return
IT	Information Technology
kEUR	kilo (thousands) of Euros
m	million(s)
M&A	Mergers & Acquisitions
n/a	not applicable
NPV	Net Present Value
OEM	Original Equipment Manufacturer
p.; pp.	page; pages
QS	Quantitative Study
R&D	Research & Development
ROA	Real Options Analysis
ROI	Return on Investment
RQ	Research Question
VC	Value Constellation
VP	Value Proposition
vs.	versus

Abstract

Driven by the current environmental challenges, the profitability of established business models is decreasingly sustainable, a circumstance that intensifies the need for business model innovation. This dissertation focuses on multi-business firms and identifies management practices, which support business unit managers in successfully realizing business model innovation. In such firms, the knowledge about business models and potentially value-creating business model innovation mainly resides within the business units as opposed to the corporate headquarters and central services. The proposed management practices build a deliberate, strategic-level management approach to the challenge of business model innovation, an approach currently lacking in most firms.

In order to arrive at this management approach, a theory-building, multiple-case study design is applied. Such a design is appropriate, since academic research on business model innovation is still in its early stages and has not yet elucidated the role of business unit managers. Before engaging in fieldwork, a "BMI-identification tool" is developed, which facilitates the selection of suitable cases. The final set of five cases covers successful and failed business model innovations in five different business units. It is selected from an initial set of nineteen proposed cases at four very large, publicly listed, European corporations. This "polar type" sample enables the combination of replication logic with failure analysis.

The within- and cross-case study of the five cases gives rise to a conceptual process of business model innovation, as well as twelve management practices, each attributable to one single phase within this process. These practices were all carried out by business unit managers in the success cases, whereas most of them were lacking in the failure cases. The case data reveals that gaining trust, being open to new processes, iterative real-world testing and active leadership are imperative to mitigate the risk in such initiatives and to overcome the rigidities in established organizations. Next to providing tangible recommendations for managers seeking business model innovation, the dissertation entails further important contributions to this emerging literature stream.

Key words: business model innovation, business unit manager, multi-business firm

1 Introduction

1.1 Research Motivation

Scholars and consultancies increasingly consider business model innovation (BMI) as a means towards profitable firm growth.[1] Innosight, a global consultancy specialized in innovation, analyzed that from the twenty-six firms founded since 1984 that have entered the *Fortune 500* between 1997 and 2007, more than half did so through innovative business models; among these are firms such as eBay, Starbucks, Qualcomm and Google.[2] Moreover, Innosight found that introducing an innovative business model may restructure entire industries and redistribute significant shareholder value.[3] In the airline industry, for example, a major part of the market value is now accounted for by those airlines that have adopted the low-cost business model,[4] once introduced by Southwest Airlines in the U.S. and Ryanair in Europe.[5] The same holds true for the retail industry, in which discounters such as Target, Walmart and Amazon meanwhile accumulate much more market value than traditional department stores.[6] In terms of business model innovators, scholars note that new business models are mostly launched by new entrants as opposed to established industry players[7] who, in the face of organizational rigidities, are said to be focused on executing their existing business model for too long.[8]

However, as a matter of fact, established firms seeking long-term success cannot abstain from BMI. Empirical evidence suggests that firm-specific returns above the industry mean, which originate from specific competitive advantages, eventually regress to the industry mean, proving the intrinsically temporary nature of competitive advantages.[9] What is more, the pace of such regression has accelerated substantially over the last few decades. Drivers such as globalization, deregulation and trade liberalization translate into a rising number of competitors inside an

---

1 See Zott et al. (2011), p. 1033.

2 See Johnson (2010), p. 19. From the twenty-six firms, Innosight classifies these as business model innovators: Amazon, AutoNation, BJ's Wholesale Club, Blockbuster, CarMax, Community Health Systems, DaVita, eBay, Express Scripts, GameStop, Google, Qualcomm, Starbucks, and Yahoo. Innosight was co-founded by Harvard Professor Clayton Christensen.

3 See Comes / Berniker (2008), p. 66.

4 See Johnson (2010), pp. 16-18, for the development of the market value distribution in the U.S. airline industry. In Europe, the market capitalization of the two "low-cost carriers" Ryanair (€ 9.920 bn) and Easyjet (€ 5.723 bn) roughly equals that of the biggest three "traditional carriers" Lufthansa (€ 7.352 bn), Air France-KLM (€ 2.050 bn) and International Consolidate Airlines Group (€ 5.767 bn), based on the share price at 20 June 2013. Source: CapitalIQ.

5 See Casadesus-Masanell / Ricart (2010), pp. 198-201; McGrath (2010), p. 252.

6 See Johnson (2010), pp. 16-18. According to Innosight analysis, discounters accumulated 76% of the market value in the U.S. retail industry in 2007, leaving 24% to department stores. In 1981, department stores still had accumulated 61% of the industry's market value.

7 See Comes / Berniker (2008), p. 66; Giesen et al. (2007), pp. 30-31; Govindarajan / Trimble (2011), p. 109; Hamel (2012), p. 86; Kuhn / Marsick (2005), p. 28.

8 See Doz/Kosonen (2010), p. 370, Govindarajan / Trimble (2011), p. 109; Sosna et al. (2010), p. 384; Wirtz et al. (2010), p. 273; Zimmermann (2011), p. 1.

9 See Pacheco-de-Almeida (2010) for an overview of the relevant empirical research.

industry which, in turn, fosters imitation, price-erosion, and commoditization.[10] Therefore, competing on the basis of mere product or process innovation within the boundaries of a mature industry only leads to revenue replacement and short term improvements.[11] In addition, technological progress may cause the convergence of formerly separate industries. Thereby, the industries' formerly standard business models are rendered obsolete.[12] Besides, the power of customers over business models in all industries has increased significantly.[13] In short, the longevity of a business model is decreasing.[14] However, by treating the business model as a variable and not a constant, BMI offers to firms a path back to returns above the industry mean. BMI allows managers to capitalize on identified business opportunities, may it be from new technology, new customer insights or a new-to-the-firm market.[15] In particular, the popular example of Apple's iPod/iTunes business model demonstrates to managers of established firms the high potential of BMI for strategic renewal and firm growth.[16]

From an academic point of view, BMI is closely tied to the business model concept.[17] This concept introduces a new perspective in strategic thinking.[18] Traditional strategic management theory refers to the notion of competitive advantage, which is a firm's ability to earn returns superior to the cost of capital, and explains it through the logic of "competitive imperfection" in product and/or factor markets.[19] The business model concept, on the other hand, does not per se provide a new source of competitive advantage, but it does suggest a different, more holistic approach to strategy design.[20] Instead of focusing on the construction of a competitive advantage through defending a certain market position or through leveraging a unique set of competencies, the business model concept is more concerned with revenues and costs.[21] GAMBARDELLA / MCGAHAN state:

---

10 See Casadesus-Masanell / Ricart (2010), p. 195; Chandrasekaran (2009), p. 12; Cliffe (2011), p. 96; Comes / Berniker (2008), pp. 71-72; Kuhn / Marsick (2005), pp. 27-28; Lindgren / Abdullah (2013), p. 116; Venkatraman / Henderson (2008), pp. 259-260.

11 See Bucherer et al. (2012), p. 183; Matzler et al. (2013), p. 30; Schlegelmilch et al. (2003), p. 117.

12 See Amit / Zott (2012), p. 42; Bieger / Krys (2011), p. 5; Bieger / Rüegg-Stürm (2002), pp. 19-22; Colvin (2013), p. 42; Jaeggi (2010), p. 5; Kaplan (2012), pp. 3-4.

13 See Roland Berger Strategy Consultants (2011), p.11.

14 See Kaplan (2012), p. xv.

15 See Cavalcante et al. (2011), p. 1328; Sinfield et al. (2012), p. 86.

16 1) For a description of Apple's iPod/iTunes BMI, see, e.g., Amit / Zott (2010), pp. 4-5; Johnson et al. (2008), pp. 51-52; Lindgardt et al. (2009), pp. 1-2, 8; Skarzynski / Gibson (2008), p. 110; Zollenkop (2006), pp. 5, 12, 336, 348.
2) Agarwal / Helfat (2009), p. 282, define the term "strategic renewal" as: "includ[ing] the process, content, and outcome of refreshment or replacement of attributes of an organization that have the potential to substantially affect its long-term prospects"; see also section 2.2.4.

17 See Zott et al. (2011), pp. 1032-1034.

18 See Hacklin / Wallnöfer (2012), p. 167; Lecoq et al. (2010), pp. 216-217.

19 See (e.g.) Barney (1986); Foss / Knudsen (2003).

20 See Ricart (2012), pp. 23-25.

21 See Demil / Lecoq (2010), p. 244; Johnson et al. (2008), pp. 52-54; Lecoq et al. (2010), p. 217; Zott et al. (2011), p. 1036.

"[The] business model is a mechanism for turning ideas into revenue at reasonable cost." [22]

Essentially, managers should seek profits from a business opportunity by designing a compelling customer value proposition in conjunction with the appropriate value constellation.[23] Once competition has caught up or markets have changed, managers should seize new business opportunities by crafting the right new business model.[24] Consequently, the business model concept leads to a less abstractive but strongly action-oriented perspective in strategic thinking.[25] As RICART states, managers of established firms tend to forget about the "entrepreneurial drive" in strategy making.[26] The business model concept and especially BMI help to restore it.

A number of current top management surveys reveal that in light of profound environmental dynamics, managers of established firms are beginning to perceive BMI as an important source of profitable growth.[27] Yet, most firms lack a deliberate approach to the task of exploring and implementing a new-to-the-firm business model.[28] In acknowledgement of the obstacles that potentially hinder successful BMI in established firms, scholars in fact deem a deliberate approach necessary.[29] In a conceptual paper, CAVALCANTE et al. argue that a traditional business model, with its underlying processes and mental models, is persistent. For this reason, BMI initiatives might be rejected by business functions impacted by the new model; or they may be initially conceived from or later adapted towards the traditional business model. As a result, the greater potential of the new opportunity does not get exploited.[30] However, the lack of a deliberate approach to BMI in most firms is primarily assignable to the absence of scientifically-derived recommendations in terms of management frameworks and methods supporting BMI.[31] One of the main findings of the above mentioned top management surveys is that, in the words of CASADESUS-MASANELL / RICART,

"[...] top management in a broad range of industries are actively seeking guidance on how to innovate in their business models to improve their ability to both create and capture value."[32]

---

22 Source: Baden-Fuller / Morgan (2010), p. 158.
23 See Teece (2010), p. 184. The term "value constellation" relates to the internal and external value chain. It is drawn from Yunus et al. (2010), p. 312. See section 2.1.3.1 for a detailed discussion of the components of a business model.
24 See McGrath (2010), pp. 248-249.
25 See ibidem; Lecoq (2010), p. 217.
26 See Ricart (2012), p. 25.
27 See Reinhold et al. (2011), pp. 81-83, 89; IBM (2006, 2008, 2010); EIU (2005).
28 See Colvin (2013), p. 42; Frankenberger et al. (2013), p. 269.
29 See Chesbrough (2010), p. 356; Tuff / Wunker (2010), p. 10.
30 See Cavalcante et al. (2011), pp. 1335-1336.
31 See Bucherer et al. (2012), p. 183; Frankenberger et al. (2013), p. 269.
32 Source: Casadesus-Masanell / Ricart (2010), p. 195.

1.2 Research Gap and Research Goal

In a recently presented review on BMI research, SCHNEIDER / SPIETH assessed the current understanding of BMI as vague.[33] In an earlier version of their paper, the authors found that the existing literature on BMI is accused of lagging behind practice.[34] As an integral part of a future research agenda as well as to address managers' frequent failure in BMI, SCHNEIDER / SPIETH suggest studying the process of conducting BMI to more deeply understand BMI's core elements. Ideally, tools and methods can be identified that support managers in their BMI efforts.[35] Likewise, MASON / SPRING call for in-depth studies to advance the knowledge of practices managers use to develop and transform business models.[36] There is empirical evidence inferring that deliberate management decisions define or, after the occurrence of emerging and surprising events, redefine the direction a business model follows.[37] Such evidence constitutes a prerequisite for engaging in this kind of research. Furthermore, SOSNA et al. argue that BMI proceeds differently in established firms as opposed to in start-ups and, hence, must be studied separately.[38]

NIPPA et al. state that the most prevalent form of established for-profit organization in both mature and emerging economies is the multi-business firm.[39] One of the very few articles that specifically addresses BMI in multi-business firms is the paper by ASPARA et al., in which they present the results from studying the strategic management of corporate business model transformation at Nokia.[40] More precisely, the authors examine the period between 1987 and 1995 when Nokia transformed from a diversified conglomerate, covering the product areas of, e.g., rubber, paper, cables, consumer electronics, telecom networks, and mobile phones, to a focused structure of two business units in the telecommunications product area: mobile phones and networks. Thereby, ASPARA et al. explicitly differentiate between the business unit level and the corporate level, as well as between a business unit's business model and the corporate business model. They found that Nokia's corporate business model, triggered by severe market changes in the early 1990s, transformed through inheritance of the routines, capabilities and managerial cognitions that existed within the then best-ranked unit-level business model(s). The

---

33 See Schneider / Spieth (2013a), p. 2. For the literature review, the authors identified articles, reviews and books; as well as working papers through the ISI Web of Knowledge's Social Sciences Citation Index (SSCI) and the Social Science Research Network, by using "business model innovation" as the key word. Publications in the English language were considered if published between 1981 and 15 May 2012, see ibidem, p. 5.

34 See Schneider / Spieth (2012), p. 3.
Zott et al. (2011), p. 1038, consider the business model literature as "young and quite dispersed".

35 See Holm et al. (2013), p. 328; Schneider / Spieth (2013a), pp. 22-23.

36 See Mason / Spring (2011), p. 1040.

37 See Cavalcante et al. (2011), p. 1337; Demil / Lecoq (2010), p. 243.

38 See Sosna et al. (2010), pp. 402-403.

39 See Nippa et al. (2011), p. 50; see also Chandler (1991), p. 31; Collis et al. (2007), p. 383.

40 See Aspara et al. (2011). This article was also included in the review of BMI research conducted by Schneider / Spieth (2013a).

transformation had been facilitated by the promotion of managers from the best-ranked business units to Nokia's corporate headquarters.

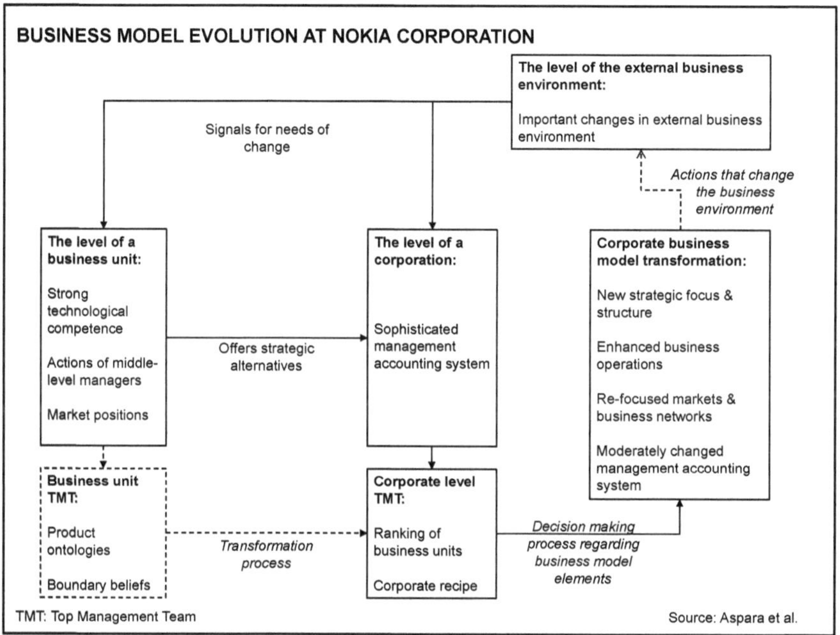

Figure 1: Business model evolution at Nokia Corporation[41]

Intriguingly, the findings of ASPARA et al. as visualized in Figure 1 emphasize the significance of business unit managers for initiating and implementing BMI. Corporate managers refer to internally existing elements when transforming the corporation's business model. Therefore, it is in the hands of business unit managers to pursue the innovation of business models in the sense of creating something new-to-the-firm. For an example of business-unit-generated BMI, ASPARA et al. refer to Nokia's "Mobira/NokiaMobile" telecom unit, which demonstrated strong technological competence already in the 1980s enabling it to anticipate the mass market prospects of GSM technology.[42]

Corporate managers and central services might have past experience or explicit knowledge of a business unit's business model, but they lack more tacit knowledge accumulated from the involvement in day-to-day business operations and continuous interaction with customers.[43] Undoubtedly, corporate managers may reserve the right

41 Source: Aspara et al. (2011), p. 641.
42 See ibidem, p. 642.
43 See Berghman (2012), pp. 21-22, 24; Santos et al. (2009), pp. 33-34, 47.

to grant permission for BMI because such efforts potentially influence the corporation's scope and risk profile. Put differently, corporate managers have the power to affect the BMI actions of business unit managers.[44] Nonetheless, business unit managers play a critical role for the realization of BMI in multi-business firms. Therefore, the research presented in this dissertation seeks to advance the understanding of how business unit managers in multi-business firms successfully conduct the innovation of business models. The research question reads as follows:

Which management practices support business unit managers in successfully realizing business model innovation in multi-business firms?

Hereby, the term "management practices" is drawn from STORBACKA. He researches solution business models and in this context defines "capabilities and management practices" as that which is necessary to design and to effectively manage such business models.[45] In strategy research, in general, "practices" includes something that guides activity, whereas "praxis" solely refers to actual activity.[46] The aim of this dissertation is to be understood as developing a strategic-level management approach to the challenge of BMI, an approach that most firms currently lack, in contrast with deriving non-generalizable, pure operational-level activity recommendations. Regarding the decision to study multi-business firms, there are two main reasons. Firstly, as mentioned above, this form of organization is the most predominant. Secondly, business unit managers in corporations usually steer their business relatively autonomously;[47] however, as described above, they are reliant on the decision-making of corporate headquarters. Hence, they enjoy less independency than, for example, the owner-managers of single business entities.[48] Therefore, it is assumed that the findings from studying BMI in business units of multi-business firms may be more easily transferable to single business entities than vice versa.

1.3 Research Method

BMI research in general is in early stages.[49] What is more, for the time being, journal articles that particularly relate to the role of business unit managers in BMI are

---

Explicit knowledge is objective and can be expressed in such forms as data or specific actions. Tacit knowledge is subjective, experiential and difficult to formalize or transact. It refers to, e.g., mental models and ideas. See Nonaka et al. (2001), p. 15.

44 See Greve (2003), p. 109; Hungenberg (2006), pp. 402-403; Santos et al. (2009), pp. 30-31.

45 See Storbacka (2011), p. 699.

46 Whittington (2006), p. 619: "Briefly, the distinction between praxis and practices follows [...] the dual sense of practice in social theory, both as something that guides activity and as activity itself. Accordingly, 'practices' will refer to shared routines of [behavior], including traditions, norms and procedures for thinking, acting and using 'things', this last in the broadest sense. By contrast, the Greek word 'praxis' refers to actual activity, what people do in practice."

47 See Dess et al. (2008), p. 345; Hungenberg (2006), p. 399.

48 See Dess et al. (2008), p. 342.

49 See Cavalcante (2012), p. 18; Frankenberger et al. (2013), p. 253; Schneider / Spieth (2013a), p. 25; Spieth et al. (2013), pp. 1-2.

relatively non-existent. Notable exceptions are the 2009 INSEAD working paper by SANTOS et al., in which business unit managers are mentioned as being important for BMI,[50] and CHESBROUGH's presumption that "general managers of specific businesses in larger firms" are suited to the task of BMI experimentation.[51] As such, there is no consistent structure of testable hypotheses, which renders it necessary to answer this dissertation's research question through an explorative and theory-building research method.

In fact, one of the most appropriate methods for learning about the dynamics present in longitudinal change events like BMI is the process of inducting theory from case studies as introduced by EISENHARDT.[52] Importantly, the research process she describes explicitly refers to aspects discussed in the context of "grounded theory".[53] According to GLASER / STRAUSS, a theory is grounded and therefore highly relevant for the respective area of research if it was discovered from systematically obtained and analyzed empirical data.[54] YIN states that case studies in general are particularly suited to examine the "how" and "why" questions inherent to contemporary, real-life events, provided that the scholar cannot manipulate those events.[55] The major advantage of case studies is that they can provide a "deep understanding".[56] Case study research is able to capture the complexity and richness of the phenomenon to a higher extent than other research methods.[57] By converging data from multiple sources in a triangulating fashion, this method allows the scholar (1) to deal with the entangled situation between phenomenon and context, and (2) to retain a holistic view of the events studied.[58] Indeed, theory developed from case studies is, meanwhile, routinely published in top-management journals, demonstrating the rising appreciation of this research method next to large-scale deductive studies.[59] Moreover, in their review on BMI research, SCHNEIDER / SPIETH find case studies to be the most often used method for empirically researching the phenomenon of BMI.[60]

With regard to the type of case study design, it must be considered that most studies that have investigated the factors influencing the success or failure of *new product development* adopted a "matched-pair" methodology. Thereby, the development phases of similar new products are examined with one being less successful than the other. This approach allows scholars to discriminate between good and poor

---

50 See Santos et al. (2009); see also sections 1.2 and 2.3.6.
51 See Chesbrough (2010), p. 361; see also section 2.3.6.
52 See Eisenhardt (1989).
53 See ibidem, pp. 532-533.
54 See Glaser / Strauss (1967), pp. 1-2.
55 See Yin (2009), pp. 8-16.
56 See Berg (2007), p. 285; Woodside (2010), p. 6.
57 See Berg (2007), pp. 283-284; Eisenhardt (1989), p. 538; Gummesson (2008), p. 38; Schöberl (2008), p. 93.
58 See Yin (2009), p. 18.
59 See Eisenhardt / Graebner (2007), pp. 25, 30; Sutton (1997), p. 98.
60 See Schneider / Spieth (2013a), p. 9.

practice, while checking for other background factors.[61] In a similar fashion to the matched-pair methodology, KOEN et al., who proclaimed their intention to identify the factors causing the failure of BMI projects at incumbent firms, also consider "paired case studies" a best-practice methodology for BMI research. For this reason, they look for companies that offer for study at least one failed and one successful BMI project.[62] Overall, GLASER / STRAUSS perceive a "general method of comparative analysis" a major strategy for the discovery of grounded theory that is a suitable subject for further testing and verifying.[63]

In theory-building case study research, the sampling of cases is crucial because only a limited number of cases can be studied.[64] To arrive at answers to the research question, the scholar engaged in intensive fieldwork that eventually resulted in the selection and in-depth analysis of five cases from five different business units. Of these, three cases contain successfully integrated BMIs, one case encompasses an integrated but financially disastrous BMI, and one case comprises a blocked BMI in an eventually sold business unit. At the time of the events, the business units were part of two different multi-business firms, both publicly listed and headquartered in Europe. Hence, this multiple-case study covers both different business units and different multi-business firms. Furthermore, this carefully selected sample of positive and negative cases enables the combination of replication logic with failure analysis. Such combination fosters a multi-faceted focus on the BMI process and also stimulates the consideration of otherwise probably unmentioned but crucial management practices.[65] In short, this "polar type" sample clearly renders possible the identification of those management practices that help business unit managers in multi-business firms in successfully realizing BMI.[66] By definition, the identified management practices have the character of propositions since they result from theory-building as opposed to theory-testing research.[67]

1.4 Contributions of the Dissertation

The dissertation elaborates significant contributions to the managerial practice and the theory of BMI in multi-business firms:

1) Derivation of managerial recommendations. This research is motivated by the fact that management in many industries is seeking guidance on how to innovate business models for profitable firm growth. Therefore, the propositions resulting from this research represent managerial recommendations for the realization of BMI in

---

61 See Tidd / Bessant (2009), p. 393.
62 See Koen et al. (2010), p. 50.
63 See Glaser / Strauss (1967), pp. 1-2.
64 See Eisenhardt (1989), p. 537.
65 See Ghezzi et al. (2010), p. 213.
66 See Eisenhardt (1989), p. 537; Eisenhardt / Graebner (2007), p. 27; Strauss / Corbin (1990), p. 109.
67 Eisenhardt (1989), p. 545: "The final product of building theory from case studies may be concepts [...], a conceptual framework, or propositions [...]." See also Dul / Hak (2008), pp. 176-177.

multi-business firms. They address, in the first place, managers of business units within multi-business firms. Nonetheless, the results are also of great interest to corporate managers, owner-managers and top-executives of established single business entities, as well as to aspiring middle-level managers in established firms.

2) Provision of a set of propositions for further theory testing. Essentially, this theory-building research results in a set of propositions that constitute an adequate basis for further empirical testing and extension of theory in the exciting field of BMI in established firms.

3) Compilation of a BMI-identification tool. Business model innovation has become the "buzzword du jour".[68] Nonetheless, definitional clarity is lacking. The fieldwork revealed that most managers had to have the exact meaning of the term BMI explained to them. The here-compiled BMI-identification tool addresses the need for an operationalized BMI definition. It integrates easily understandable criteria and indicators, enabling managers to qualify events as BMI. It can therefore be used for further empirical research into BMI. As for this dissertation, it enabled the selection of five cases out of nineteen initially proposed cases.

4) Linking BMI in multi-business firms with Corporate Entrepreneurship. Recent literature on BMI in established firms has not conclusively clarified whether the concept can be grounded in already existing and therefore more solid theoretical streams. In response, this dissertation presents points of contact between BMI in multi-business firms and the broad research arena of Corporate Entrepreneurship.

5) Identification of further contributions to BMI literature. This dissertation's theoretical foundation incorporates the greater part of extant BMI literature. Such thorough preparatory work enables the scholar to indicate how the findings contribute to other open topics discussed in the context of BMI.

1.5 Structure of the Dissertation

Overall, the dissertation is divided into seven chapters. Following this introduction, Chapter 2 lays the theoretical foundation for the fieldwork. Section 2.1 elaborates a working definition for the concept of BMI in multi-business firms and operationalizes it through the corresponding BMI-identification tool. Section 2.2 indicates links between this concept and the arena of Corporate Entrepreneurship. Section 2.3 identifies managerial activities or behaviors mentioned in extant BMI literature that serve as an early orientation for the initial interviews with managers. Chapter 3 explicates the course of action taken by the scholar in the empirical case study work to eventually identify management practices that support business unit managers in successfully realizing BMI. Sections 3.1 to 3.3 elucidate how the scholar arrived at the five cases constituting the findings' empirical basis. Section 3.4 explains how the findings have

---

68 See Abraham (2013), p. 31.

been induced from the cases. Section 3.5 summarizes the measures for ensuring the findings' validity and reliability.

Chapter 4 provides an in-depth understanding of the five BMI cases from which answers to the research question are derived. Each case description portrays the traditional and the new business model, illustrates how the new business model qualifies as successful or failed BMI, and describes from the business unit manager's point of view the process from the idea to the final integration of the new business model. Chapters 5 and 6 present the dissertation's findings. Chapter 5 introduces a conceptual BMI process model. This model abstracts from the concrete course of action in each BMI and is therefore of a more general character. Chapter 6 presents the management practices induced from the five cases, which together build an approach for business unit managers to successfully realize BMI in multi-business firms. Chapter 7 concludes the dissertation. Section 7.1 summarizes the findings and the steps taken by the scholar to reach them. Sections 7.2 and 7.3 illuminate the dissertation's implications for managerial practice and theory. Finally, section 7.4 discusses limitations and avenues of further research. Figure 2 illustrates this structure.

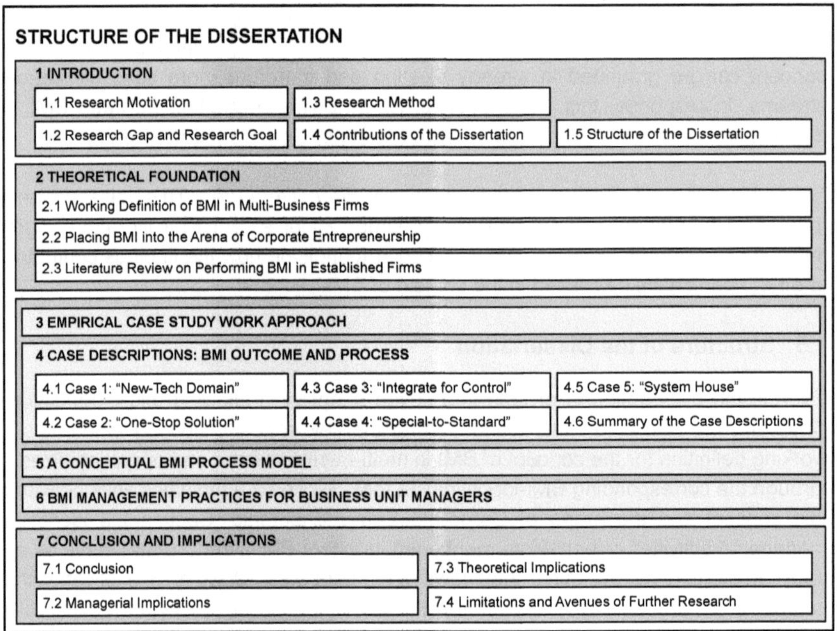

Figure 2: Structure of the dissertation[69]

[69] Source: own Figure

2 Theoretical Foundation

Case study research requires the development of a theoretical foundation, independent of whether the case study's purpose is to build or to test theory.[70] This chapter addresses such requirement. Firstly, the concept of BMI in multi-business firms is defined (2.1). Along with the working definition, a set of measures and indicators is brought forward in the form of a BMI-identification tool that allows the concept's operationalization. The term "operationalization" can be understood as the process of deciding how to translate abstract concepts such as BMI in multi-business firms into something more concrete and directly observable.[71] It constitutes an important prerequisite for the selection of cases worth being studied in order to answer the research question. Secondly, a recommendation is made to place the concept of BMI in multi-business firms, as defined in section 2.1, into the arena of Corporate Entrepreneurship (2.2). Ultimately, this leads to the suggestion that the dissertation's findings complement this broad and well-established research field. Thirdly, by working through the existing literature on BMI, activities or behaviors are identified that possibly turn out to be relevant for business unit managers to perform BMI (2.3). EISENHARDT contends that the a-priori specification of theoretical constructs helps to shape the initial design of theory-building research. In this respect, ex-ante identified activities can serve as an early orientation in the field, especially when conducting the initial interviews. However, a-priori specified constructs are only of a tentative character in theory-building research. They are not guaranteed a place in the resultant theory.[72]

2.1 Working Definition of BMI in Multi-Business Firms

2.1.1 Motivation and Method

Overall, a common BMI language has not yet evolved. SCHNEIDER / SPIETH note that, in practice, the term "business model innovation" appears to be commonly used despite not being consciously defined.[73] One of the reasons is that authors often have not defined the concept of BMI at all, or not thoroughly, within their publications.[74] Another reason is that authors applied idiosyncratic definitions to suit the purpose of the particular study or paper.[75] Hence, as of this writing, a single definition scholars can draw on is not available.[76] However, with respect to the case selection it is crucial for this research to have the concept of BMI in multi-business firms defined and operationalized.

---

[70] See Yin (2009), p. 35.
[71] See De Vaus (2002), p. 14.
[72] See Eisenhardt (1989), p. 536; Lasinger (2011), p. 14.
[73] See Schneider / Spieth (2013a), p. 26.
[74] See Wirtz (2011), p. 203.
[75] See Björkdahl / Holmén (2013), p. 218.
[76] See Schneider / Spieth (2013a), p. 2; Zott et al. (2011), p. 1034.

For achieving the goal of developing and operationalizing a working definition, three steps were carried out. Firstly, existing literature on BMI was reviewed with the aim of identifying phrases that hint at a definition or an explanation of BMI. The identified phrases were then analyzed according to apparent consensus, on the one hand, and more conflicting views, on the other. The former were to be integrated into the working definition, whereas the latter required a well-grounded decision by the scholar as to which view to follow. In addition, the articles containing those phrases were examined with regard to whether and – if yes – how the BMI definition or explanation was operationalized. Secondly, an initial working definition was put forward, together with a set of criteria and indicators building a BMI-identification tool. The overall guiding question for developing this tool was: *How to identify a BMI in multi-business firms?* As suggested by HAUSCHILDT / SALOMO, the working definition was formed along the five dimensions inherent to the notion of innovation. These five dimensions include the following: content, intensity, subjective, process-related, and normative dimensions.[77] Thirdly, the BMI-identification tool was applied in the field. Pre-talks were held with senior managers in four corporations to identify cases suitable to be studied for answering the research question.[78] Out of those pre-talks – leading to the selection of nine cases from nineteen initially proposed cases – two additions to the BMI-identification tool evolved: business model experiments and M&A.

2.1.2 Review of Existing BMI Definitions or Explanations

It is commonly acknowledged that the business model is a new unit of innovation that is distinct from products (hereby used interchangeably with services) or processes.[79] The business model's degree of abstraction and its inherent complexity is higher in comparison with products or processes.[80] BMI has an overarching impact on a business and therefore requires systemic and holistic thinking.[81] ZOTT et al. point out that the business model can be both a vehicle for innovation and a subject of innovation. In the first case, a new business model is understood as the means to commercialize an innovative idea or technology. In the second case, an already existing business model is being renewed.[82] Hence, although distinct, BMI can be interrelated with other topics of innovation.[83] However, besides this common acknowledgement, BMI literature is diffuse and lacking in clarity. As mentioned above, no commonly accepted language and understanding of BMI has yet been reached.[84] On the other hand, the BMI concept is in an emergent phase with numerous contributing authors who are convinced of the concept's usefulness.

77 See Hauschildt / Salomo (2011), p. 5.

78 See section 3.1.

79 See Bucherer et al. (2012), p. 183; Lindgardt et al. (2013), p. 292; Zott et al. (2011), p. 1038.

80 See Wirtz (2011), p. 206.

81 See Amit / Zott (2012), p. 47.

82 See Zott et al. (2011), pp. 1032-1034; see also Teece (2010), p. 176.

83 See Horn / Brem (2013), pp. 946-947; Wirtz (2011), p. 207.

84 See Berglund / Sandström (2013), p. 282; Björkdahl / Holmén (2013), pp. 218-219; Schneider / Spieth (2013a), p. 5; Skarzynski / Gibson (2008), p. 111; Spieth et al. (2013), pp. 1-2.

Therefore, definitional and conceptual agreement cannot be expected at this stage.[85] Still, existing BMI definitions or explanations as well as their operationalization shall be reviewed with the aim of providing an initial theory basis for the working definition and the BMI-identification tool.

Existing business model and BMI literature – in the form of academic and practitioner-oriented management journals, books, and working papers – was searched for via the journal databases "ABI/INFORM Complete" and "EBSCOhost", as well as the search engine "Google Scholar". Also, the "Business Model Community" website was included in this search.[86] Library catalogs and Amazon facilitated the search for books. In addition, proceedings with reference to BMI from the EURAM conferences 2012 and 2013 were included.[87] In fact, WEBSTER / WATSON recommend adding selected conference proceedings to the source material of a literature review.[88] Most of the collected BMI literature was published in English; the remainder in French or German. In order to avoid translation issues, only the body of English literature was then scanned for phrases hinting at a definition or explanation of BMI. Table 1 illustrates the results of this scan. The 30 identified definitions are sorted chronologically by year of publication. Within one year, they are sorted alphabetically by the source's name. The definitions presented in the conference papers can be found at the end of the table.

Apparent Consensus and Conflicting Views

Table 1 reveals that, indeed, the existing definitions or explanations provide a heterogeneous perception of BMI. Often, different aspects of BMI are being touched upon, rendering the consolidation of all of them problematic. Also, the level of detail varies among existing definitions. The statements that can be drawn from them are shown in Table 2 and listed below.

- BMI is essentially a process and should be studied as such.
- BMI leads to value enhancement for the firm.
  This statement includes phrases describing BMI as a source of profit as well as a means to create and capture new, better, superior, or increased value.
- BMI is about changing an existing business model.
- BMI is about creating a new business model.
- BMI entails a new value constellation.
  The term "value constellation" is drawn from the definition by YUNUS et al. Similar terms used in other definitions are "value architecture", "value (creation) logic", "organizing logic", "activity (system) reconfiguration", "new skills", or "design of organizational structure".

---

85 See Zott et al. (2011), p. 1034.

86 The Business Model Community is a platform for authors from any discipline to submit and exchange their studies on business models; see www.businessmodelcommunity.com, last accessed 14 July 2013.

87 EURAM: European Academy of Management.

88 See Webster / Watson (2002), p. xvi.

- BMI entails a new value proposition.
- BMI entails a new revenue model.

Each of the above statements occurs multiple times in the set of collected BMI definitions or explanations. Hence, these statements seem to gain broader consensus among the research community and should be integrated into the working definition.

However, other aspects are seen as being more controversial; for example, the question as to BMI should be:

- new-to-the-industry (e.g., Santos et al.), or
- new-to-the-firm (e.g., Bock et al., Björkdahl / Holmén).

Moreover, the views deviate on:

- whether BMI is manifested in stand-alone changes of one business model component such as a new value constellation, a new value proposition, a new revenue model (e.g., Abdelkafi et al., Bock et al., Santos et al., Schneider / Spieth), or
- whether BMI is manifested in a novel combination of business model components (e.g., Comes / Berniker, Matzler et al., Velamuri et al., Yunus et al.).

With regard to these more controversial aspects, a decision by the scholar is required as to which view to follow in the working definition. This decision must be well-grounded in existing theory.

Operationalization
Table 3 illustrates that, out of the 30 identified definitions, 20 have been applied in field research on BMI in established firms.[89] In summary, the main forms to operationalize the BMI concept are the following:

- Case study:
    - (CS1) Description of BMI detailing the new state compared to the former state;
    - (CS2) Description of BMI with the help of a business model framework consisting of predetermined business model components;
    - (CS3) Description of BMI based upon analyzing if activities are new or changed;
- Quantitative study (QS): Measure novelty on the level of the entire business model or, more deeply, in predetermined business model elements.

89 See section 3.1 for a definition of the term "established firm".

#	Source	Definition / Explanation of BMI
1	Mitchell & Coles (2004), p. 17	"By business model innovation, we mean business model replacements that provide product or service offerings to customers and end users that were not previously available. We also refer to the process of developing these novel replacements as business model innovation."
2	Markides (2006), p. 20	"Business-model innovation is the discovery of a fundamentally different business model in an existing business."
3	Giesen et al. (2007), p. 27	*"[...]* we first identified three main types of business model innovation, which can be used alone or in combination: innovations in industry models, in revenue models and in enterprise models."
4	Comes / Berniker (2008), p. 73	"The core of business model innovation lies in the new answers to the following two questions – the key answers that guide any business: 1. What value is the company providing to its customers? 2. How does providing this value profit the company?"
5	Skarzynski / Gibson (2008), p. 111	*"[...]* business model innovation is about creating fundamentally new kinds of businesses, or about bringing more strategic variety into the business you are already in – the kind of variety that is highly valued by customers."
6	Liedtka / Meyer (2009), p. 2	"Business model innovation [...] is about producing value-creating outcomes for customers."
7	Lindgardt et al. (2009), p. 2	"Innovation becomes BMI when two or more elements of a business model are reinvented to deliver value in a new way."
8	Santos et al. (2009), p. 14	"Business model innovation *[...]* is a reconfiguration of activities in the existing business model of a firm that is new to the product/service market in which the firm competes."
9	Aspara et al. (2010), p. 47	[*Two indicators for measuring a firm's strategic emphasis on BMI:*] 1. *"[...]* initiatives to create novel value by challenging existing industry-specific business models, roles, and relations in certain geographic market areas." 2. *"[...]* initiatives to provide entirely new value to certain people and/or organizations (customers)."
10	Bock et al. (2010), p. 10	"Business model innovation is new-to-the-firm changes in the design of organizational structures."
11	Gambardella / McGahan (2010), p. 263	"In this conceptualization, business-model innovation occurs when a firm adopts a novel approach to commercializing its underlying assets."
12	Jaeggi (2010), p. 39	"A business model innovation is any new business model or redesign of an existing business model that leads to superior value creation for the client, business or partner, and that enables to appropriate the value created over a longer period of time."
13	Johnson (2010), p. 13	"Seizing the white space requires new skills, new strengths, new ways to make money. It calls for the ability to innovate something more core than the core, to innovate the very theory of the business itself. I call that process business model innovation."
14	Osterwalder / Pigneur (2010), p. 5	"Ultimately, business model innovation is about creating value, for companies, for customers, and society."
15	Yunus et al. (2010), p. 312	"Business model innovation is about generating new sources of profit by finding novel value proposition / value constellation combinations."
16	Sorescu et al. (2011), p. 57	"We define a RBM [*Retail Business Model*] innovation as a change beyond current practice in one or more elements of a retailing business model *[...]* and their inter-dependencies, thereby modifying the retailer's organizing logic for value creation and appropriation."
17	Amit / Zott (2012), p. 44	"Business model innovation can occur in a number of ways: 1. by adding novel activities *[...]*; 2. by linking activities in novel ways *[...]*; 3. by changing one or more parties that perform any of the activities *[...]*."

Table 1: (continued)

#	Source	Definition / Explanation of BMI
18	Bucherer et al. (2012), p. 184	"We define business model innovation as a process that deliberately changes the core elements of a firm and its business logic."
19	Kaplan (2012), p. 108	"Business model innovation is a better way to create, deliver and capture value."
20	Lindgren (2012), p. 55	"BMI can *[…]* both be valuable and focused on BM on the way to the market (TO BE) BM and in the market (AS IS) BM *[…]*."
21	Abdelkafi et al. (2013), p. 13.	"A business model innovation happens when the company modifies or improves at least one of the value dimensions *[value proposition, communication, creation, delivery, capture]*."
22	Berglund / Sandström (2013), p. 276	"A BMI can thus be thought of as the introduction of a new business model aimed to create commercial value."
23	Björkdahl / Holmén (2013), p. 214.	"A business model innovation is the implementation of a business model that is new to the firm. […] Specifically, the business model innovation phenomenon includes both creating value for customers and users, and capturing value for the firm."
24	Frankenberger *et al.* (2013), p. 253	"At root, a business model innovation can be defined as a novel way of how to create and capture value, which is achieved through a change of one or multiple components in the business model."
25	Günzel / Holm (2013), pp. 1-2.	"As a process, and not merely a management concept, business model innovation encompasses developing novel value chain architectures in different ways, from new product developments to new delivery and marketing patterns, as well as innovative re- source acquisition and application. The novelty presented by new business models can potentially result in superior value creation."
26	Matzler et al. (2013), p. 31	"Business model innovation results when a company increases customer value and simultaneously creates a new value creation and revenue model that allows the company to capture some of the value created in a new way."
27	Velamuri et al. (2013), p. 4	*"[…]* We define business model innovation as having a novel combination of (1) value propositions (i.e., perceived usefulness for customers), (2) value chain architectures (i.e., internal processes to deliver products or services), and (3) revenue streams (i.e., the manner incomes are generated) that are difficult to imitate. "
28	Fielt (2012), p. 3 – EURAM	"Business model innovation refers to organizations rethinking their dominant value logic and coming up with new ways of creating value for their customers and themselves."
29	Klang / Hoffmann (2012), pp. 6-7 – EURAM	"In this study, we understand business model innovation as intentional changes in the specific activity system that is conducted to satisfy the perceived needs of the market and the specifications of the parties that form and conduct this activity system."
30	Rauter et al. (2012), p. 10 – EURAM	"In this paper, we treat business model innovation as an approach of changing the business model; therefore business model innovation is seen as the process itself and not as the result of the ongoing changes."
31	Schneider / Spieth (2013b), p. 17 – EURAM	"Consequently, business model innovation is defined as a conscious and significant change of at least one dimension of a firm's or a business units' business model *[value offering, value creation architecture, revenue model logic]*."
32	Mezger et al. (2013), p. 4 – EURAM	*"[…]* business model innovation defines new concepts for firms to create and capture value; new business models represent new architectures and logics of conducting business, novel ways of creating revenues and defining value propositions for customers; It redefines a firm's activities within a business ecosystem of stakeholders and describes new transactions that essentially lead to increased value creation *[…]*."

Table 1: Identified definitions or explanations of BMI[90]

[90] Source: own Table.

BMI ...	Occurrence	Source (see Table 1)																													
		1	2	3	4	5	6	7	8	9	10	11	12	13	14	15	16	17	18	19	20	21	22	23	24	25	26	27	28	29	30	31	32
is a process	5x	X												X					X							X					X		
leads to value enhancement for the firm	13x									X			X	X	X	X				X			X	X	X	X	X		X				X
is about changing an existing BM	12x		X			X			X			X	X				X		X		X	X			X						X	X	
is about creating a new BM	4x					X							X								X		X										
entails a new value constellation	16x				X			X	X		X	X		X		X	X	X				X				X	X	X		X		X	X
entails a new value proposition	13x	X			X		X						X			X						X		X		X	X	X	X			X	X
entails a new revenue model	5x			X																							X	X				X	X
is new-to-the-industry	1x								X																								
is new-to-the-firm	3x										X	X												X									

Table 2: Statements in identified definitions or explanations of BMI[91]

[91] Source: own Table.

Contains operationalization of BMI for field research				Form of operationalization for field research on BMI at established firms		
				Case studies		Quantitative study via standardized questionnaire
Source (see Table 1)	No: Conceptual or no own data	Yes: Not-for-profit businesses	Yes: Established firms	Description of BMI	Description of BMI via ex-ante specified framework	
1			X	X		
2	X					
3			X		IBM's framework for BMI / CEO Study 2006	
4			X	X		
5			X	X		
6	X					
7			X	Not disclosed how firms were segmented into business model, product, or process innovators		
8			X		4 forms of reconfiguration of activities	
9			X			X
10	X					
11			X	X		
12			X	X		
13			X		Four-box business model framework	
14			X		Business model canvas (9 building blocks of a BM)	
15		X				
16			X		6 design themes for retail BMI	
17			X		3 design elements and 4 value drivers/ design themes	
18			X	X		
19			X	X		
20			X		7 building blocks of a BM	
21	X					
22	X					
23	X					
24			X	X		
25			X		Modified business model canvas	
26	X					
27			X		Novel combination of 3 business model components	
28	X					
29	X					
30	X					
31			X			X
32			X			X
Occurrence	**10x**	**1x**	**21x**	**8x**	**9x**	**3x**

Table 3: Forms of BMI concept operationalization for field research[92]

[92] Source: own Table.

(CS1) The most common form of operationalization is to describe the BMI in terms of what it entails and how it compares to the former state.[93]

(CS2) JOHNSON, GÜNZEL / HOLM, LINDGREN, OSTERWALDER / PIGNEUR, and VELAMURI et al. generically define a business model as being constituted of certain building blocks or components. In order to identify and to explain the BMI, they analyze each building block of the new business model and compare it to the respective building block of the former business model. Put differently, BMI is recognized ex-post by identifying changes within predetermined business model components. According to the IBM framework, BMI can consist of one or more of the three innovation types: industry model innovation (i.e. creating or moving into new industries), revenue model innovation (i.e. a new way of revenue generation), and enterprise model innovation (i.e. a redefined role within a value chain). For BMI identification, IBM uses case summaries to assess ex-post to which degree the three innovation types occurred.[94]

(CS3) AMIT / ZOTT, SANTOS et al., and SORESCU et al. perceive business models as activity systems. AMIT / ZOTT understand a business model as resulting from the design of three different elements: content, structure and governance. Change in one or more of these elements, e.g., by adding novel activities ("content"), by linking activities in new ways ("structure"), or by changing the parties that perform any of the activities ("governance") potentially represents BMI. Moreover, AMIT / ZOTT suggest four major value drivers of business models. These are called design themes because they guide the design of the activity's content, structure and governance. Summarized by the acronym "NICE", the themes are *n*ovelty, lock-*i*n, *c*omplementarities, and *e*fficiency.[95] SORESCU et al. relate to "NICE" when defining six design themes for retail business models. They analyze retailers' business models and classify them as BMI if one or more of the six design themes can be recognized.[96] SANTOS et al. manifest BMI in the reconfiguration of activities that can take the form of: relinking, repartitioning, relocating, or reactivating. In a case study approach, they investigate whether one or more of the four pre-defined reconfiguration types has or have been implemented in a firm's business model.[97]

(QS) ASPARA et al. carry out a quantitative study wherein BMI is operationalized by two indicators that both focus on novel value creation. These indicators remain on the level of the entire business model and do not specify single business model elements more deeply.[98] Similarly, the quantitative study by MEZGER et al. presented at the EURAM 2013 conference, measures BMI by asking to what extent –

93 "Description of BMI" as a method of operationalizing the definition of BMI is representatively illustrated in Bucherer et al. (2012), p. 187.
94 See Giesen et al. (2007), pp. 27-32.
95 See Amit / Zott (2012), pp. 44-46; see also Amit / Zott (2001).
96 See Sorescu et al. (2011), pp. S7-S11.
97 See Santos et al. (2009), p. 15.
98 See Table 1.

on a five-point Likert scale – new business models have been implemented or are being developed.[99] By contrast, the quantitative study by SCHNEIDER / SPIETH, presented at the EURAM 2013 conference, uses nine business model elements from three business model dimensions to measure how strongly a firm's business model has changed. Table 4 discloses these business model dimensions and elements, as well as each corresponding item in the questionnaire.

Innovated business model dimension and element	Item in questionnaire
Value offering: target customer	Target customers have changed.
Value offering: product and service offering	The product and service offering has changed.
Value offering: firm's competitive positioning	The firm's positioning in the market has changed.
Value architecture: core competences and resources	The firm's core competencies and resources have changed.
Value architecture: internal value creation	Internal value creation activities have changed.
Value architecture: partners in value creation	Role and involvement of partners into the value creation process have changed.
Value architecture: distribution	Distribution has changed.
Revenue model: revenue mechanisms	Revenue mechanisms have changed.
Revenue model: cost mechanisms	Cost mechanisms have changed.

Table 4: Business model innovation items used by SCHNEIDER / SPIETH[100]

2.1.3 Developing a Working Definition

Based upon (1) the collected body of literature, (2) the results from the review of existing BMI definitions or explanations, and (3) the pre-talks with senior managers in four corporations,[101] the following subsections define the concept of BMI in multi-business firms for the purpose of this dissertation. Simultaneously, a set of criteria and indicators building the BMI-identification tool is put forward in order to operationalize the working definition. The overall guiding question for developing this tool is: *How to identify a BMI in multi-business firms?* As suggested by HAUSCHILDT / SALOMO, the working definition is formed along the five dimensions inherent to the notion of innovation, i.e. the content, intensity, subjective, process-related, and normative dimensions.[102] Criteria or indicators in the BMI-identification tool, which evolved from the pre-talks, are marked as such.

---

[99] See Mezger et al. (2013), p. 37.
[100] Source: Schneider / Spieth (2013b), p. 36.
[101] See section 3.1.
[102] See Hauschildt / Salomo (2011), p. 5.

2.1.3.1 Content Dimension: What is new?

The statements drawn from the review in section 2.1.2 relating to the content dimension of BMI are listed below.

- BMI entails a new value constellation.
- BMI entails a new value proposition.
- BMI entails a new revenue model.

This subsection clarifies how they are integrated into the working definition.

As stated above, the subject of innovation in BMI is the business model. The origins of the term "business model" can be traced back to Peter Drucker's classic 1954 book, *The Practice of Management.*[103] As a concept, the business model gained popularity in the 1990s with the upsurge of the commercial internet and advances in information and communication technology. The internet triggered the emergence of the new economy and created an array of new business models. In response, academic literature focused on explaining the characteristics of profitable e-business models. Subsequently, the business model concept has also been adopted by practitioners in the old economy and is now being applied more broadly in the corporate world.[104] Academics from a wide range of disciplines found a connection and contributed to the development of business model literature. However, these many different perspectives on the business model concept make it difficult to find a commonly accepted definition.[105] In order to visualize the current polyphony related to this term, Table 5 lists several meta-sources of business model definitions published in 2010 or later, i.e. authors who collected different, elsewhere-published definitions. In addition to the name of the source and the number of definitions, Table 5 indicates whether a meta-source also analyzes the business model components that certain definitions contain. Hereby, the term "component"[106] is used interchangeably with "element"[107], "dimension"[108], "domain"[109], or "building block"[110].

With the aim of finding common ground across the different business model definitions, SHAFER et al. developed an affinity diagram including twelve definitions and forty-two business model components. Based on their analysis, they suggest:

> *"[The] business model [is] a representation of a firm's underlying core logic and strategic choices for creating and capturing value within a value network."*[111]

---

103 See Casadesus-Masanell / Ricart (2010), p. 197; Dahan et al. (2010), p. 328.
104 See Dahan et al. (2010), p. 328; Lecoq et al. (2010), p. 219; Nielsen / Bukh (2011), p. 258; Teece (2010), p. 174.
105 See Brette et al. (2011), p. 240; Dahan et al. (2010), p. 328; Nenonen / Storbacka (2010), p. 44; Shafer et al. (2005), p. 200; Yunus et al. (2010), p. 311.
106 See (e.g.) Skarzynski / Gibson (2008), p. 112.
107 See (e.g.) Mitchell / Coles (2003), p. 16.
108 See (e.g.) Bieger / Reinhold (2011), pp. 31-34
109 See (e.g.) Wirtz et al. (2010), p. 274.
110 See (e.g.) Osterwalder / Pigneur (2010), p. 15.
111 Source: Shafer et al. (2005), p. 202.

This definition comprises the key terms "core logic", "strategic choices", "creating and capturing value", and "value network", which deserve further explanation. Firstly, the business model is not a strategy. Business strategy refers to the choices about how the firm wishes to compete. The business model, by contrast, is a reflection of the chosen strategy.[112] It is through business models that firms compete in a marketplace.[113] Put differently, strategy can be seen as the plan for how to move to a desired state. The business model is the comprehensive description of a state.[114] The major cause-and-effect relationships that physically work in a business model constitute the core logic.[115] Secondly, strategic choices are imperatively linked to value creation and value capture. For-profit firms must simultaneously create value for their customers and, monetarily, capture a part of it in order to survive.[116] Finally, a value network can be understood as the context within which a firm establishes a cost structure and operating processes, and within which it works with suppliers and channel partners.[117]

Meta-Source	Number of Collected BM Definitions	Analysis of BM Components
Baden-Fuller / Morgan (2010), p. 158 Long Range Planning special issue on business models	9	No
Bieger / Reinhold (2011), pp. 18-19 Definitions translated into German language	12	Yes
Bucherer (2010), pp. 16-18	9	Yes
Jaeggi (2010), pp. 18-20	7	No
Moingeon / Lehmann-Ortega (2010), pp. 294-297	50	No
Nenonen / Storbacka (2010), pp. 46-47	12	Yes
Neubauer (2011), pp. 338-350 Author also provides the research context behind each definition.	24	Yes
Rauter et al. (2012), pp. 7-9 (EURAM)	9	Yes
Wirtz (2011), pp. 66-69	21	No
Zott et al. (2011), p. 1024 Authors name papers that cite a certain definition.	8	No
Sahut et al. (2013), p. 70 Authors indicate how other authors contribute to the business model concept.	20	No

Table 5: Meta-sources of business model definitions[118]

112 See Casadesus-Masanell / Ricart (2010), p. 203; Casadesus-Masanell / Ricart (2011), p. 107.
113 See Nenonen / Storbacka (2010), p. 53.
114 See Dahan et al. (2010), p. 328.
In a similar conception, Casadesus-Masanell / Ricart (2010), p. 203, view strategy as the contingent plan as to which business model to use.
115 See Shafer et al. (2005), p. 202.
116 See ibidem.
117 See Christensen / Raynor (2003), p. 44.
118 Source: own Table.

Notably, scholars have repeatedly attached a subjective dimension to the business model concept. DOZ / KOSONEN, for example, emphasize that business models also stand as cognitive structures providing the firm's management with a theory on how the firm relates to its environment, how it creates value, and how it organizes its internal structure and governance.[119] Likewise, the business model framework by ASPARA et al. stresses the importance of intangible, cognitive structures that exist in the minds of people at different levels of the corporation.[120] Above all, CHESBROUGH / ROSENBLOOM convincingly concluded from research on Xerox, which failed to capture the value from multiple new technologies invented at its Palo Alto Research Center (PARC), that the extant business model logic – the "dominant logic" - potentially constrains the sense-making task required to discover the most appropriate business model for a new technology.[121] Eventually, CAVALCANTE et al. highlight with regard to business model dynamics, that business model changes require managers to question their mental models of how the firm does business and how it should be organized.[122]

Discussion has evolved on the question of how to further conceptualize the core logic of a business model.[123] As already indicated in the review, the below two major approaches exist.

- *"Ex-ante BM framework approach":* The first major approach consists of specifying ex-ante generic core components of a business model. Representative for this approach is the business model canvas by OSTERWALDER / PIGNEUR and the four-box business model framework by JOHNSON. Both are often-cited.[124] The business model canvas resembles a painter's canvas preformatted with nine blocks: customer segments, value propositions, channels, customer relationships, revenue streams, key resources, key activities, key partnerships, and cost structure. These nine building blocks cover the "four main areas of a business": customers, offer, infrastructure, and financial viability.[125] OSTERWALDER / PIGNEUR state that their tool is intuitively understandable while not oversimplifying the complexities of how enterprises function. It has been developed to facilitate the description and discussion of business models.[126] JOHNSON conceptualizes a business model through four interlocking elements:

[119] See Doz / Kosonen (2010), p. 371.
[120] See Aspara et al. (2011), p. 623.
[121] See Chesbrough / Rosenbloom (2002), p. 550; see also Chesbrough (2010), pp. 358-359. Originally, the term "dominant general management logic" was coined by Prahalad / Bettis (1986), p. 490, and defined as "the way in which managers conceptualize the business and make critical resource allocation decisions".
[122] See Cavalcante et al. (2011), p. 1335.
[123] See Abdelkafi et al. (2013), p. 10.
[124] See (e.g.) Abraham (2013), pp. 33-36; De Reuver et al. (2013), p. 3; Günzel / Holm (2013), p. 4; Leavy (2010), pp. 5-12.
[125] See Osterwalder / Pigneur (2010), pp. 14-51.
[126] See ibidem, p. 15.

customer value proposition, profit formula, key resources, and key processes. Taken together, those elements create and deliver value.[127]

- "*Activity system approach*": The second major approach to business model conceptualization is to perceive the business model as an activity system. In particular, ZOTT / AMIT contend that the activity system should be the level of business model analysis, and the single activity should be the unit of analysis. Thereby, an activity is to be understood as the engagement of resources belonging to any party involved in the business model (e.g., the focal firm, customers, or partners), serving a specific purpose for the accomplishment of the business model's overall objective. Linking those activities leads to the activity system. The firm's activity system may exceed the focal firm's boundaries to include the involved external parties, but remains firm-centered to enable the focal firm to capture a share of the mutually created value. For managers, the identification of distinct activities can be "conceptually challenging" because activities can be repeatedly broken down, further creating a large number of potential activities. However, the definition of activities at subsequent levels of aggregation may facilitate this task.[128] Quite similarly, CAVALCANTE et al. conceptualize the business model by the core processes necessary for a firm to perform its business. A core process is "a set of related activities repeatedly carried out to meet a priori specified goals".[129] Consequently, the authors argue that business model changes are changes in the core processes, which become visible through different working practices.[130]

One of the key advantages of the "*ex-ante BM framework approach*" to business model conceptualization is that changes in those pre-defined components can be measured consistently over time and across firms. What is more, normative definitions may offer valuable guidance as to what managers should consider when designing business models. On the other hand, this approach assumes that the same components are equally core in all firms. Besides, normative definitions might indirectly impose limits on what characterizes a complete business model.[131] The major advantage of the more inductive "*activity system approach*" to business model conceptualization is that it allows the unrestricted "decoding" of what a business model really is about.[132] In contrast, comparisons of business models over time and across firms may be challenging.[133]

As a way of combining the advantages of both approaches, DEMIL / LECOQ propose to ex-ante specify only a few core business model components. Through

[127] See Johnson (2010), pp. 21-46; Johnson et al. (2008), pp. 52-53.
[128] See Zott / Amit (2010), pp. 217-219.
[129] See Cavalcante et al. (2011), pp. 1328-1329.
[130] See ibidem, p. 1333.
[131] See Casadesus-Masanell / Ricart (2010), p. 201; Demil / Lecoq (2010), p. 231.
[132] See ibidem.
[133] See Mezger / Enkel (2012), p. 8.

this, business model comparisons would still be possible while within a core component the more inductive approach can be used to thoroughly analyze the particularities of a business model.[134] Indeed, several authors have promoted conceptualizing a business model with just two core components (Table 6).

COMES / BERNIKER view the fundamentals of a business model as constituted by the value a firm is providing to its customers, and by the way the firm serves those customers at a profit.[135] MCGRATH endorses a similar view on the business model. She argues that the business model results from two sets of managerial choices. Firstly, managers have to choose a particular "unit of business". Such a unit refers to the products and services a firm offers and for which customers pay. Secondly, managers have to choose the "key metrics" standing for the activities and processes set up by the firm to profitably sell those units. In essence, the key metrics reflect the business architecture.[136] MEZGER / ENKEL as well as GÜNZEL / HOLM divide the nine building blocks into the two main categories: *front-end of the business model* – comprising of the value proposition, distribution channel, revenue model, and customer relationship; and *back-end of the business model* – including the resources, key activities, partnerships, and cost structure.[137]

Authors promoting business model conceptualization with only two components	
Source	**Components**
Comes / Berniker (2008), p. 73	1. Value, a firm is providing to its customers 2. Way, the firm serves those customers at a profit
McGrath (2010), p. 249	1. Managers choose a "unit of business" (products/services) 2. Managers choose "key metrics" (business architecture)
a) Moingeon / Lehmann-Ortega (2010), p. 271 b) Yunus et al. (2010), p. 312	1. Value proposition made to the clients 2. Value constellation (named value architecture in a))
Mezger / Enkel (2012), p. 9 (EURAM)	1. Customer front-end of the business model 2. Back-end of the business model
Günzel / Holm (2013), pp. 4-5	1. Front-end of the business model 2. Back-end of the business model

Table 6: Authors promoting only two business model components[138]

Another similar view is presented by MOINGEON / LEHMANN-ORTEGA. They conceptualize the business model through three components: the value proposition, the value constellation and the profit equation (Figure 3). The value proposition describes the offer a firm brings to its clients. The value constellation then comprises the tasks put into action by the firm to deliver the offer to the clients. This involves both the firm's own value chain and its value network with suppliers and partners.

[134] See Demil / Lecoq (2010), p. 231.
[135] See Comes / Berniker (2008), p. 73-79.
[136] See McGrath (2010), p. 249-252.
[137] See Günzel / Holm (2013), pp. 4-5.
[138] Source: own Table.

The profit equation, by contrast, is the combined result of the two previous components. Sales revenues reflect the value proposition's success with clients, whereas the cost structure and the capital employed mirror the made decisions in reference to the value constellation. In order to generate profits, the value proposition and the value constellation must be consistent with each other.[139] In a case study research, MOINGEON / LEHMANN-ORTEGA used this business model conceptualization to assess if a potentially new business model classifies (ex-post) as BMI[140]. Since the scholar faces a similar task in this research, their conceptualization shall be incorporated into the working definition and BMI-identification tool.

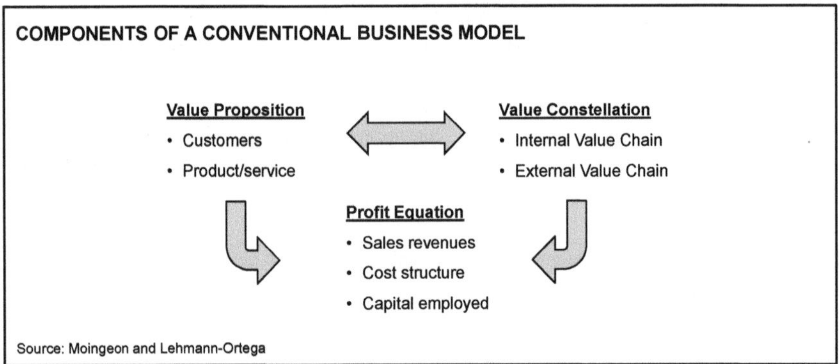

Figure 3: Components of a conventional business model[141]

Applying MOINGEON / LEHMANN-ORTEGA's business model conceptualization relates to the statements drawn from the review in section 2.1.2 as follows:

- BMI entails a new value constellation. – *integrated*
- BMI entails a new value proposition. – *integrated*
- BMI entails a new revenue model. – *not integrated*

The revenue model shall not be integrated as an additional distinct criterion for identifying BMI, because the revenue and cost mechanisms are considered to be resultant from the choices on the value proposition and the value constellation.

Table 7 illustrates the two criteria and the respective indicators in the BMI-identification tool that represent the content dimension of BMI. The first criterion emphasizes the importance of a new value proposition. By drawing on JOHNSON, a customer value proposition consists of the customer needs addressed by the firm and the offering (product and/or service) that satisfies those customer needs.[142]

---

139 See Moingeon / Lehmann-Ortega (2010), pp. 270-271; Yunus et al. (2010), p. 312.

140 See Moingeon / Lehmann-Ortega (2010), pp. 271-275.

141 Source: Yunus et al. (2010), p. 312.

142 See Johnson (2010), p. 24. Johnson employs the term "job-to-be-done" instead of "customer needs addressed" because, in his opinion, "customer needs" are often defined too broadly. On the

Similar indicators were used by SCHNEIDER / SPIETH in the business model dimension "value offering".[143] In order to meet the criterion, at least one of these two indicators must be new or changed-to-become-new. The second BMI criterion relates to the development of an innovative value constellation. MOINGEON / LEHMANN-ORTEGA argue that innovativeness of the value constellation may originate from the creation or suppression of several activities in the value chain, from changes to several activities, and/or from changes in the order of activities.[144] The implementation of a new set of activities leads to a new set of daily routines which become visible through different working practices.[145] Put differently, the criterion is met if employees, attached to the business model that potentially classifies as BMI, at some point, physically do something other than those in the traditional business model. SCHNEIDER / SPIETH employ a similar indicator in the business model dimension "value architecture". They ask for changes in internal value creation activities.[146]

Criteria for classifying a business model as BMI in the multi-business firm	Indicators
New or changed-to-become-new value proposition	- Customer need(s) addressed, and/or - Offering (product/service)
Innovative value constellation: New, and/or changed, and/or suppressed working practices to fulfill the value proposition	May apply to the activities of, e.g., - product/service design - finding customers - quoting - retaining customers - sourcing - inbound logistics - product manufacturing or service provision - delivery/distribution - claim management

Table 7: BMI identification criteria: *What is new?*[147]

2.1.3.2 *Intensity Dimension: How is it new?*

The major finding from the review in section 2.1.2 that relates to the intensity dimension of BMI is the need to clarify the point:

- whether BMI is manifested in stand-alone changes of one business model component, or
- whether BMI is manifested in a novel combination of business model components.

The intensity dimension covers the degree of innovativeness, i.e. the extent to which an innovation is new. It relates to the assessment of how or how much a new

other hand, the more mainstream term "customer needs addressed" is easy to understand by practitioners and shall hence be integrated into the BMI-identification tool.

143 See Table 4.

144 See Moingeon / Lehmann-Ortega (2010), p. 273.

145 See Cavalcante et al. (2011), p. 1333.

146 See Table 4.

147 Source: own Table.

situation differs from the former one, whereby the new situation is the innovation or that which arose out of the innovation. Typically, innovations are placed on a continuum between incremental and radical. The position on this continuum can be assessed with the help of, e.g., multi-categorical scoring.[148] With regard to BMI, the intensity dimension raises the question of how much a business model shall differentiate itself from an existing business model in order to qualify as BMI.[149]

SOSNA et al. answer this question by drawing on the characteristic that renders the business model concept unique: its dual focus on value creation and value capture.[150]

> *"The business model perspective is unique in one crucial respect: it embraces system wide changes that include both value creation and value exploitation [...]."*[151]

To them, a business model qualifies as BMI if it incorporates new transaction content, structure and governance configurations that lead to novel ways of both value creation and capture.[152] Likewise, SORESCU et al. argue that BMI modifies the firm's organizing logic for value creation and appropriation by changes in business model elements and their interdependencies. They highlight that:

> *"[...] innovations in [...] business models are system-wide changes; even though the change may originate in just one element of the business model, it also triggers changes to other parts of the system."*[153]

Furthermore, TUFF / WUNKER demand that system-wide changes constitute a BMI requirement. In detail, the authors define ten types of innovation covering four major innovation categories: finance, process, offering and delivery. To qualify as BMI, a new business model must contain six or more innovation types with at least one type coming from each of the four innovation categories.[154] A similar statement is made by MITCHELL / COLES. They define BMI as consisting of a business model replacement plus or including new product/service offerings to customers. Thereby, a business model replacement means a change in at least four out of seven business model elements.[155]

Hence, when transferring this line of argumentation to the working definition and BMI-identification tool, both criteria related to business model content are to be met. Put

---

[148] See Hauschildt / Salomo (2011), pp. 11-18; Jensen (2012), p. 16.
[149] See also Jensen (2012), p. 33.
[150] See Sosna et al. (2010), p. 401; see also Zott et al. (2011), p. 1037.
[151] Source: Sosna et al. (2010), p. 401.
[152] Content, structure and governance have been proposed by Zott / Amit as the design elements of a business model; see section 2.1.2.
[153] Source: Sorescu et al. (2011), p. S7.
[154] See Tuff / Wunker (2010), pp. 3-4.
[155] See Mitchell / Coles (2004), p. 17.

differently, in order to classify as BMI, the business model under examination must show a new value proposition and, simultaneously, a new value constellation. Certainly, the initial innovation idea can target just one of these two major business model components. Ex-post, however, changes in both components should be noticeable.

An argument against perceiving BMI as a system-wide change may be that such a perception would not recognize those business models as BMI that only feature either a new value proposition or a new value constellation.[156] Other scholars could argue that such a perception would, for example, deny that Taco Bell's "K-Minus" (Kitchen Minus) initiative in the late 1980s, which has been recognized as BMI, does not qualify as BMI anymore. As to this specific case, other scholars have so far focused on the management's decision to turn the restaurants' kitchens into a mere heating and assembly unit of pre-cooked food; this permitted smaller kitchens and more customer space in each restaurant. It enabled Taco Bell to capture more value through a different set of working practices without changing the offer to the customer.[157] Indeed, the offering did not change. Nonetheless, that decision was accompanied by a re-conception of the customer need addressed by Taco Bell, as evidenced in the company CEO's comment on K-Minus:

> *"One of the things that struck us was, perhaps we needed to figure out a different way to go about this [...]. We're really not in the business of making food. We're in the business of feeding people."*[158]

With this information, Taco Bell's new business model classifies as BMI even when adopting the perception of BMI as system-wide change, since it in fact contains both a new value constellation and a new value proposition.

Besides, an emphasis on just one of these two business model components makes it more difficult to draw the line between BMI on the one side and product or process innovation on the other. Likewise, SCHNEIDER / SPIETH propose to differentiate in this context business model innovation from business model development:

> *"While business model development emphasizes the status quo of a firm's current business model and focuses on adjustments and incremental innovations within the established business model framework, business model innovation removes itself from the status quo [...]."*[159]

Table 8 depicts that a yes or no assessment is sufficient to meet a criterion incorporated into the BMI-identification tool. Admittedly, this evaluation method

156 Wirtz (2011), p. 206, classifies a business model as BMI if it features either a new value proposition or a new value constellation.
157 See Amit / Zott (2010), p. 8; Santos et al. (2009), pp. 16-17, 21.
158 Source: Delong et al. (2001), p. 3 [HBS Case: Taco Bell Inc. (1983-1994)].
159 Source: Schneider / Spieth (2013a), p. 26.

inhibits a gradual judgment process of whether the business model represents an incremental or radical BMI. TARAN actually developed a three-dimensional business model innovation scale to measure a BMI's radicality.[160] The latter is a function of the number of affected building blocks and the type of change within each affected building block. As for the type of change, TARAN offers these two options: existing/familiar vs. new/unfamiliar. However, TARAN conceptualizes a business model through seven building blocks and considers any change in one of them as BMI, which obviously makes further judgment on radicality desirable. By contrast, in this dissertation BMI is already understood as a system-wide change. With this in mind, the main purpose of the here-developed BMI-identification tool is to help in assessing whether or not a business model qualifies as BMI, rather than whether the BMI is incremental or radical.

Criteria for classifying a business model as BMI in the multi-business firm	Indicators	**Assessment** (Yes/No)
New or changed-to-become-new value proposition	- Customer need(s) addressed, and/or - Offering (product/service)	Yes
Innovative value constellation: New, and/or changed, and/or suppressed working practices to fulfill the value proposition	May apply to the activities of, e.g., - product/service design - finding customers - quoting - retaining customers - sourcing - inbound logistics - product manufacturing or service provision - delivery/distribution - claim management	Yes

Table 8: BMI identification criteria: *How is it new?*[161]

2.1.3.3 Subjective Dimension: New to whom?

The major finding from the review in section 2.1.2 that relates to the subjective dimension of BMI is the need to clarify the point:

- whether BMI must be new-to-the-industry, or
- whether BMI must be new-to-the-firm.

One of the prerequisites for dealing with innovation is determining on what terms something is considered innovative. In the corporate world, management defines what is seen as innovation from the firm's perspective. Typically, it has to decide whether innovation is something that is new-to-the-firm or new-to-the-industry.[162]

---

[160] See Taran (2012), pp. 84-85, 90-93; see also Taran et al. (2009), p. 8.
[161] Source: own Table.
[162] See Hauschildt / Salomo (2011), pp. 18-20.

Such a decision must be made for product and process innovation as well as for BMI. Hence, the BMI-identification tool must clarify on this choice.

Scholars see this particular aspect of BMI as rather controversial. SANTOS et al., for example, underline that a firm's new business model can be imported from another industry but it must be new-to-the-focal-industry to qualify as BMI.[163] MARKIDES embodies the same opinion when stating that BMI redefines an existing industry, although to him, BMI is synonymous with strategic innovation.[164] JOHNSON et al. even argue that instituting a new business model, which is not in some way game-changing to the industry, would be a waste of time and money.[165] ABDELKAFI et al. mention that among start-ups the business model's level of newness within the industry determines whether it qualifies as BMI.[166]

AMIT / ZOTT, on the other hand, emphasize that a new business model does not need to disrupt an industry to be classified as BMI. What is important is that it yields substantial benefits to the focal firm. Taco Bell's K-Minus program was not game-changing for the fast-food industry, but it allowed the restaurant chain to improve its bottom-line.[167] And since this dissertation's aim is to support managers in achieving profitable growth through BMI, the new-to-the-firm perspective, rather than the new-to-the-industry perspective, shall be adopted. With respect to multi-business firms, the new-to-the-firm criterion disallows those business models used by the firm in the past from being classified as BMI, as well as those currently existing in other business units (Table 9).

Another argument for adopting the new-to-the-firm perspective on BMI is that replicating another firm's business model is not a trivial task. Copying a novel product or process is relatively easier.[168] Of course, at a superficial level it may be simple to copy the basic "idea" behind a business model. But it is difficult for outsiders to understand in sufficient detail how a business model is implemented, and how activities are linked both within the firm and between the firm and its environment.[169] The numerous failures of established airlines to replicate the business model of Southwest Airlines illustrate the challenge of copying business models.[170] In this regard, WINTER / SZULANSKI found that even attempts to replicate business models from within a firm often fail:

163 See Santos et al. (2009), p. 14.
164 See Markides (2006), pp. 19-20.
Section 2.2.4 indicates how strategic innovation differs from BMI.
165 See Johnson et al. (2008), p. 57.
166 See Abdelkafi et al. (2013), p. 13.
167 See Amit / Zott (2010), p. 8.
168 See Amit / Zott (2010), p. 5.
169 See Matzler et al. (2013), p. 36; Teece (2010), pp. 181-182.
Sosna et al. (2010), p. 401, use the term "meta-model" in this context.
170 See Chatterjee (2013), p. 109; Santos et al. (2009), p. 9.

"Growth by replicating [a business model] requires the capability to recreate complex, imperfectly understood, and partly tacit productive processes in carefully selected sites, with different human resources every time, facing in many cases resistance from proud, locally autonomous agents."[171]

Replicating a business model takes time and effort because its complex interdependencies can only be discovered by "doing".[172] Hence, replicators usually try to copy the best parts of a number of different activities with the goal of creating something better.[173]

Criteria for classifying a business model as BMI in the multi-business firm		**Indicators**	**Assessment** (Yes/No)
Established firms	New-to-the-firm (corporation)	As opposed to: - copied from what the firm did in the past - copied from one of the firm's other business units	Yes
Start-ups	New-to-the industry		

Table 9: BMI identification criterion: *New-to-whom?*[174]

2.1.3.4 Process-related Dimension: Where does BMI end?

The statements drawn from the review in section 2.1.2 relating to the process-related dimension of BMI are listed below.

- BMI is essentially a process and should be studied as such.
- BMI is about changing an existing business model.
- BMI is about creating a new business model.

Innovation is perceived as the process of turning ideas into reality and capturing value from them. This process begins with the more or less deliberate resolution to further pursue an idea that can come from, e.g., R&D, copying, regulations, competitor behavior, market signals, or "Eureka" moments. The trigger idea's potential must then be translated into something new and launched in an internal or external market. The process ends when the innovation is transferred to operational management and thus becomes part of the daily routine.[175] Hence, for a new business model to classify as BMI it must be integrated into the firm.

171 Source: Winter / Szulanski (2001), p. 731.
172 See ibidem.
173 See Szulanski / Winter (2002), p. 64.
174 Source: own Table.
175 See Hauschildt / Salomo (2011), pp. 20-21; Tidd / Bessant (2009), p. 19.

Figure 1 by ASPARA et al. indicates that one business unit operates one business model.[176] In fact, JOHNSON argues that a business unit should not adopt and operate more than one business model at a time.[177] However, MARKIDES / OYON point out that firms have succeeded in playing "two games" at once in the same market without separating the business models into two units. They recommend analyzing on the activity level the extent to which separation is required.[178] Building on this recommendation, HARREN conducted simulation studies which show that the organizational structure for managing two business models depends on the type of interdependencies between them. Only in case of independence, separation into two different organizational units leads to superior long-term performance.[179] Moreover, SCHALLMO emphasizes that some products or services marketed by the focal business unit may require a different business model.[180]

Bearing this in mind, there are four different generic options for realizing BMI (Figure 4), whereas only three of them are considered as relevant for this dissertation. Firstly, the new business model can be integrated by a new business unit – and legal entity – that adds to those already existing. Secondly, BMI can be integrated by the redesign of an existing unit's traditional business model. Thirdly, the new business model can be integrated within an existing unit where it adds to the unit's traditional business model, i.e. the business model established before the BMI. In this case, the business unit would operate more than one business model. Similar to corporate functions, such a business unit could set up activities shared by its business models, for instance, controlling, purchasing or maintenance. Nevertheless, revenues and a certain cost structure must be allocable to each business model.[181] The arrows in Figure 4 symbolize the fact that knowledge about potentially value-creating BMI resides within the business units as opposed to within the corporation's headquarters.[182] The fourth option – foundation of a new firm by a third party outside of the corporation's larger scope of financial consolidation – is another way to implement BMI. For example, firms such as 3Com or Adobe were founded by former Xerox employees outside of Xerox. Those firms' business models represented BMIs. However, apart from license fees, Xerox did not capture the greater value from those BMIs, although its investments enabled the underlying technological inventions.[183] Therefore, in this dissertation, such a scenario is not considered as BMI in multi-business firms.

---

176 See Figure 1.
177 See Johnson (2010), p. 167.
178 See Markides / Oyon (2010), pp. 26-27, 29; see also Harren (2012).
179 See Harren (2012), pp. 145-149.
180 See Schallmo (2013), pp. 31-33.
181 See section 2.1.3.5.
182 See section 1.2.
183 See Chesbrough / Rosenbloom (2002), pp. 542-545.

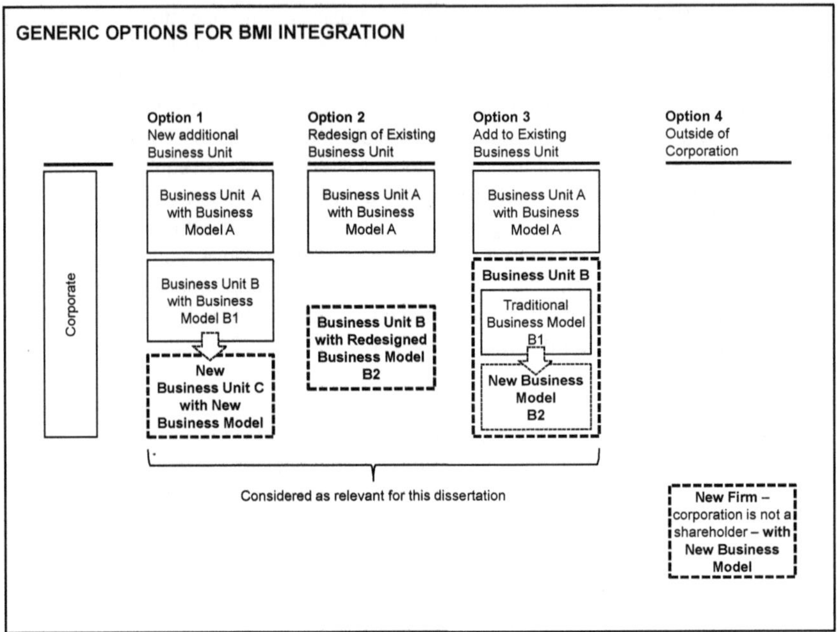

Figure 4: Generic options for BMI integration[184]

Additional indicator for BMI identification evolved out of the pre-talks
The criterion that a new business model must be integrated into the firm excludes business experiments to qualify as BMI. If a new business model is still in the trial phase, if it does not have some kind of profit and loss statement, and/or if a special status is still attached to it; for the purpose of this dissertation it will not be considered as an idea converted into reality. Table 10 illustrates the process-related BMI identification criterion.

Criteria for classifying a business model as BMI in the multi-business firm	Indicators	Assessment (Yes/No)
Integrated into the firm	As opposed to: - business experiment (in trial phase)	Yes

Table 10: BMI identification criterion: *Where does BMI end?*[185]

2.1.3.5 Normative Dimension: Is BMI successful?

The statement from the review in section 2.1.2 relating to the normative dimension of BMI is listed below:

- BMI leads to value enhancement for the firm.

[184] Source: own Figure.
[185] Source: own Table.

One of the constitutive characteristics of innovation is success. From the assessor's point of view, for inventions to become innovations, they must be successful in the markets in which they were launched.[186] The review of existing BMI definitions has shown that, similar to product or process innovation, a new business model must be value enhancing to qualify as BMI.[187] However, the extant literature on BMI does not provide a clear guideline on which measures to use for determining the success of new business models in multi-business firms. Notably, one measure of success to consider according to JOHNSON et al. is the payback time of the investment in a new business model.[188] Besides, the success and failure (S/F) measures applied in the context of *new product development* may also be relevant in BMI since new business models encompass new value propositions. GRIFFIN / PAGE identified the sixteen most appropriate S/F measures in product development. They were drawn out of a total of seventy-five measures used by academics and firms, and assigned to four different dimensions. These are:

- *Financial Performance Measures*: break-even time (from start of project), attain margin goals, attain profitability goals, IRR/ROI;
- *Customer Acceptance Measures*: customer acceptance, customer satisfaction, met revenue goals, revenue growth, met market share goals, met unit sales goals;
- *Product-Level Measures:* development cost, launched on time, product performance level, met quality guidelines, speed to market; and
- *Firm-Level Measures:* % of sales by new product.[189]

Nonetheless, the task of determining the success of a new business model is not straightforward. Essentially, measuring success should not be conducted based upon one single criterion. It is recommended to use a combination of measures ideally from different dimensions.[190] The benchmark for assessing the financial success of a new business model could be the firm's or the business unit's current and expected overall financial performance. Most likely, shareholders of multi-business firms would classify a new business model with margins above the firm's average as successful. The financial results of industry competitors might also be a suitable benchmark.[191] With respect to the business model's lifecycle, success could be determined three to five years after the model's integration.[192] Another issue related to innovation success concerns the possible influence of other factors.[193] In fact, the business model is a rather holistic construct. Still, unpredictable exogenous events beyond a

186 See Hauschildt / Salomo (2011), pp. 21-22; Tidd / Bessant (2009), p. 76.
187 See section 2.1.2.
188 See Johnson et al. (2008), p. 59.
189 See Griffin / Page (1993), pp. 307-308.
190 See ibidem, p. 295.
191 See Schneider / Spieth (2013b), p. 14.
192 With reference to product development success, Griffin / Page (1993), p. 307, propose the measure "% of sales/profits provided by products less than 5 years old". Skarzynski / Gibson (2008), p. 218, suggest as a measure for innovation output: "percentage of revenue coming from products or services introduced in the last three years".
193 See Tidd / Bessant (2009), p. 76.

firm's control might have a financial impact that must be considered when classifying business models as BMI. Moreover, measuring the success of a new business model depends on the data that, on the one hand, the firm generates and that, on the other hand, the firm agrees to make available (especially less aggregated financial figures firms may want to hold back).[194] Table 11 visualizes the criterion related to the normative dimension of innovation which is to be incorporated into the BMI-identification tool.

Criteria for classifying a business model as BMI in the multi-business firm	**Indicators**	**Assessment** (Yes/No)
Financial success	Benchmark against, e.g., - shareholder expectation - firm/business unit's average financial performance - industry competitors	Yes

Table 11: BMI identification criterion: *Is BMI successful?*[195]

2.1.3.6 M&A dimension: Is BMI created via M&A?

Additional criterion for BMI identification evolved out of the pre-talks

Both JOHNSON and ZOLLENKOP consider the acquisition of other companies as a means to achieving BMI. Without regard to the dangers of a too high takeover premium or cultural clashes hindering integration, acquisitions allow a corporation to quickly gain access to new business models. Firms such as General Electric, Procter & Gamble, Johnson & Johnson or Cisco make extensive use of M&A to acquire new technologies and to enlarge their business model portfolio.[196] In contrast, SINFIELD et al. view acquisitions and BMI as two different growth paths.[197] Therefore, the working definition and BMI-identification tool must state whether or not acquisitions can be accepted as a form of BMI.

As a matter of fact, some of the most often-cited cases of BMI did not involve M&A. Dow Corning, for example, the chemical manufacturer and global leader in silicone-based products launched a new self-service business model in 2002 without the help of acquisitions. The firm's traditional business model was intended for high margin products sold together with extensive technical support. After it realized that many customers no longer needed technical services, but commodity products at low prices, Dow Corning created in-house a web-based business model, which it branded Xiameter. Price reductions were achieved through strict product and

---

[194] See Griffin / Page (1993), p. 304.
[195] Source: own Table.
[196] See Johnson (2010), pp. 150-154; Zollenkop (2011), p. 209.
Moreover, Doz / Kosonen (2010), p. 380 mention acquisitions as a means to business model transformation.
[197] See Sinfield et al. (2012), p. 85.

process standardization.[198] Another often-cited BMI is Hilti's internally developed fleet-management program. The Lichtenstein-headquartered company is a manufacturer of high-end power tools for the construction industry. Interaction with customers showed Hilti that construction crews found it difficult to manage the tools by themselves. In times of tools being increasingly commoditized, Hilti seized the chance and became the industry's first manufacturer to offer this form of tool leasing.[199] Furthermore, Nespresso represents a BMI conducted by Nestlé without involving acquisitions. The food giant built this new business model that is more typical of a luxury goods manufacturer than a provider of fast-moving consumer goods internally.[200] Therefore, the view of SINFIELD et al. is adopted here. New-to-the-firm business models acquired through M&A will not be included in the scope of this dissertation (Table 12).

Criteria for classifying a business model as BMI in the multi-business firm		Indicators	Assessment (Yes/No)
This dissertation	Created without M&A	As opposed to: - acquiring an externally existing business - acquiring a share in an externally existing business	Yes

Table 12: BMI identification criterion: *Is BMI created via M&A?*[201]

2.1.4 Summary of the Working Definition

This chapter's first purpose is to develop a working definition of the concept of BMI in multi-business firms. This task is obligatory considering that neither a common BMI language nor a single definition scholars can draw on has yet evolved. The overall guiding question for this task was: *How to identify a BMI in multi-business firms?*

Based upon (1) the collected body of literature, (2) the results from the review of existing BMI definitions or explanations, and (3) the pre-talks with senior managers in four corporations, the working definition and the corresponding BMI-identification tool were built along the five dimensions inherent to the notion of innovation as suggested by HAUSCHILDT / SALOMO, i.e. the content, intensity, subjective, process-related and normative dimension. In addition, an M&A-related criterion was embraced.
The working definition reads as follows:

198 See (e.g.) Bucherer (2010), p. 43; Comes / Berniker (2008), pp. 74-75; Johnson et al. (2008), pp. 58-59; Koen et al. (2011), pp. 54-55.
199 See (e.g.) Björkdahl / Holmén (2013), p. 213; Bucherer (2010), p. 44; Johnson et al. (2008), pp. 54-57; Johnson (2010), pp. 64-69; Löwer (2011), p. 59.
200 See (e.g.) Koen et al. (2011), pp. 54-57; Markides / Charitou (2004), p. 25; Matzler et al. (2013), pp. 34-36; Skarzynski / Gibson (2008), pp. 181-183; Zollenkop (2011), p. 207.
201 Source: own Table.

Business model innovation is the process for the integration of a value enhancing, new-to-the-firm business model comprising a new value proposition and value constellation – here: without involving M&A.

The criteria and indicators in the BMI-identification tool allow assessing whether or not a business model qualifies as BMI in multi-business firms (Table 13). This tool renders it possible to select those cases worth studying to appropriately answer the research question. For presentation purposes, the "Financial success" criterion is placed at the end. If a business model meets all criteria, it classifies as BMI success.

Criteria for classifying a business model as BMI in the multi-business firm		Indicators	Assessment (Yes/No)
1	New or changed-to-become-new value proposition	- Customer need(s) addressed, and/or - Offering (product/service)	Yes
2	Innovative value constellation: New, and/or changed, and/or suppressed working practices to fulfill the value proposition	May apply to the activities of, e.g., - product/service design - finding customers - quoting - retaining customers - sourcing - inbound logistics - product manufacturing or service provision - delivery/distribution - claim management	Yes
3	New-to-the-firm (corporation)	As opposed to: - copied from what the firm did in the past - copied from one of the firm's other business units	Yes
4	Integrated into the firm	As opposed to: - business experiment (in trial phase)	Yes
5	Created without M&A	As opposed to: - acquiring an externally existing business - acquiring a share in an externally existing business	Yes
6	Financial success	Benchmark against, e.g., - shareholder expectation - firm/business unit's average financial performance - industry competitors	Yes

Table 13: BMI-identification tool[202]

[202] Source: own Table.

2.2 Placing BMI into the Arena of Corporate Entrepreneurship

2.2.1 Motivation and Method

TEECE remarks that the study of business models is an interdisciplinary topic, but – despite its importance – the concept itself lacks an "intellectual home" in economics or business studies. Mainstream textbook economics conclude from such theoretical assumptions as fully developed spot and forward markets, strong property rights, costless information transfer and perfect arbitrage; that markets are problem-solving. In consequence, economic science considers the step of figuring out business models for a new or existing product to be unnecessary. Strategic or marketing science has explored topics that somehow relate to business models, in particular the topics of competitive advantage and new organizational forms such as the modern corporation. However, business models have only recently appeared as a distinct research area in business studies.[203] The same difficulty exists for the currently emerging research on BMI. SOSNA et al. state:

> *"While dynamic business model evolution has been recognized by several scholars, it lacks theoretical grounding in the established literature which would [...] move the still shaky conceptual frameworks of business model development and innovation to more solid theoretical ground."*[204]

Equally, SCHNEIDER / SPIETH assert that an appropriate underlying theoretical grounding of BMI has not yet been determined.[205] Since such grounding would help academics to advance their understanding of BMI, SCHNEIDER / SPIETH discuss the explanatory support of three extant theoretical streams for research on BMI: (1) the resource-based view – "How to employ extant resources and competencies?"; (2) the dynamic capabilities view – "How to develop extant resources and competencies?"; and (3) strategic entrepreneurship – "How to explore and exploit opportunities?". Firstly, they distinguish BMI from business model development. The latter embraces improvements and continuous adjustments to a firm's established business model, whereas BMI emphasizes a firm's removal from the status quo. Secondly, they propose that the resource-based and, in extension thereof, the dynamic capabilities view provide appropriate theoretical grounds for business model development, while strategic entrepreneurship appears to be the suitable theoretical ground for BMI. However, they declare their theoretical framework to be of tentative character only.

Continuing this discussion, this section shows links between the here-studied concept of BMI in multi-business firms, as defined in section 2.1, and Corporate Entrepreneurship (CE). By comparing theory on BMI and CE, this section indicates that the arena of CE might be an "intellectual home" for the concept of BMI in multi-

---

203 See Teece (2010), pp. 175-176.
204 Source: Sosna et al. (2010), p. 385.
205 See Schneider / Spieth (2013a), pp. 2, 15-21.

business firms, and that the dissertation's findings may complement this broad and well-established research field. In the following subsections, the arena of CE is shortly introduced before aspects linking BMI in multi-business firms with CE are explained.

2.2.2 The Arena of Corporate Entrepreneurship

Scholars started to research CE about four decades ago.[206] Importantly, "corporate entrepreneurship" must be differentiated from "independent entrepreneurship", which is not undertaken within the context of an existing organization.[207] Over time, the way of depicting CE has varied considerably and so far, a universally agreed-upon definition of the term does not exist.[208] In an effort to reconcile the confusing terminology, SHARMA / CHRISMAN propose to view CE quite broadly as

> *"[...] the process whereby an individual or a group of individuals, in association with an existing organization, create a new organization or instigate renewal or innovation within that organization".*[209]

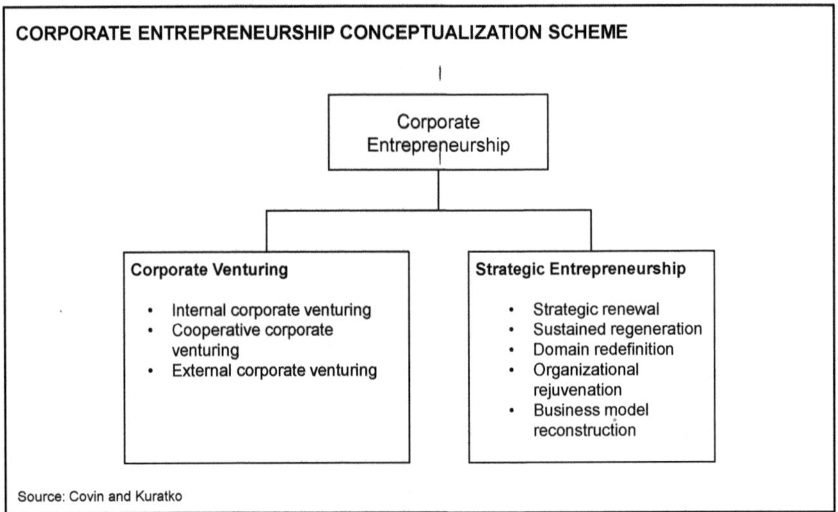

Figure 5: CE conceptualization scheme[210]

Such a view promotes the idea that CE does not only exist in the form of corporate venturing, but also includes organizational renewal. ZESCHKY points out that a common theme underlying the numerous different definitions of CE is that they all

---

206 See Covin / Kuratko (2009), p. 207.
207 See Sharma / Chrisman (1999), p. 18.
208 See Covin / Duratko (2009), p. 207.
209 Source: Sharma / Chrisman (1999), p. 18.
210 Source: Covin / Kuratko (2009), p. 208; see also Morris et al. (2011), p. 88.

link to innovative behavior by the established firm.[211] COVIN / KURATKO argue that it is less important to establish an objectively "correct" meaning of the term. It is more important to have a "CE conceptualization scheme" that captures the essence of the CE arena as currently discussed within the literature, and is one that CE scholars and practitioners implicitly agree with. In this sense, COVIN / KURATKO promote two domains as currently constituting the CE conceptualization scheme: corporate venturing and strategic entrepreneurship (Figure 5).

The first domain, Corporate Venturing, refers to the entrepreneurial act by which an established firm enters into a new business that adds to the existing businesses. Internal corporate venturing means to create a new business within the corporation, whereas external corporate venturing implies the acquisition of a new business that was created outside of the corporation. Cooperative corporate venturing denotes the joint creation of a new business together with external development parties. Usually, cooperative ventures exist outside of the organizational boundaries of the founding partners. Whether a venture can be labeled "new business" depends on the novelty degree of its product/market combination.[212]

The second domain, Strategic Entrepreneurship, is a young field that has existed as a relatively concerted research effort for only about a decade or so.[213] This research field was officially introduced with the *Strategic Management Journal's* 2001 special issue on "strategic entrepreneurship".[214] Its central idea is to merge the opportunity-seeking perspective in entrepreneurship with the advantage-seeking perspective in strategic management. Accordingly, firms must, in order to maximize wealth creation, continuously discover new opportunities (entrepreneurship), but they must pursue only the best opportunities and pursue these with discipline (strategic management).[215] Thereby, wealth creation can stem from discovering and exploiting a few massive, but short-lived opportunities or from many small, long-lived ("sustainable") opportunities.[216] COVIN / KURATKO note that, in comparison to corporate venturing, strategic entrepreneurship involves a broader array of entrepreneurial initiatives that "can happen anywhere and everywhere in the company". They can take one of the following five forms:[217]

- *Strategic renewal*: Adoption of a new strategy resulting in a fundamental repositioning of the firm within its competitive space.

---

211 See Zeschky (2010), p. 6. An overview of existing CE definitions is provided by (e.g.) Sharma / Chrisman (1999), pp. 14-15.
212 See Covin / Kuratko (2009), pp. 208-209.
213 See Foss / Lyngsie (2011), p. 1.
214 See Hitt et al. (2001).
215 See Foss / Lyngsie (2011), p. 8; Hitt et al. (2001), p. 488.
216 See Foss / Lyngsie (2011), p. 8.
217 See Covin / Kuratko (2009), pp. 210-211.

- *Sustained regeneration:* Introduction of a new product into a pre-existing product category or introduction of an existing product into a new-to-the-firm but pre-existing market.
- *Domain redefinition:* Creation of new or reconfiguration of existing product categories or market space.
- *Organizational rejuvenation:* Enactment of a major, internally focused innovation, such as business process reengineering, aimed at improving strategy implementation.
- *Business model reconstruction:* Design of a new or redesign of an existing business model in order to improve operational efficiencies or to be otherwise differentiated from industry competitors.

In the case of multi-business firms, the entrepreneurial event can happen in one or more of the firm's businesses.[218]

2.2.3 Link to Internal Corporate Venturing

Internal corporate venturing refers to the internal creation of a new business that resides within the corporate structure and adds to the existing businesses.[219] SANTOS et al. contend that BMI is not synonymous with internal corporate venturing. For them, the essence of entrepreneurialism is to match new products or new technologies with opportunities in the marketplace. Internal corporate venturing could only potentially lead to BMI. In order to exemplify their argumentation, SANTOS et al. mention an act of internal corporate venturing within Mars. The firm's R&D matched a new printing technology with an existing product, M&M candies, to create a new product, M&M candies printed with personalized messages. Marketing this new product at a profit required a new business model, entailing customized, small batch production and direct distribution. The authors conclude that BMI only followed internal corporate venturing.[220] However, the idea of personalized M&Ms could not have been realized without BMI. If the goal of internal corporate venturing is to implement a profitable new business into the firm (here in the sense of a new product/market combination), and if this goal involves the creation of not only a new-to-the-firm value proposition but also a new-to-the-firm value constellation, BMI would then become an integral part of the internal corporate venturing process.

A similar conclusion can be drawn from CHESBROUGH's research on several technology companies spun off from the Xerox Corporation in the 1980s. Xerox funded significant R&D activity at its own Palo Alto Research Center (PARC) on man-machine interfaces and other technologies later used in the personal computer industry. In cooperation with Xerox's CTO, CHESBROUGH looked at 35 R&D projects that the company had stopped supporting, and found that some of these

---

218 See Covin / Kuratko (2009), p. 211.
219 See section 2.2.1.
220 See Santos et al. (2009), p. 21.

projects became very valuable outside of Xerox: namely, 3Com, Adobe and SynOptics. Remarkably, none of these valuable projects used a business model similar to that of Xerox. At the time, Xerox's business model fostered technologies that allowed for faster copiers, the handling of very high copy volumes and maximum machine availability. Xerox stopped funding those new technologies it could not profit from within the boundaries of its existing business model.[221] In other words, Xerox was not willing or capable of designing new business models that would have enabled it to successfully exploit several of its new, in-house-developed technologies. Therefore, it can be concluded that BMI, in some cases, must be integrated into the process of internal corporate venturing in order to add a profitable new business to the firm. In consequence, this dissertation's findings on management practices supporting business unit managers in successfully realizing BMI may complement research on internal corporate venturing.

2.2.4 Link to Strategic Entrepreneurship

Strategic Entrepreneurship does not necessarily entail new businesses being added to the firm. Nonetheless, BMI, as the process towards a new-to-the-firm value proposition and value constellation, can be achieved by redesigning an existing business model.[222] Hence, there are also aspects that link BMI with strategic entrepreneurship, in particular with the following two forms: business model reconstruction and strategic renewal.

Business model reconstruction is perceived as the redesign of an existing business model aimed at improving operational efficiencies. Common activities within business model reconstruction include outsourcing and, to a lesser extent, vertical integration.[223] By definition, business model reconstruction is clearly not BMI. However, the fact that such an activity may lead to a new-to-the-firm value constellation constitutes a point of contact between both phenomena.

Strategic renewal is purposely defined broadly by AGARWAL / HELFAT as:

> *"[...] includ[ing] the process, content, and outcome of refreshment or replacement of attributes of an organization that have the potential to substantially affect its long-term prospects."*[224]

This definition emphasizes refreshment and replacement as opposed to other types of change and focuses on a firm's long-term prospects. As for the types of strategic renewal, AGARWAL / HELFAT distinguish between discontinuous strategic transformation, which encompasses the fundamental alteration of a firm's strategy; and incremental renewal, which, if pursued on a regular and proactive basis, reduces

221 See Chesbrough (2010), pp. 355-356; see also Chesbrough / Rosenbloom (2002).
222 See section 2.1.
223 See Covin / Kuratko (2009), p. 212.
224 Source: Agarwal / Helfat, p. 282.

the need for a much larger transformation later on.[225] The authors mention IBM as a company that successfully underwent strategic renewal twice: first, when it moved from electromechanical accounting equipment to electronic computing during the period 1940 to 1965; and second, when it moved to business computing services in the 1990s.[226]

In contrast, COVIN / KURATKO promote a narrower view of strategic renewal. They argue that firms only undergo strategic renewal if the newly adopted strategy represents a fundamental repositioning of the firm within its competitive space that deviates from accepted industry standards. These firms are then "playing new strategic games", also referred to as the outcome of "strategic innovation".[227] In their seminal 2001 paper on the topic of strategic innovation, GOVINDARAJAN / GUPTA conceive it as a change in "the rules of the game" by finding new answers to at least one of the three questions:

1. *Who are my target customers?*
2. *What value do I want to deliver to them?*
3. *How will I create it?*

Thereby, changes to one of these three "business model arenas" may have implications for the other two.[228] Indeed, some authors, e.g., BUZZAVO, GEBAUER et al., or MARKIDES, deem "strategic innovation" synonymous with "business model innovation".[229] Nevertheless, it is essential to note that three important aspects distinguish the phenomenon described as strategic innovation from BMI as defined in section 2.1. Firstly, strategic innovation by definition can only happen in an existing industry.[230] Secondly, a newly introduced business model is only considered strategic innovation if it is new-to-the industry as opposed to new-to-the-firm.[231] Third, a newly introduced business model only qualifies as strategic innovation if it enlarges the market by either encouraging existing customers to consume more, or by attracting new customers into the market.[232] Hence, Dell's direct sales approach in the personal computer industry or Amazon's e-business approach in the book retail industry, for instance, are considered as strategic innovations; whereas the above mentioned transformation of IBM in the 1990s is not.[233] Nevertheless, there is overlap between strategic innovation and BMI in multi-business firms. Both research streams have a business model focus and may therefore, to a certain extent, cross-fertilize each other. With specific regard to AGARWAL / HELFAT's broader conception of strategic renewal, MOINGEON / LEHMANN-ORTEGA point out that

---

225 See ibidem, p. 283.
226 See ibidem, pp. 285-288.
227 See Covin / Kuratko (2009), p. 211.
228 See Govindarajan / Gupta (2001), pp. 3-4.
229 See Buzzavo (2012); Gebauer et al. (2011), Markides (2006).
230 See Markides (2006), p. 20; Schlegelmilch et al. (2003), p. 118.
231 See Buzzavo (2012), p. 28; Markides (2006), p. 20.
232 See Markides (2006), p. 20.
233 See ibidem.

research on BMI may contribute to the knowledge of strategic renewal, which still remains largely to be acquired.[234]

2.2.5 Summarizing Remarks

This chapter's second purpose consists of the determination of whether to place the concept of BMI in multi-business firms, as defined in section 2.1, into the arena of CE. This undertaking has been motivated by the implicit need to place research of BMI in established firms into a broader, already recognized research field. In summary, this section demonstrates links of BMI in multi-business firms with three forms of CE: internal corporate venturing, business model reconstruction and strategic renewal. These three forms cover both of CE's currently constituting domains: corporate venturing and strategic entrepreneurship. Thus, it is suggested that this dissertation's findings on management practices supporting business unit managers in successfully realizing BMI complement the research on CE.

2.3 Literature Review on Performing BMI in Established Firms

2.3.1 Motivation and Method

EISENHARDT suggests that the a-priori specification of "constructs" is a valuable step before engaging into fieldwork. Derived from extant literature, those "constructs", or theoretical perspectives, add to the research question and help to shape the initial research design.[235] In her theory-building case study research, LASINGER experienced that a-priori specified theory served as an early orientation when conducting the first interviews with managers.[236] Likewise, with respect to generating grounded theory, STRAUSS / CORBIN point out that reading through existing literature may help scholars create questions they might want to ask respondents.[237] Consequently, the existing literature on BMI in established firms was reviewed, with the aim of identifying activities or behaviors authors recommend as possibly relevant to managers for performing BMI. Thereby, the term managers does not relate to a specific group of managers, such as business unit managers, but to all managers acting in for-profit organizations. Section 2.1.2 describes how the body of literature was collected. Importantly, academic or practitioner-oriented articles, working papers, or books were only integrated in the review if the text contains the phrase "business model innovation".

Without claiming mutual exclusivity, the identified activities have been subsumed into the following five "principles": (1) proactiveness, (2) experimentation, (3) autonomy, (4) conflict management, (5) leadership commitment and alignment. The term "principle" is used by COMES / BERNIKER in the very context of conducting BMI and

---

234 See Moingeon / Lehmann-Ortega (2010), pp. 285-286.
235 See Eisenhardt (1989), p. 536.
236 See Lasinger (2011), p. 14.
237 See Strauss / Corbin (1990), p. 51.

shall therefore be adopted here.[238] However, research on BMI is in its early stages and has not yet established any sort of fundamental truths.[239] Many literature-mentioned managerial activities or behaviors may be categorized as rather general suggestions and do not stem from formal studies.[240] That is why the term "principle" shall be put in quotation marks throughout this section. Furthermore, the activities identified in this literature review are not assured a place in the resultant theory. They are only of a tentative and preliminary character. Most importantly, it is notable that preordained theoretical perspectives should neither bias nor limit the findings of the fieldwork.[241] In the following subsections, the five "principles" containing the identified activities shall be described.

2.3.2 Proactiveness

Proactiveness refers to a firm's effort to anticipate new opportunities and to act upon them ahead of the competition. Proactive firms adopt a forward-looking perspective when searching for new possibilities for profitable growth and development.[242] With respect to BMI, MCGRATH emphasizes that managers must recognize threats to a business model before the model's ability to generate value is completely eroded. Managers must then mobilize resources to address the new situation by, e.g., BMI. In reality, leaders easily overlook how environmental changes undermine the viability of a successful business model. As a means for managers to notice in time whether a particular business model is under threat of erosion, MCGRATH proposes "critical conversations". Firstly, these conversations can include leading technologists in- or outside the firm, whose job it is to think about future possibilities. Secondly, they can involve "oblique-competitors", i.e. firms that are competing only indirectly with a focal firm for customers. Thirdly, such conversations can address potential future customers.[243] Likewise, DOZ / KOSONEN point out that anticipation and foresight give managers the time for deliberate reforms of business models. Besides applying standard forecasting tools to monitor known risks, managers may actively explore future usage concepts to anticipate how end-users would deploy a firm's future products.[244] Similarly, CHESBROUGH finds it important to undertake active tests to probe nascent markets with potential configurations of new business models as they allow a firm to learn ahead of the competition.[245]

Moreover, LINDGARDT et al. note that BMI, when approached proactively to explore new growth avenues, is more powerful than BMI, when pursued defensively to protect a dying business.[246] Correspondingly, TEECE argues that it is preferable for a

---

238 See Comes / Berniker (2008), p. 79.
239 See section 2.1.
240 See Holm et al. (2013), p. 328.
241 See Eisenhardt (1989), p. 536; Yin (2009), p. 69.
242 See Dess et al. (2008), pp. 434-435.
243 See McGrath (2010), pp. 256-258.
244 See Doz / Kosonen (2010), pp. 371-372.
245 See Chesbrough (2010), p. 359.
246 See Lindgardt et al. (2013), p. 293.

firm to initiate business model changes itself, instead of it becoming necessitated by external events. During the late 2000s financial crisis, for example, those U.S. investment banks that did not disappear entirely were forced to convert themselves into federally chartered commercial banks if wishing to survive, which caused significant business model changes and presumed lower profitability.[247] Furthermore, NUNES / BREENE firmly advocate the "principle" of proactiveness in BMI. Managers need to take action towards reinvention while revenues and profits from the current business model are still robust. Firms do not fail to generate new growth because they are bad at fixing what is broken, but because they wait too long before fixing it. In this sense, the authors state:

> *"[Successful firms] turn conventional wisdom on its head and learn to focus on fixing what doesn't yet appear to be broken."*[248]

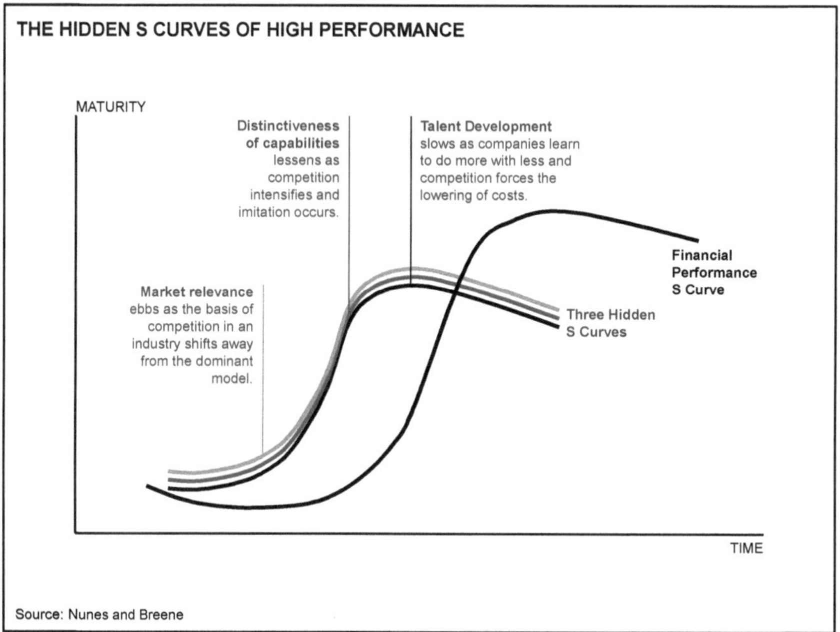

Figure 6: The hidden S curves of high performance[249]

NUNES / BREENE explain their argument by presenting three S curves – tracking the basis of competition in an industry, the renewal of capabilities and the nurturing of talent - hidden behind the financial S curve that displays to managers the profits

[247] See Teece (2010), pp. 177-178, 187.
[248] Source: Nunes / Breene (2011), p. 82.
[249] Source: Nunes / Breene (2011), p. 84.

generated by a particular business model (Figure 6).[250] These three curves visualize business aspects that decline earlier than financial performance and hence require particular management attention. Accordingly, successful firms anticipate changes in customer needs and create a new basis of competition in their industry before existing businesses have peaked. In the cell phone industry, for instance, the basis of competition has changed from that of price to that of network coverage, design, branding and apps. High performers also consider that the distinctiveness of capabilities linked to genuine offerings vanishes before it becomes apparent by the financial S curve. Building the capabilities needed for new distinct offerings may take years. What is more, successful firms understand that they need to develop the talent that drives new growth. Efforts to make existing operations leaner and less costly should not turn those people away, which the firm could rely on for reinvention.[251]

A seemingly different view is brought forward by SOSNA et al. From analyzing the single case of Naturehouse, they conclude that established firms initiate BMI as a *reaction* to difficulties.[252] Naturehouse is the brand name of a chain of franchised retail outlets that offer dietary and beauty products; it belongs to the Spanish family-owned Kiluva Group founded in 1986. Initially, Kiluva operated a wholesale business model typical of distributors of dietary products in Spain. The authors stress that only after the competitive intensity heightened due to domestic market liberalization in 1991, did Kiluva's owner-manager begin to experiment with the new Naturehouse business model. However, it took Kiluva five years, from 1992 to 1997, to explore and fine-tune the business model until it was rolled out on a larger scale. Throughout this period, sales revenues from the existing wholesale business only slightly decreased from € 5.5 m in 1992 to € 4.8 m in 1997,[253] which presumably, as profit numbers have not been disclosed, allowed Kiluva to experiment over such a long time.[254] Put differently, the creation of Naturehouse does not represent a drastic business model change in the short term dictated by external events to avoid immediate extinction. Kiluva actually started experimentation early enough to finally integrate a fine-tuned and well-tested, new successful business model. Therefore, it is also possible to classify Naturehouse as *proactive* BMI.

2.3.3 Experimentation

MCGRATH perceives experimentation as central for performing BMI successfully. She argues that existing business models are effective within the boundaries set by particular constraints. At the time of one of these constraints being lifted, due to, e.g., the emergence of a new technology, shifting customer preferences or regulatory

---

250 The S curve refers to the lifecycle of a product, business model, or industry typically entailing the stages of introduction, growth, maturity and decline; see (e.g.) Dess et al. (2008), pp. 176-183; Zollenkop (2006), pp. 167-203.
251 See Nunes / Breene (2011), pp. 83-84.
252 See Sosna et al. (2010), pp. 388-391.
253 This sales development translates into a Compound Annual Growth Rate (CAGR) of -2.7%; see ibidem, p. 389.
254 See also ibidem, p. 402.

changes, new business models emerge. It may be possible to detect such trends or changes, but it is hard to figure out ex-ante how to best take advantage of them via BMI. In many cases, the new constraints, or at least some of them, are not yet known when critical resource allocation decisions need to be made. In those cases, marketplace experimentation can be valuable to resolve the uncertainty.[255] As CHESBROUGH highlights, experimentation can create the data necessary to justify an investment decision. While it might be clear to managers that the old model cannot be applied, it is often far from clear what the new business model will turn out to be.[256]

TEECE adds that entrepreneurial managers may, to a certain extent, be able to intuit a new model, especially when understanding some "deep truths" about what customers want. However, the likely existence of "tacit components" prevents the ability to fully rationalize the new model upfront, which in turn requires learning by, e.g., experimentation. In other words, a business model draft cannot be assessed in the abstract, but must be assessed against a particular business environment or context. Assumptions about costs, customers, competitors, distributors or suppliers have to be validated or adapted by testing them in a real business context.[257] Felix Revuelta, for example, Kiluva Group's owner-manager, designed the first draft of the Naturehouse business model based on his professional experience in the Spanish dietary industry, as well as on some ideas he had collected from the industries in the U.S. and Europe. As those ideas had been previously untested in Spain, he engaged in a long period of trial-and-error experimentation accompanied by constant business model adaptation to eventually eliminate uncertainty about the outcomes of introducing Naturehouse.[258]

Similarly, YUNUS et al. understand experimentation as the preferable route towards the required learning if other sources of information are non-existent or unavailable. Because of the "fundamental nature" of BMI, simple market studies or client surveys might be ineffective for determining whether a new business model will work out. Instead, a series of small business model experiments would then allow for maximum learning at minimal risk.[259] Likewise, DOZ / KOSONEN view experiments as useful when performing BMI, especially if important insights cannot be generated via forecasting tools or scenario planning. Besides validating core business assumptions, experiments may also pilot change in established firms.[260] By functioning as a form of "early action", business model experiments may ease the cognitive act of reframing a firm's dominant logic.[261] Moreover, KAPLAN strongly

---

255 See McGrath (2010), p. 253.
256 See Chesbrough (2010), p. 357.
257 See Teece (2010), pp. 187-188, 191.
258 See Sosna et al. (2010), pp. 391-393.
259 See Yunus et al. (2010), pp. 315-316.
260 See Doz / Kosonen (2010), p. 373.
261 See Chesbrough (2010), p. 361.

promotes real world experiments as crucial to the BMI process. He strikingly formulates:

> *"We spend far too much time thinking and planning and nowhere near enough time experimenting in the real world to see what works. We need to try more stuff."*[262]

In his opinion, leading organizations should have several business model experiments going on at all times.[263]

With respect to effective experimentation, CHESBROUGH underlines the importance of an experiment's fidelity. Highest fidelity can be achieved if a new business model is tested on real customers in real economic transactions. Other important parameters for planning experiments include the cost of conducting them, the time until the learning occurs and, essentially, the amount of information learned. Even failed experiments are valuable as long as they yield some new knowledge that might help to distinguish between what works and what does not work. On the other hand, experiments teaching nothing new are considered "mistakes" since they were either poorly planned or badly conducted.[264]

CHESBROUGH further suggests that managers construct business model maps before committing to specific investments in reality. Visualization may help to clarify the configuring elements as well as the core processes of new business model proposals. Therefore, maps may facilitate simulation and, after adding initial experimental results, may support the design of new experiments.[265] With regard to business model ideation, HOFFMANN et al. found that groups using the business model canvas[266] generated ideas of higher quality and were able to select the best idea, whereas groups using brainstorming formulated ideas of lower quality and were not able to select the best idea they had generated. However, brainstorming led to higher group satisfaction and a bigger number of ideas.[267] EPPLER et al. conclude that, in practice, a combination of creativity triggering methods with more structured methods such as the business model canvas could be best when trying to find novel business model ideas.[268]

Another significant aspect relating to experimentation in the course of BMI concerns the financial valuation of investment decisions. According to MCGRATH, decisions on investing in business model experiments should be based on real options reasoning as opposed to more deterministic approaches such as economic value

---

262 Source: Kaplan (2012), p. xvii.
263 See ibidem.
264 See Chesbrough (2010), p. 360; Sosna et al. (2010), p. 392.
265 See Chesbrough (2010), p. 359.
266 See section 2.1.3.1.
267 See Hoffmann et al. (2012), p. 4; see also Eppler et al. (2011), p. 1334.
268 See Eppler et al. (2011), p. 1336.

added or net present value (NPV).[269] Real options analysis (ROA) transfers the valuation techniques of financial options to the assessing of investment opportunities in real assets that entail embedded options. Real assets include, for instance, land, buildings, plant or equipment. If an opportunity to invest in a real asset can be seen as a series of sequential steps, whereby at each step the investor has the option to expand, reduce, abandon or defer the investment, ROA potentially can be employed. These embedded options reflect the investor's flexibility and may add significant value that the standard NPV approach, which uses a single, risk-adjusted discount rate, can hardly take into account. Therefore, applying ROA may turn a previously unattractive business model experiment into an attractive one.[270] What is more, ROA may foster many smaller investments with a deliberately limited downside risk, but still with the chance of accumulating significantly positive returns over time, instead of putting all financial resources into the one project with the highest NPV. The latter approach typically depicts a pattern of high negative cumulated cash flow in the short term, on the hopeful assumption that the project will unfold as planned. This pattern is often referred to as the "hockey stick" approach, whereas an options-oriented investment strategy depicts a pattern of several "little hockey sticks" (Figure 7).[271]

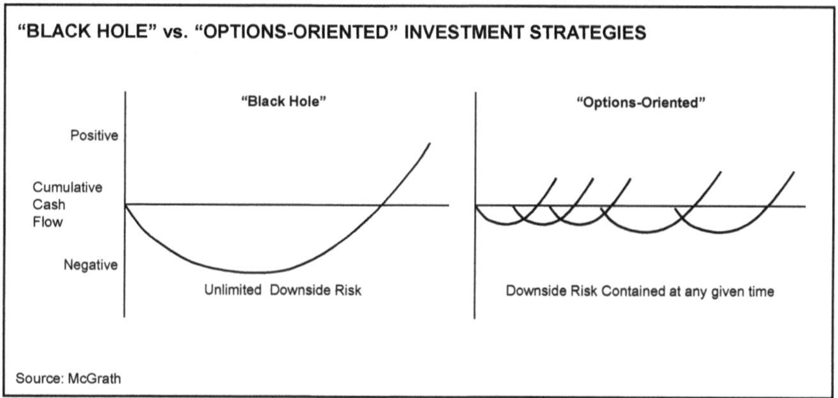

Figure 7: "Black Hole" vs. "Options-Oriented" investment strategies[272]

2.3.4 Autonomy

COMES / BERNIKER view autonomy as a "guiding principle" of BMI.[273] In essence, autonomy represents a type of empowerment. It refers to the authorization of individuals or teams to act independently, with the aim of carrying a business opportunity forward.[274] Thereby, independence relates to the situation in which the

[269] See McGrath (2010), pp. 255-256.
[270] See Dess et al. (2008), pp. 428-429; Hull (2006), pp. 713-727.
[271] See McGrath (2010), p. 256.
[272] Source: ibidem.
[273] See Comes / Berniker (2008), p. 79.
[274] See also Dess et al. (2008), pp. 432-433.

team charged with developing the new business model is not bound by the rules, metrics or notions of an existing model. TEECE emphasizes that adopting a neutral perspective is critical for shaping a new business model.[275] As indicated above, firstly, the value proposition should be designed in a way aimed at truly satisfying specific customer needs. Secondly, the value constellation must be composed so as to deliver the value proposition at a profit for the firm.[276] As a means to gaining a neutral perspective when creating new business models, DOZ / KOSONEN advise firms to integrate people from the outside, e.g., independent external directors or new hires among senior managers, consultants, or academic researchers.[277]

In fact, not keeping BMI efforts free of interference from the existing business may cause the new business model to be adapted to the existing one. In this case, a new opportunity's full potential might not be exploited.[278] Managers who keep the existing business model going daily and who are simultaneously charged with advancing a BMI initiative often try to leverage core capabilities whether or not these serve the new model.[279] Eastman Kodak, for instance, initially tried to "cram" digital photography into its established chemical film business model focused on having high quality pictures developed in retail stores; whereas other entrants in the digital imaging business such as Hewlett-Packard, Canon or Sony created completely new products that enabled consumers to print images at home.[280] On the contrary, Nestlé granted operational independence to the team charged with developing Nespresso and benefited from it. Remarkably, the team found that Nespresso needed other coffee beans than those used for Nescafé to optimize the new value proposition. This finding was pursued although it inhibited cost synergies in the area of purchasing.[281]

Another aspect related to the autonomy "principle" touches the budgeting process imposed on the BMI initiative. COMES / BERNIKER cite the example of a BMI team that was expected by corporate headquarters to present and justify its numbers on a quarterly basis, as with every other business unit. Headquarters then compared those numbers with the performance of the team's peer established business units. The pressure to constantly defend investment requests swallowed a considerable part of the team's time and energy and also led to wrong investment decisions. As a result, the BMI initiative was abandoned. This is why different evaluation metrics than those for established businesses should be applied to BMI initiatives.[282] JOHNSON notes that new business models should show their ability to generate profits rather quickly. However, an overeager push for scale and lack of patience with a process

---

275 See Teece (2010), p. 190.
276 See Johnson et al. (2008), pp. 54-55.
277 See Doz / Kosonen (2010), p. 374; see also Comes / Berniker (2008), p. 81.
278 See Cavalcante et al. (2011), p. 1336.
279 See Johnson (2010), p. 164.
280 See ibidem, p. 158; see also Gilbert (2001), pp. 3-4; König (2009), pp. 35-36.
281 See Comes / Berniker (2010), pp. 80-81.
282 See ibidem, pp. 79-80.

that needs time can put an end to the best-conceived BMI initiatives.[283] This "credo" for measuring success can be summarized with

> *"patien[ce] for growth, but impatien[ce] for profits".*[284]

One of the firms used by JOHNSON to exemplify the autonomy "principle" for performing BMI is Dow Corning. In June 2001, the firm's Executive Committee gave Don Sheets a certain amount of financial resources, a title and a deadline, to build a team whose purpose was to turn the idea of a low-cost, web-based business model into a reality. Sheets was a member of the task force of mid-level executives requested to come up with new ideas to stimulate growth.[285] This autonomy allowed Sheets and his team to figure out which conditions would permit such a model to be profitable. Substantially differing from Dow Corning's established business, these conditions included highly standardized products and lead times, more risk-taking salespeople, a new brand (Xiameter) and a very low overhead structure.[286] Initially, Xiameter's operation was limited to a small scale. Still, after going live in March 2002, it paid back Dow Corning's investment within three months, proving the new business model's profitability.[287]

2.3.5 Conflict Management

In the BMI process, conflicts can arise from employees and middle managers who are affected by a business model redesign, or who are supposed to support a new additional business model with the aim of exploiting synergies. CAVALCANTE et al. underline that employees who are asked to change their working practices try to make sense of it, which may be interpreted as resistance to change.[288] Typically, the knowledge about the BMI and its potential positive impact is known at first to only a small group of people, usually including top management. This knowledge must be integrated into the organization and involve people at all levels. In short, managers should establish a collectively shared understanding about the BMI's content and effects when implementing it.[289] As a way to achieve that, OSTERWALDER / PIGNEUR suggest conducting a highly visible, multi-channel internal communication campaign announcing and explaining the new business model. Such a campaign should make use of stories and visualizations to help people understand the BMI's rationale.[290]

---

283 See Johnson (2010), p. 142.
284 Source: Comes / Berniker (2010), p. 80.
285 See Kashani / Francis (2011), p. 7 (IMD Case: Xiameter: The Past and Future of a "Disruptive Innovation"); Johnson (2010), pp. 54-55.
286 See Johnson (2010), pp. 58-62.
287 See Johnson et al. (2008), p. 59.
288 See Cavalcante et al. (2011), pp. 1333-1334.
289 See Sosna et al. (2011), p. 393.
290 See Osterwalder / Pigneur (2010), p. 257.

One specific source of resistance is rooted in employees' fear of not having the skills required to execute the new working practices.[291] For instance, Hilti's sales force was used to selling power tools on the spot to the purchasing manager of construction sites. With the introduction of Hilti's fleet-management program, the sales force was asked to build partnerships with their customers' top management, which is indeed a completely different task. Hilti noticed its sales force's fear and committed significant resources to training and instruction.[292] Moreover, resistance may stem from employees being worried that the BMI renders their existing skill-set entirely obsolete. In this regard, CHESBROUGH notes that the vice president of a field sales organization might take strong exception to introducing online sales of the same products, regardless of the possible positive impact on the firm.[293] Such a conflict constitutes a barrier to BMI, unless it is addressed.

What is more, resistance to BMI may also be caused by cannibalization concerns of the established distribution channels, including the firm's internal sales force.[294] COMES / BERNIKER rank the latter as the most rigid of all corporate groups because sales people could see any effort to change the revenue structure as a threat to reaching their respective personal target agreement, especially if the current best customers are not those addressed by the new business model. In effect, failure to persuade the existing distribution channels to pursue the new business model might put an end to the BMI efforts.[295] Bearing this in mind, Dow Corning's management, when integrating Xiameter, adjusted the individual targets and performance incentives of its sales force so as to reflect total company performance and not just that of Dow Corning's brand.[296]

Before actually integrating the BMI, JOHNSON recommends identifying potential points of conflict by comparing the blueprint of the new business model with that of the existing one. Conflicts may arise at those places where the expectations and entrenched habits of the existing business model interfere with the success of BMI efforts.[297] Similarly, MARKIDES / OYON contend that an established firm intending to introduce a new business model should ask itself which activities it can operate together against the background of potential synergies, and which activities it must separate or redesign. In essence, separation should be considered if conflict seems inevitable.[298] Consequently, managers should also have a thorough understanding of

[291] See Bucherer et al. (2012), p. 191. The authors discuss a "lack of willingness" and "a lack of knowledge".
[292] See Johnson (2010), p. 67.
[293] See Chesbrough (2010), p. 358.
[294] See Comes / Berniker (2008), pp. 81-83; Johnson (2010), p. 160; Kaplan (2012), pp. 44-45; Teece (2010), p. 182; Zollenkop (2011), p. 206.
[295] See Comes / Berniker (2008), pp. 81-83.
[296] See Kashani / Francis (2011), p. 9 (IMD Case: Xiameter: The Past and Future of a "Disruptive Innovation").
[297] See Johnson (2010), p. 134.
[298] See Markides / Oyon (2010), p. 30.

the current business model(s). Otherwise, the extent of the BMI's impact cannot be determined.[299]

> *"We must first peel away the veneer of everyday operations and come to understand the [existing] business model at the core of our efforts – how it works, what it enables, and what it inhibits."*[300]

With respect to conflict management, TUFF / WUNKER add that focused pilots enable managers to test existing employees' flexibility.[301] In exactly this sense, Don Sheets conducted an experimental war game to test how Dow Corning's staff and systems would react to the requirements of Xiameter's business model.[302] Beyond that, OSTERWALDER / PIGNEUR propose to have people from throughout the organization participating in the BMI process long before the actual integration. Such a participatory approach may uncover conflicts before the new model's integration is even planned.[303] On the other hand, such an approach may contradict the benefits of the autonomy "principle".

2.3.6 Leadership Commitment and Alignment

In general, leadership refers to the act of transforming an organization from what it is to what the leader(s) would have it become. This definition implies that leadership is more than custodial management to keep the organization afloat. Rather, leadership is about improving the status quo through the design and implementation of a creative vision.[304] And as BMI is understood as the process of introducing a value enhancing new business model, several authors emphasize that performing BMI requires leadership.

KAPLAN, for example, clearly states that BMI must be led from the top because it requires the authority to act outside of the interests of the current business model.[305] BMI will not happen if senior leaders are satisfied with the existing business model and therefore want employees to solely focus on refining it. Likewise, DOZ / KOSONEN argue that BMI would not be possible without a top management team committed to taking the risks necessary to advance into new or redesigned business models.[306] Moreover, SOSNA et al. stress that the commitment and the resilience of the owner-manager and the top management team of Kiluva Group to repeatedly engage in business model experiments were critical to the success of Naturehouse. If leaders with significant decision power are obstructive to BMI, it would be almost

---

299 See Cavalcante et al. (2011), p. 1338; Santos et al. (2009), p. 44.
300 Source: Johnson (2010), p. 150.
301 See Tuff / Wunker (2010), p. 7.
302 See Johnson et al. (2008), p. 58.
303 See Osterwalder / Pigneur (2010), p. 257.
304 See Dess et al. (2008), pp. 378-379.
305 See Kaplan (2012), pp. 40, 131.
306 See Doz / Kosonen (2010), p. 376.

impossible for other managers to perform BMI.[307] JOHNSON similarly asks how leaders can expect anyone else in the company to engage in BMI when they themselves feel uncomfortable pursuing ideas for new business models.[308] What is more, from analyzing data of the IBM CEO Study 2006, BOCK et al. found that CEO responsibility for innovation is positively associated with an organization's engagement in BMI (b=0,36). This correlation proved significant at the 99% confidence level.[309]

With specific reference to multi-business firms, CHESBROUGH presumes that the general managers of business units are ideally suited to the task of leading BMI, unless they are being rotated to another position every 2-3 years. Unlike functional heads, business unit managers typically have the authority across all of the business unit's functions including, e.g., product design, manufacturing, marketing or sales, which is necessary for conducting business model experiments.[310] Besides, business unit managers possess a greater extent of knowledge behind the current business models and of potential value enhancing BMI; this is because, in contrast with corporate headquarters and central services, they continuously interrelate with customers and are deeply involved in daily operations.[311]

Nevertheless, as SANTOS et al. point out, BMI may require corporate approval, since such initiatives potentially alter the scope and risk profile of the corporation. Furthermore, it may be the case that BMI in one business unit impacts the strategic operations of other business units, leading to potential conflicts that may require corporate direction.[312] Beyond that, business unit managers who do not have sufficient financial resources to pursue a BMI idea will have to involve corporate headquarters anyway. And with reference to this kind of situation, a number of authors request firms to create a context of openness, trust and organizational justice. DOZ / KOSONEN indicate that business unit managers should be given the feeling of "personal safety"; otherwise they may not reveal their deeper motives and concerns.[313] Equally, SANTOS et al. note that business unit managers need "psychological safety" in which they can offer BMI ideas to corporate managers without the fear of punishment or personal rejection in case an idea is not approved.[314] KAPLAN adds that CEOs and their senior leadership teams should make explicit to the organization whether they are open to BMI – and, if so,

---

307 See Sosna et al. (2010), p. 400.
308 See Johnson (2010), p. 168.
309 See Bock et al. (2012), p. 297.
310 See Chesbrough (2010), p. 361.
311 See Santos et al. (2009), pp. 33-34.
In the context of "strategic innovation", Berghman (2012), pp. 21-22, emphasizes that the people who are interwoven with current business activities are also those who detect promising customer needs. Section 2.2.4 discusses the relationship between BMI and strategic innovation.
312 See Santos et al. (2009), p. 30.
313 See Doz / Kosonen (2010), p. 377.
314 See Santos et al. (2009), p. 36.

encourage ideas – or whether they want the organization to solely focus on optimizing current business models.[315]

Another aspect in regard to the relationship between corporate and business unit managers when performing BMI concerns the alignment of incentives. Business unit heads who are charged with advancing a BMI initiative should feel that it is both in their personal and their organization's best interest to embrace the new business model. Often, BMI projects carry differing expectations concerning growth and profitability than the existing business models do; a fact that should be reflected in managers' compensation packages, bonuses and promotions. Thereby, incentives targeting the near-term success of the broader firm may be counterproductive since BMI can take years to reach fruition.[316] Furthermore, alignment and consensus on the limitations, freedoms and financial targets of the business unit pursuing a BMI should be reached very early, in order not to divert managers' efforts on these struggles.[317] Next to pure financial incentives, a compelling mission and values statement shared by all managers to provide an inner cultural compass can be deployed to promote BMI.[318]

Moreover, OSTERWALDER / PIGNEUR argue for a strong, sustained and visible commitment by the board and/or top management for BMI efforts in the form of project sponsorship. Such project sponsorship signals the importance and legitimacy of the BMI and should be in place from the beginning.[319] Likewise, COMES / BERNIKER contend that each BMI initiative should be "spearheaded" by at least one member of senior management to infuse enthusiasm (although the authors do not exactly specify senior management).[320] At Nestlé, Camillo Pagano, the then senior executive vice president in charge of several world-wide strategic product divisions and business units, strongly supported the Nespresso initiative. He commented:

> *"People thought I was a 'nut' to spend so much time on this small thing and to support the idea. Nespresso is so different from what the company does in its day-to-day business. [...] You need champions at the top for a new idea. You need to give an idea support against criticism."*[321]

Business units, on the other hand, should regularly demonstrate to senior managers the BMI's progress in order to not lose their support due to a perceived lack of productivity.[322]

---

315 See Kaplan (2012), p. 40.
316 See Johnson (2010), pp. 165-166.
317 See Comes / Berniker (2008), p. 81.
318 See Doz / Kosonen (2010), p. 378.
319 See Osterwalder / Pigneur (2010), pp. 251, 257.
320 See Comes / Berniker (2008), p. 81.
321 Source: Kashani / Miller (2003), p. 5 (IMD Case: [...] The Nespresso Story).
322 See Osterwalder / Pigneur (2010), p. 253.

2.3.7 Summarizing the Results

This chapter's third purpose is to review the existing literature on BMI in established firms with the aim of identifying activities or behaviors that may turn out to be relevant for business unit managers to perform BMI. Without claiming mutual exclusivity, the identified activities have been subsumed into five "principles" and described accordingly. It is important to mention that numerous recommendations within the literature reviewed do not stem from formal studies, and not all recommendations are free of inconsistencies.[323] Nonetheless, the activities add to the research question and provide early orientation for initial interviews with managers. Notably, they are only of a tentative and preliminary character and not guaranteed to occur in the results of this theory-building, case study research. Moreover, it is to be mentioned that preordained theoretical perspectives may neither bias nor limit the findings of the fieldwork. Figure 8 summarizes the outcome of the literature review.

LITERATURE-MENTIONED ACTIVITIES OR BEHAVIORS FOR PERFORMING BMI IN ESTABLISHED FIRMS

Proactiveness	Experimentation	Autonomy	Conflict Management	Leadership Commitment and Alignment
• Take BMI action when revenues and profits are still robust. • Seek "critical conversations" to find out about erosion of the current BM. • Be aware of the three "hidden S curves" declining earlier than the financial S curve. • Actively conduct tests to probe new BMs in nascent markets. • Self-initiate BMI instead of having it dictated by external events.	• Experiment to find out how to best take advantage of detected trends and changes. • Experiment to collect data that justifies investment decisions if other information sources are not available. • Experiment in the "real world" as a new BM cannot be assessed abstractly. • Experiment because "early action" eases the act of reframing the dominant logic. • Use real options analysis.	• Adopt a neutral perspective when shaping a new BM. • Keep the BMI initiative free of interference from the existing BM to avoid inappropriate adaption. • Authorize teams charged with pursuing a BMI to act independently. • Leverage existing competencies only if they serve the new BM. • Apply different evaluation metrics: "patience for growth, but impatience for profits".	• Transfer knowledge about the BMI to people at all levels. • Establish a shared understanding about the BMI's content and effects. • Identify points of conflict before the implementation by comparing the activities of the new BM to the existing BM. • Provide training to employees anxious about not having the right skill set. • Resolve cannibalization concerns of existing sales channels.	• As a senior leader, clearly state your openness for BMI. • As a senior leader, provide a context of "personal safety" for managers to offer BMI ideas. • Devise a mission promoting BMI. • As a senior leader, grant authority to act outside the interests of the current BM. • Align the personal incentives of managers pursuing a BMI initiative. • As a senior leader, act as project sponsor of BMI initiatives.

Figure 8: Summary of the literature-mentioned activities or behaviors[324]

[323] See sections 2.3.1 and 2.3.5 (e.g., the recommendation to involve employees from throughout the organization early in the BMI process to uncover conflicts vs. the autonomy principle).

[324] Source: own Figure.

3 Empirical Case Study Work Approach

This chapter describes the course of action in the empirical case study work undertaken by the scholar in 2012 and 2013 to eventually identify management practices that support business unit managers in successfully realizing BMI. As suggested by EISENHARDT, information about the procedures of data collection and analysis is provided in order to enhance the readers' confidence in the results' validity.[325] Figure 9 illustrates an overview of the four steps that comprise the case study work and that build upon the theoretical foundation established in chapter 2. The following sections explain each step in greater detail. Sections 3.1 through 3.3 elucidate the method pursued by the scholar to arrive at the five cases that have been subject to an in-depth study. Section 3.4 explicates how the findings have been induced from the cross-case analysis. Finally, section 3.5 summarizes how the scholar worked to ensure the validity and reliability of the case study findings.

STEPS IN THE EMPIRICAL CASE STUDY WORK

Pre-Empirical Work	Case Study Work			
	Step 1: Initial Contact and Rough Case-Screening	**Step 2:** Begin Interviewing and Fine Case-Screening	**Step 3:** Final Interviewing and Data Collection	**Step 4:** BMI Process Model and Identification of Practices
Research motivation Research question Theoretical Foundation • Definition of BMI in multi-business firms • BMI-identification tool • „Principles" for performing BMI mentioned in extant literature	Make initial contact with four multi-business firms willing to support the research Pre-talks with one experienced manager at each of the four firms: • Explanation of the research goal • Collection of suitable cases Results from the rough case-screening: • Number of proposed cases: 19 • Thereof eliminated during the same pre-talks through the BMI-identification tool: 10 • Thereof remaining for study: 9 Determine which business unit managers to contact for interviews	Contact the business unit managers involved in the nine remaining cases If the business unit managers had left the focal firm, other deeply involved senior unit managers were contacted instead. Begin interviewing and fine case-screening: • Number of declined interview requests: 1 • Number of cases that turned out to not correspond to the here-defined BMI criteria: 3 • Number of remaining cases for further in-depth study: 5	Interview a second and if possible a third senior unit manager involved in the BMI for each of the five cases Collection of further publicly available and internal documents or archival records for "triangulation" Multiple follow-up telephone calls or emails to interviewees for clarification purposes	Within-case analysis • (1a) BMI process phases • (2a) Open coding of practices Cross-case analysis • (1b) General BMI process model • (2b) Literal and theoretical replication ⇩ Identification of management practices that support business unit managers in successfully realizing BMI

Figure 9: Overview of the steps in the empirical case study work[326]

3.1 Step 1: Initial Contact and Rough Case-Screening

The term "established firms" refers to organizations that emerge as survivors in an industry. In at least a minimal fashion, they satisfy some market demands and

[325] See Eisenhardt (1989), p. 548.
[326] Source: own Figure.

attempt to develop a competitive advantage over other firms seeking to offer products to the same market. Moreover, they create an internally consistent set of throughput processes that ensure that output and competitive advantage demands are met.[327] Typically, an organization is considered as established after fifteen years of existence which indicates that it has overcome the liabilities of newness and adolescence, reaching some form of stability.[328] Established multi-business firms are distinguished from single business entities by having a separate corporate headquarters and multiple relatively autonomous and discrete operating units. These business units are organized in functional departments with the business unit managers having profit responsibility. Corporate managers focus on monitoring, firm-level planning and resource allocation. Additionally, they handle the firm's external relations with shareholders and legislatures. Other group or division levels between the business units and the actual corporate offices usually function as part of the corporate headquarters.[329]

Initial Contact

The fieldwork began by studying the investor presentations of publicly listed companies headquartered in Europe. The goal was to detect indications of BMI. From this exercise, thirteen companies were identified as promising "research candidates" and therefore initially contacted. Out of this sample, four companies expressed an initial willingness to support this research. All of them fulfill the above described characteristics of a multi-business firm. Their fictive names shall be:

ChemCorp; ElectricCorp; OilCorp; TechCorp.

ChemCorp produces basic chemicals and intermediates from raw materials such as oil, gas, water and metal, as well as more downstream, application-specific chemicals for a wide range of industries. The product portfolio includes, for instance, construction chemicals, herbicides, food additives, ingredients for personal care items, catalysts, battery materials, chemicals for mining and water treatment, plastics and coatings. *ChemCorp* employs tens of thousands of employees and realizes annual sales of multiple tens of billions of Euros.

ElectricCorp's multiple business units engage in the design, manufacturing and marketing of products in the area of electrical engineering and serve a broad range of business-to-business markets where they face the effects of intense global competition. *ElectricCorp* is active around the globe and employs tens of thousands

---

327 See Ahuja / Lampert (2001), p. 525.

328 See Brüderl / Schüssler (1990), pp. 530-547. The term "liability of newness" refers to the reasons for higher "death rates" of new organizations compared to old ones. These reasons include the costs for inventing and learning new roles and tasks, the lack of an informal information structure, and unstable links to customers. "Liability of adolescence" adds that the highest risk of disbandment is not found at the very beginning of an organizational life due to an initial stock of resources, and because gathering sufficient information about an organization's performance needs time.

329 See Chandler (1991), pp. 31-35; see also Collis et al. (2007), p. 383; Santos et al. (2009), p. 29.

of people. The corporation's annual sales exceed the one billion Euros mark as of 2012.

OilCorp is one of world's largest integrated oil and gas companies. It engages in all aspects of the petroleum industry that entail upstream activities such as the exploration and production of oil and gas, as well as downstream activities such as refining, manufacturing, marketing, trading and the supply of crude oil, petroleum and petrochemical products. It runs a large, international retail network of service stations and also invests in alternative energy sources. With its tens of thousands of employees, *OilCorp* currently generates annual sales of more than one hundred billion Euros.

TechCorp is a global leader in electrical engineering and electronics that divides its activities into several divisions. For example, the Energy division is a supplier of products and services for the generation and transmission of power; the Healthcare division is one of the world's largest providers of imaging system and laboratory diagnostics; and the Industry division provides automation technologies, as well as software solutions for industrial customers. Other divisions offer mobility solutions or power distribution equipment. As of 2012, *TechCorp* has hundreds of thousands of employees and annual sales of tens of billions of Euros.[330]

This case study research relies upon managers revealing profound information that they may consider strategically sensitive. For this reason, it was determined that the managers' initial willingness to contribute to this research could be augmented by using fictive instead of real firm names. Indeed, many managers insisted on anonymity. The processing of all data in an anonymized form shall prevent any unintentional disclosure of competitively relevant information.

Multi-Business Firm	Position of Respondent	Form of Pre-Talk
ChemCorp	- Head of Strategic Controlling - Corporate headquarters - Job tenure: >10 years	via telephone
ElectricCorp	- Senior Project Manager - Corporate strategy department - Job tenure: >10 years	face-to-face
OilCorp	- Head of New Energies and Product Quality - National headquarters - Job tenure: >10 years	face-to-face
TechCorp	- Head of TechCorp in Region A - Group headquarters - Job tenure: >10 years	via telephone

Table 14: Position of respondents in pre-talks[331]

[330] The information for these four company descriptions is drawn from the firms' website.
[331] Source: own Table.

After the four firms' initial positive responses, the scholar requested from each firm to be referred to a long-tenured manager acting on the corporate-level who has an overview of recent intra-firm developments that could qualify as BMI. Notably, one of the reasons to focus on more recent events was to prevent, or at least attenuate, potential retrospective bias of the surveyed managers.[332] After short coordinative email or personal exchanges, appointments for pre-talks between the scholar and one experienced manager at each of the four firms were arranged. The pre-talks lasted between 30 and 45 minutes and were conducted face-to-face or over the phone (Table 14).

The overall objective of these talks was to assess, together with the senior managers, the availability of recent BMI cases, both those which succeeded or failed, for in-depth studying. However, after explaining the research goal, it was already clear that the managers were neither sure about the meaning of the term "business model innovation" nor about the criteria that are used to classify an event as BMI. Although assumable from the IBM CEO studies that found BMI to be on the CEOs' priority list,[333] this term is currently not present in the daily language of the surveyed firms. The pre-talks revealed:

- At *TechCorp* the term as such is not used in strategy discussions. Instead, *TechCorp* is looking for opportunities that potentially change *"the rules of the game"* in existing businesses.[334] The firm is constantly screening the competitive landscape to identify targets that complement its business portfolio. The implementation of new-to-the-firm business models is mostly achieved by acquiring other established firms.

- At *OilCorp,* senior managers frequently use the notion of *"blue ocean strategy"* when debating about strategic options.

  [This notion was coined by KIM / MAUBORGNE and refers to making the competition irrelevant by creating a new market space – the blue ocean – where there are no competitors. In contrast, red oceans represent today's known market space in which companies try to outperform their rivals with the aim of grabbing a greater share of existing demand. As the space gets ever more crowded, increasing competition turns the water bloody.[335] In their earlier work, KIM / MAUBORGNE called the logic that is inherent to the blue ocean strategy "value innovation".[336] In principle, it promotes a rethinking of existing products or

---

332 Retrospective bias occurs if events or situations are looked back upon with a preference towards a particular perspective or ideology. They may be attributable to faulty memory or to attempts to cast past behaviors in a positive light; see Golden (1992), pp. 848-860; Yin (2009), p. 102.
333 See Pohle / Chapman (2006), p. 34; IBM (2008), p. 47; IBM (2010), p. 28.
334 See section 2.2.4 on "strategic innovation".
335 See Kim / Mauborgne (2004), p. 77; Kim / Mauborgne (2005), p. 106.
336 See Kim / Mauborgne (1997), p. 103.

services.[337] BMI, on the other hand, is understood as a system-wide change comprising of both a new-to-the-firm value proposition and constellation.[338]]

- At *ElectricCorp*, managers link innovation with new products or processes. Linking innovation with new business models appeared to be a concept not used by the senior manager with whom the pre-talk was held.

- At *ChemCorp*, the term BMI as such is not used either. Though, the notion of "white space" can be found in recent capital market presentations. It refers to new business ventures. Furthermore, one category within the firm's innovation controlling scheme is called "new business model". It refers to a new application for a more or less existing chemical.

Rough Case-Screening
Nonetheless, the explanation of the BMI classification criteria, as introduced in section 2.1, rendered the concept of BMI in multi-business firms more tangible and enabled all of the four respondents to think of recent events, developments or innovations that could qualify as a BMI case. The respondents initially proposed nineteen cases, including those with both positive and negative outcomes (Table 15).

BMI Cases		*ChemCorp*	*ElectricCorp*	*OilCorp*	*TechCorp*	#
Initially proposed		2	10	5	2	19
Reasons for elimination	M&A	1			1	2
	"Only" product innovation		3	1		4
	"Too early"		1	2		3
	Conjoined with other case		1			1
Remaining		1	5	2	1	9

Table 15: Results from rough case-screening during step 1[339]

The content of each case was shortly discussed. By applying the BMI-identification tool, ten cases were already eliminated for further in-depth study during these talks. These eliminations were due to the below three main reasons.

Firstly, in some of the cases, the implementation of the new-to-the-firm business model was achieved by acquiring another established company. For example, in 2007, *TechCorp* finalized the acquisition of a software development house for the product lifecycle management (PLM) industry with a global workforce of more than 7,000 employees. Products included CAx software packages for product design (i.e.

337 See Zollenkop (2006), p. 140.
338 See section 2.1.3.2.
339 Source: own Table.

CAD, CAE, CAM), collaborative product data management software, as well as software for the planning and simulation of entire manufacturing processes, a concept termed "digital factory". *TechCorp* integrated the company into the division that supplies factory automation control architecture such as programmable logic controllers. The target's complementary product portfolio enabled *TechCorp* to become the first integrated provider of software and hardware across a complete product lifecycle. Tying the PLM software together with the controllers unifies virtual and physical domains and offers customers a shorter time-to-market for new product developments. Back then, competitors of *TechCorp* did not have own PLM software expertise. For this reason, *TechCorp* publicly described this acquisition as a "game changer". It was one of the firm's most successful M&A projects in recent years and, essentially, this was why this case was brought up for discussion during the pre-talk.[340]

Secondly, some of the proposed case contained a product innovation instead of a business model innovation. For instance, *OilCorp* introduced a new product to be sold at service stations that essentially failed to deliver positive results. However, the working practices that were necessary to manufacture and distribute this new product did not differ from already established working practices. Moreover, the firm could use its existing asset base. The same holds true for a case initially proposed during the pre-talk with *ElectricCorp*. One of its business units introduced a product with new-to-the-world technical characteristics that was sold to a new-to-the-firm customer group. Undoubtedly, with this move the firm realized a new value proposition. However, in order to deliver the new value proposition, the business unit leveraged the resources and processes in-place. As long as a new product or service does not entail a new-to-the firm value constellation, the innovation is not considered to be a BMI.[341]

Thirdly, in certain cases, it was too early to tell whether an innovation failed or succeeded. As argued in section 2.1.3.5, the success of a BMI could be determined three to five years after its integration. Some of the proposed cases were not yet in this stage. *OilCorp,* for example, works at developing an infrastructure that allows service stations to independently produce and distribute hydrogen for fuel cell vehicles. A very limited number of *OilCorp* service stations already run some prototype hydrogen pumps that, until now, have not generated any financial profits. Clearly, this project is a BMI to the effect that it encompasses a new value proposition and constellation. Overall, however, it is still being developed; a major roll-out has not yet taken place. Another similar example at *ElectricCorp* features the development of fiber-optic splitters, an important passive component in data networks. Certain lead customers have already received prototype versions and are eager to order more of this product. However, independent of whether it is a BMI or product innovation, it is too early to objectively assess the project's financial

[340] Sources: pre-talks' interview minutes and additional documents accessible via the internet.
[341] Sources: pre-talks' interview minutes and the firms' websites.

success.[342] Eventually, the pre-talks helped to identify nine cases that appeared suitable to be studied for answering the research question (Table 15). For all of these cases, the respondents were asked for the contact details of the involved business unit managers and of other senior unit managers or key participants.

3.2 Step 2: Begin Interviewing and Fine Case-Screening

Begin Interviewing

The identified business unit managers and other key participants were emailed with the request for an interview appointment. Attached to the email were a cover letter and one slide indicating the interview's content. The cover letter briefly described the significance of BMI for established firms, as well as the research goal. Furthermore, the letter showed why and how the managers were chosen for an interview. In order to enhance the managers' motivation to participate in this research, confidentiality and a free copy of the final results were offered. The slide attached to the email highlighted the fact that the interview would be about investigating the BMI's outcome and on how the manager had witnessed the BMI process. In three cases, the responsible business unit managers had left the firm and the pre-talk respondents did not know how to reach them. Instead, other experienced managers who were deeply involved in the events were contacted. One of them did not work for the focal firm anymore, but was still willing to share her point of view on what had happened.

Figure 10 displays the guideline for the semi-structured interviews; an interview mode that is especially effective with "busy executives".[343] The guideline's purpose was to ensure the rudimental comparability of interviews.[344] The shaded "essential questions" cover the BMI outcome and process. These questions were raised in all interviews and served as a path towards the discussion of, firstly, the BMI outcome and, secondly, the BMI process, with the latter being the core research problem.[345] The "sub-questions" functioned as a reminder to the scholar to learn about those aspects during the interview. They stem from the theoretical foundation set in chapter 2 and were only raised if the interviewee had not yet mentioned the underlying aspects during her narration. The actual stream of questions was rather fluid than rigid as the scholar attempted to create a trustful and open atmosphere comparable to a normal conversation.[346] In contrast to structured surveys, semi-structured interviews allow for some flexibility in the course of the conversation which helps to bring up new issues that the scholar had not preconceived.[347] Thanks to the nonrigid structure, unexpected facts or interesting details could be pursued easily.[348]

342 Source: pre-talks' interview minutes.
343 See Aaker et al. (2011), p. 166.
344 See Schnell et al. (2005), p. 387.
345 The term "essential questions" is drawn from Berg (2007), p. 100, who defines them as those which concern the central focus of the study. König (2009), pp. 158-159 uses the term "problem-focused questions" that similarly cover the core research problem.
346 See Sims (2007), p. 117; Yin (2009), p. 121.
347 See Axinn / Pearce (2006), p. 6.
348 See Aaker et al. (2011), p. 166.

Essentially, a case study interview is not only a matter of data collection but also of data creation. Before this type of interview, the data collected usually had not existed in such a form.[349]

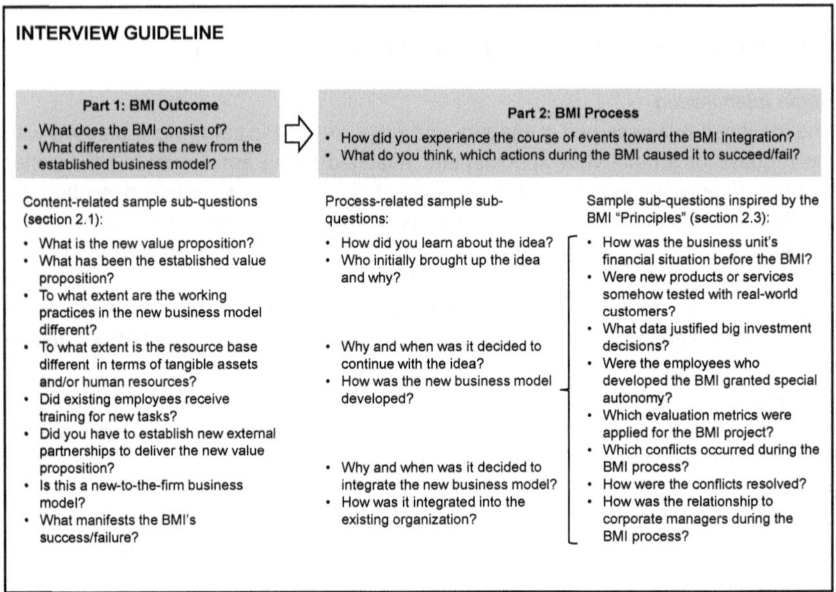

Figure 10: Interview guideline[350]

Table 16 shows that the step "begin interviewing" comprised of eight interviews. Seven of them were conducted face-to-face and one via telephone. One interview request was refused. Due to the sensitivity of the information, only two interview partners permitted voice recording. Instead, the scholar took notes during the interviews. On average, each interview lasted approximately 1.5 hours. Transcripts and better readable interview minutes were compiled within a maximum of two days after the interview using Microsoft Word.[351]

Step 2: Begin Interviewing	*ChemCorp*	*ElectricCorp*	*OilCorp*	*TechCorp*	#
No. of conducted first interviews	1	5	2	0	8
No. of rejected first interviews				1	1

Table 16: Overview of interviews during step 2[352]

349 See Sims (2007), p. 117.
350 Source: own Figure.
351 See Schnell et al. (2005), p. 388.
352 Source: own Table.

Fine Case-Screening

At this point, it must be noted that during the shorter pre-talks the outcome of the proposed cases could not be assessed as profoundly as necessary to classify each of them undoubtedly as BMI. Often, the pre-talk respondents knew about those cases without being directly involved in them. The interviews with key participants then revealed that, of the formerly nine remaining cases, four had to be excluded.

Number of cases excluded during step 2: 4 out of 9					
Criteria for classifying a business model as BMI in the multi-business firm		**Excluded Cases**			
		ElectricCorp "New End-User"	*OilCorp* "Energy Optimization"	*OilCorp* "Power to E-Vehicles"	*TechCorp* "Strategy Project"
1	New or changed-to- become-new value proposition	Yes	Yes	Yes	No permission for disclosure
2	Innovative value constellation: New, and/or changed, and/or suppressed working practices to fulfill the value proposition	No	Yes	Yes	
3	New-to-the-firm (corporation)	Yes	Yes	Yes	
4	Integrated into the firm	Yes	Yes	No	
5	Created without M&A	Yes	No	Yes	
6	Financial success	(n/a)	(n/a)	(n/a)	

Table 17: Reasons for excluding four proposed cases during step 2[353]

Table 17 visualizes the fact that three cases did not correspond to the BMI criteria and that one interview request was refused. Hence, this first round of interviews also helped to fine-screen suitable cases. The reasons for eliminating the three cases are explained below. As for the interview refusal, the contacted business unit manager wanted to check with corporate headquarters before sharing any information about this case with the scholar. Corporate headquarters denied permission. Thus, the interview was canceled. Indeed, as stated above, BMI case studies may contain strategically sensitive data. Therefore, it is of course understandable when managers do not wish to discuss such topics so as to protect the firm from any unintentional disclosure of information considered secret. Scholars researching on BMI must adapt to this.

353 Source: own Table.

Excluded Case "New End-User":

The case "New End-User" failed the criterion "innovative value constellation".[354] In detail, the business unit developed a product system that enabled a better state-of-the-art electrical connection between passenger rail cars. By considering that this product system was especially designed for one OEM customer and that the entire firm had not supplied the rolling-stock market before, this case definitely entailed a new-to-the-firm value proposition.[355] Nonetheless, for delivering the new value proposition, the business unit could leverage its existing resources and processes, i.e. its present value constellation, in the following ways:

- The product engineers with their know-how at hand were capable of, firstly, designing the product system according to specifications given by the OEM customer, and secondly, of further improving it over time.
- Partly, the business unit had to procure and to process a different set of raw materials. Nevertheless, the working practices on the shop floor, which were necessary to create the product system, remained the same.
- Remarkably, one manufacturing step was assigned to an external contractor. However, at the time, this contractor was already an established partner of the business unit and was hired for other product lines as well.
- Indeed, unusual to the established business was the fact that the unit's management had to handle a new contractual situation when entering into the rolling-stock market. In place of the usual sales agreements in product business transactions, the management initially signed a development contract with the OEM customer. However, the firm's legal department supporting the contract negotiations had dealt with this kind of contract before. It was not new-to-the-firm.

In short, delivering the new value proposition did not bring about a system-wide change for the business unit and the case can therefore not be classified as BMI. Interestingly, about four years after the successful entry into the rolling-stock market, the business unit insourced the manufacturing services formerly done by the contractor. But this move cannot be regarded as a system-wide change either because the value proposition did not alter. Overall, this case falls into the category of business model development as opposed to business model innovation.[356]

Excluded Case "Energy Optimization":

The case "Energy Optimization" failed the criterion "Created without M&A".[357] "Energy Optimization" is the disguised name of a new business unit that operates an absolutely new-to-the-firm business model. Therein, the business unit approaches manufacturing companies of all sizes with the promise of optimizing their overall energy consumption and energy cost per unit. Firm-internal research confirmed that

---

[354] Source: interview with "New End-User" business unit manager.

[355] Rolling-stock generally comprises of all the vehicles that move on a railway.

[356] See section 2.1.3.2.

[357] Sources: interview with "Energy Optimization" business unit manager and firm's website.

almost every company has untapped energy saving potential. The value proposition includes, e.g., on-site visits and tests, analysis software and the breakdown of current energy bills. *OilCorp* then generates profits in two ways: Firstly, it claims a minor share of the customers' annual energy cost savings that result from the "Energy Optimization" services. These profits are directly related to the new business model.

> *"The new business model is a great chance for [OilCorp] to offset the expected sales decline of petroleum products through the sale of services."*[358]

Secondly, it has the chance to convince customers to cover parts of their energy needs with *OilCorp* in the future. The profits from cross-selling energy from oil, gas, or alternative sources to those customers are then indirectly linked to the new business model. In fact, *OilCorp's* general business rationale is to market as much petroleum, petrochemical or gas-based products as possible in order to reach maximum asset utilization. The new business model enables the firm to get in touch with potential customers for some of its existing product lines, which eventually may increase asset utilization. However, of importance to the case selection is that *OilCorp* implemented the new business model by acquiring a stake in an established provider of energy consulting services. This information was only revealed during the interview with the business unit manager.

Excluded Case "Power to E-Vehicles":

The case "Power to E-Vehicles" failed the criterion "Integrated into the Firm".[359] After the pre-talk, this case was supposed to contain a failed BMI. But during the interview with the business unit manager, the case turned out to contain a business model experiment that yielded a great deal of learning for the firm. It covers *OilCorp's* first experience with supplying power to electric vehicles. In the 2000s, when it became obvious that vehicles with electric or hybrid drives will gradually replace vehicles with conventional internal combustion engines, the business unit manager responsible for *OilCorp's* network of service stations decided to have charging columns installed at a very limited number of existing service stations. Those stations were situated in areas with a relatively high density of electric vehicles. Globally, no other integrated oil and gas company had ever installed charging columns at service stations before. With respect to new working practices, the business unit had to accustom to the charging technology and it had to find a supplier of charging columns. *OilCorp's* engineers had to determine how to put up charging columns so that the service station still complied with the industry's high safety standards. As for the supply of electricity and the billing to drivers, *OilCorp* cooperated with a major utility company. However, after 18 months, the business unit uninstalled all the charging columns because it literally had not sold any power. There were the below three main reasons for this outcome.

---

358 Source: business unit manager in interview "Energy Optimization".

359 Source: interview with "Power to E-Vehicles" business unit manager.

- Firstly, the number of electric vehicles out on the streets compared to the number of available charging points was too small. Especially in metropolitan areas, utility companies had put up their own public charging points, usually in parking lots at places of employment, hotels, airports or shopping centers.
- Secondly, drivers of electric vehicles behave differently in terms of refilling. They do not wait until the battery is depleted before plugging the vehicle into a charging point. Instead, they recharge the vehicle wherever and whenever it is possible in order to maintain the maximum cruising range at all times. Actually, many of the early drivers of electric vehicles have charging points at home allowing overnight battery recharging.
- Thirdly, it can take hours to completely recharge a battery. Drivers could not spend all that time at a service station waiting until their vehicle was recharged.

OilCorp experienced in the real world that their first approach to supplying power to electrical vehicles does not work. However, the total investment did not exceed several thousand Euros, for which not even a business case was calculated. Purchasing a market research report instead could have been more expensive. Besides, internal business unit structures were not adapted during these 18 months. Therefore, this case describes a business model experiment. Undoubtedly, the management had initially hoped for better results. But the actual results triggered the management into considering other business model options in the context of electric mobility.

> *"Now, we know much more about the electricity market, the behavior of electric car drivers, and the safe installation of charging columns at service stations."*[360]

3.3 Step 3: Final Interviewing and Within-Case Analysis

The first round of interviews gave rise to five cases containing BMI-related content consistent with the BMI identification criteria. They constitute the empirical basis for the discovery of answers to the research question. All of the five cases took place within different business units of *ChemCorp* and *ElectricCorp*. Table 18 displays that three cases comprise of successfully integrated BMIs, one case describes an integrated but financially disastrous BMI, and one case encompasses a blocked BMI in an eventually sold business unit, which represents another type of BMI failure.

For each of the five cases, a second and if possible a third key participant was interviewed (Table 19). Thereby, multiple points of view on what had happened and on what should be considered as an important management practice were gathered. The answer to who would be a suitable second manager to contact about the respective case became obvious during the first interviews and corresponded to the names mentioned in the pre-talks. Those managers were emailed with the request for an interview appointment, again with the email enclosing a cover letter and a slide

[360] Source: business unit manager in interview "Power to E-Vehicle".

on the interview's content. YIN contends that interviewers must be able to interpret the information as it is being collected in order to know immediately if several sources of information contradict one another.[361] Therefore, in preparation for the second case interview, the notes and other documents received from the first interview were examined intensively. Thus, seeming contradictions or different views appearing in the second or third interview could be noticed and further investigated. In addition, those points that remained unclear after the first case interview could be raised again during the second and third interview. Similarly to the first round of interviews, voice recording was only permitted by two managers. Where voice recording was not permitted, notes were taken and converted into a better readable electronic document right after each interview.

<table>
<tr><th colspan="2">Criteria for classifying a business model as BMI in the multi-business firm</th><th>BMI Success "New Tech-Domain"</th><th>BMI Success "One-Stop Solution"</th><th>BMI Success "Integrate for Control"</th><th>BMI Failed "Special-to-Standard"</th><th colspan="2">BMI Blocked "System House"</th></tr>
<tr><td>1</td><td>New or changed-to-become-new value proposition</td><td>Yes</td><td>Yes</td><td>Yes</td><td>Yes</td><td rowspan="6">The BM option "System House" was under discussion but not pursued. Instead, the business unit was sold.</td><td>Yes</td></tr>
<tr><td>2</td><td>Innovative value constellation</td><td>Yes</td><td>Yes</td><td>Yes</td><td>Yes</td><td>Yes</td></tr>
<tr><td>3</td><td>New-to-the-firm (corporation)</td><td>Yes</td><td>Yes</td><td>Yes</td><td>Yes</td><td>Yes</td></tr>
<tr><td>4</td><td>Integrated into the firm</td><td>Yes</td><td>Yes</td><td>Yes</td><td>Yes</td><td>Yes</td></tr>
<tr><td>5</td><td>Created without M&A</td><td>Yes</td><td>Yes</td><td>Yes</td><td>Yes</td><td>Yes</td></tr>
<tr><td>6</td><td>Financial success</td><td>Yes</td><td>Yes</td><td>Yes</td><td>No</td><td>n/a</td></tr>
</table>

Table 18: Applying the BMI criteria to the five final cases[362]

The data gathered from all interview rounds was then examined with the aim of identifying further contradictory or open points within the cases that needed clarification by the surveyed managers. In consequence, several follow-up questions were forwarded to the affected managers, and they were responded to either via telephone or email. Hence, data collection and data analysis partly overlapped, which EISENHARDT denotes as a striking feature of theory-building case study

[361] See Yin (2009), pp. 71-72.
[362] Source: own Table.

research.[363] In the context of grounded theory, STRAUSS / CORBIN also point out that data collection and data analysis are interwoven processes because analysis can direct further data collection.[364] During the interviews, each manager was asked for additional internal documents or archival records not available to the public that would allow for a better understanding of the process and the outcome of the BMI. In fact, additional documents, such as internal strategy presentations, archived emails, board meeting minutes, business plans or financials, were provided for each of the five cases (Table 19). In one interview, the scholar was shown internal documents as proof of the interviewee's argumentation, but was not granted copies of them due to confidentiality concerns. In relation to two BMI success cases, the scholar received guided on-site tours covering the new manufacturing cell or the new office building. Overall, these tours helped obtain an even clearer picture of the BMI's content. Indeed, YIN lists "direct observations" as another source of evidence in a case study.[365] In addition, publicly available information was collected. Among this type of data source were the firms' websites, annual reports, investor presentations as well as press articles from newspapers and magazines. Public sources were mainly used as a complement or confirmation of what was already provided during and after the interviews. As proposed by YIN, all textual data including the interview minutes were entered into a case study database.[366]

In general, the sampling of cases is very important in theory-building case study research, since only a limited number of cases can be studied.[367] This "polar type" sample presented here is carefully selected. It combines replication logic with failure analysis and therefore stimulates a multi-faceted focus on the process of conducting BMI. It fosters both the clearer identification, as well as the consideration of otherwise unmentioned management practices.[368]

3.4 Step 4: BMI Process Model and Identification of Practices

The heart of building theory from case studies is data analysis, which is also the most difficult part.[369] EISENHARDT recommends separating data analysis from multiple cases into the two subsequent key steps within- and cross-case analysis. The first key step is crucial to the generation of insight and typically consists of compiling in-depth case descriptions. They help scholars to cope with the large volume of data early in the analysis process and enable them to become intimately familiar with each case as a stand-alone object. Within-case analysis allows the patterns of each case to emerge before searching for patterns across cases. In essence, a rich familiarity with each case can stimulate a fertile cross-case comparison. The main goal of the

363 See Eisenhardt (1989), p. 538.
364 See Strauss / Corbin (1990), p. 59.
365 See Yin (2009), p. 109.
366 See Yin (2009), pp. 118-122.
367 See Eisenhardt (1989), p. 537.
368 See Eisenhardt (1989), p. 537; Eisenhardt / Graebner (2007), p. 27; Ghezzi et al. (2010), p. 213; Strauss / Corbin (1990), p. 109.
369 See Eisenhardt (1989), p. 539.

second key step is then to reveal patterns that exist across cases and thus set the basis for generalizing the evidence and for deriving hypotheses.[370]

Case	Primary data	Internal secondary data	Public secondary data
New-Tech Domain	- Pre-talk - Two personal interviews 1) Business unit manager 2) Senior sales manager - Three "follow-ups"	- Initial business plan - Financials of business unit	- Firm's website - Annual reports
One-Stop Solution	- Pre-talk - Two personal interviews 1) Business unit manager 2) Head of new business model - Three "follow-ups"	- Strategy and marketing presentations - Speech manuscripts - Copy of sales contract - Financials of business unit	- Firm's website - Annual reports
Integrate for Control	- Pre-talk - Three personal interviews 1) Account manager 2) Department head 3) R&D manager - Two "follow-ups"	- Annual reports from the 1990s	- Firm's website - Annual reports - Investor presentations - Press articles accessed via Factiva[371]
Special-to-Standard	- Pre-Talk - Two personal interviews 1) Assistant to the business unit manager 2) Plant manager - One "follow-up"	- Strategy presentation - Employee newspaper	- Firm's website - Annual reports - Shareholder newsletter - Press articles accessed via Factiva[363]
System House	- Pre-Talk - Two personal interviews 1) Plant director 2) Senior project manager	- Positioning paper - Strategy presentations - Controlling reports - Board meeting minutes - Archived personal notes - Archived email communication - Financials of business unit	- Firm's website - Annual reports

Table 19: Overview of input for data analysis[372]

[370] See ibidem, p. 540.
[371] See www.factiva.com. Factiva provides access to more than 10,000 sources of business information, such as "The Wall Street Journal".
[372] Source: own Table.

Notably, a commonly agreed standard does not exist regarding the type of analytical technique to be used for obtaining valid and reliable results when pursuing a multiple-case design.[373] EISENHARDT, for example, lists three different techniques: The first one is to select categories or dimensions stemming from the research problem, existing literature or the scholar "and then to look for within-group similarities coupled with intergroup differences". The second technique is to take pairs of cases and to list similarities and differences before proceeding to the next case study. Such forced comparisons can result in new and unanticipated categories. The third technique is to divide the data by data source, to exploit the unique insights from each source of evidence, and then to compare whether the same patterns emerge from different sources. Alternatively, the case studies can be split into groups, focusing on one group of cases initially, while later turning to the remaining cases.[374] KÖNIG used analytical replication by testing whether explanations induced from one case were literally or theoretically replicated by the other cases.[375] As described below, a technique utilizing facets of both EISENHARDT's and KÖNIG's methods was applied in this dissertation.

Independent of any specific technique, YIN stresses that high-quality data analysis requires attending to all the evidence collected and presenting the evidence free of any interpretation.[376] The use of multiple sources of evidence for corroborating the same facts is frequently called triangulation.[377] BERG lists important advantages of data triangulation:

> *"By [triangulation], researchers obtain a better, more substantive picture of reality; a richer, more complete array of symbols and theoretical concepts; and a means of verifying many of these elements."*[378]

Table 19 displays the collected primary and secondary data, sorted by case and source, which was analyzed for eventually identifying management practices that support business unit managers in successfully realizing BMI.

BMI Process Model

The entire collected data was analyzed several times on a case by case basis. Firstly, the data was analyzed with the goal of becoming familiar with the BMI's outcome. For each case, it was assessed how the new business model meets the BMI identification criteria and why the case is suited for theory induction with respect to the research question. Secondly, the data was analyzed with the goal of thoroughly understanding the process from the idea to the final integration of the new business model. As for the two non-successful BMIs, the process description spans

373 See ibidem, p. 539; Yin (2009), p. 127.
374 See Eisenhardt (1989), pp. 540-541.
375 See König (2009), p. 167.
376 See (Yin), p. 126.
377 See Eisenhardt (1989), p. 538; Yin (2009), pp. 114-117.
378 Source: Berg (2007), p. 5.

up to the dissolution or divestment of the business unit. Hereby, single events were arrayed into a chronological order and then merged into broader, discrete phases. With such phases in hand, it was possible to draw a clearly laid-out process model for each case. Thirdly, the process models were compared across cases. The similarities and differences between them were determined, which partly led to an adaption and alignment of the phases' wording. Fourthly, the single-case process models could be integrated into one conceptual BMI process model covering all of the studied cases. Importantly, chronologies do not only support in attaining a holistic understanding of the events; they also support in identifying cause-and-effect relationships, since the basic sequence of a cause and its effect cannot be temporally inverted.[379] The conceptual BMI process model facilitated the delineation of distinct management practices and enabled their attribution to single phases.

Identification of General Management Practices

The subsequent goal of data analysis was to induce generalizable management practices. All of the cases were examined one by one, over two successional rounds. The first round of data analysis followed the method of "open coding", as described by STRAUSS / CORBIN. It is defined as "the process of breaking down, examining, comparing, conceptualizing, and categorizing data."[380] Essentially, codes in the form of tags or labels are assigned to discrete happenings, events, and other instances of phenomena.[381] These codes summarize the meaning given to certain "chunks" of the data collected during the fieldwork.[382] Similar discrete happenings are given the same code.[383] Later, similar codes can be grouped under a higher-order, more abstract code, called a category.[384] As characteristic of the open coding process, the codes are not pre-determined, but rather resultant from the open coding. The name chosen for a code is usually the one that appears most logically related to the empirical data it represents. Among other sources, the code names can be inspired by extant literature or by the words and phrases used by the informants themselves, called "in vivo" codes.[385]

The first round of data analysis began by grouping the cases into successes and failures. In the success cases, codes were assigned to any form of management action, whereby coherent textual statements expressed either by the interviewees or by other sources represented the unit of analysis.[386] In this sense, a code represents a management practice. In the failure cases, codes were assigned to situations and statements indicating problems, deficiencies or concerns.

379 See Yin (2009), p. 148.
380 See Strauss / Corbin (1990), p. 61.
381 See ibidem.
382 See Miles / Huberman (1994), p. 56.
383 See Strauss / Corbin (1990), p. 63.
384 See ibidem, p. 65.
385 See ibidem, pp. 67-69.
386 See König (2009), p. 163; Miles / Huberman (1994), p. 56; Strauss / Corbin (1990), p. 72.

Notably, the coding was conducted with the help of the computer software NVivo® which was specially designed to support qualitative data analysis.[387] Of course, the intellectual analysis work still remains with the scholar, but by using this kind of software, speed, clarity and traceability of the analysis are improved.[388] Importantly, NVivo® allowed all of the collected data to be imported.[389] After the open coding of each case, the entire initial set of codes was reviewed with the aim of consolidating similar codes within and across cases, i.e. codes encompassing similar content, into one code. In consequence, a coding scheme evolved that guided the second round of data analysis. Again, one code represents one management practice.

During the second round of data analysis, the coding scheme was applied to the source material, once more on a case by case basis starting with the success cases. In this group of cases, coherent textual statements were assigned to a code if they expressed the execution of the respective underlying management practice. Across the success cases, literal replication was sought, which aims at finding the same explanations for those BMIs with successful outcomes.[390] Then, in the group of failure cases, textual statements were assigned to a code if they indicated that the respective underlying management practice was not carried out. Hence, across the failure cases, theoretical replication was sought, which refers to the occurrence of contrasting results due to predictable reasons.[391] Iteratively, over the course of this second round of data analysis, adaptations were made to the wording of the practices. The resulting coding scheme is displayed in the appendix.[392] Figure 11 visualizes the coding scheme's structure with an example.

According to MAYRING, the coding scheme is at the heart of structural content analysis because it allows scholars to concentrate analysis on the most relevant aspects and augments the comparability of results. It should list the precisely defined codes, and for each code at least one anchoring example from the source material and the coding rule. The latter determines which textual statements are to be assigned to which codes.[393] Figure 11 depicts that each management practice is attributed to one BMI process phase, which enhances orientation. Moreover, due to the fact that both success and failure cases were coded, anchoring examples for both case types are given. Based on the logic of theoretical replication, the coding rules for failure cases are opposite to the ones for success cases.

---

387 NVivo® version 10 was used.

388 See Kuckartz (2007), p. 13; Yin (2009), pp. 127-130.

389 Yin (2009), p. 129, underlines that the entire data collection must be imported for the computer-assisted qualitative data analysis to be most effective.

390 See ibidem, p. 140.

391 See ibidem.

392 See appendix.

393 See Mayring (2010), pp. 602-603, 608.

STRUCTURE OF CODING SCHEME

#	BMI Process: Phase	BMI Process: Sub-phase and Block	Definition of Management Practice	Anchoring example from success cases	Coding rule	Anchoring example from failure cases	Coding rule
4	Realization Phase	*Sub-Phase:* Development *Block:* Value Proposition	Business unit managers should support flexibility and iterative testing directly with customers when developing the most promising new value proposition. *Test iteratively in the real world*	"The cable engineering and installation requirements were relatively small in this first project. [...] It can be seen as a test with customers."	Code if it indicates a flexible and/or iterative approach to real-world testing of the new value proposition.	"[...] they promised a lot to the customer. They strongly emphasized the firm's existing skill set."	Opposite to coding rule for successful cases

See appendix for full coding scheme.

Figure 11: Structure of coding scheme[394]

3.5 Validity and Reliability of the Case Study Findings

All empirical research must meet certain quality criteria.[395] As for theory-building case study research, EISENHARDT explicitly refers to YIN in this regard, who stresses that validity – i.e. construct, internal and external validity – as well as reliability are criteria for assessing the quality of case study findings.[396]

Construct validity is ensured if correct operational measures for the concepts being studied are employed. One of the here-adopted tactics for increasing construct validity consists of using multiple sources of evidence allowing for triangulation.[397] Another tactic is to have the draft case study report reviewed by key informants.[398] In this dissertation, several follow-up emails and telephone calls were exchanged with the surveyed managers in order to confirm the scholar's correct understanding of the events under study.

Internal validity relates to the "truth value" of the case study findings, in addition to the question of whether the findings make sense to the people under study and to the readers.[399] In general, to the extent that other potentially relevant variables can be excluded, a greater "truth value" can be assigned to the discovered relationships between dependent and independent variables.[400] The main tactic used in this

394 Source: own Figure adapted from Mayring (2010), p. 608.
395 See Gummesson (2008), p. 39.
396 See Eisenhardt (1989), p. 534; Yin (2009), pp. 40-45.
397 See Yin (2009), pp. 41-42.
398 See ibidem.
399 See Miles / Huberman (1994), p. 278.
400 See Yin (2009), pp. 42-44.

dissertation to address internal validity was analytical replication, which YIN discusses in the context of pattern matching.[401] In detail, it was tested whether explanations induced from one case could be literally or theoretically replicated by the other cases. Moreover, the semi-structured interviews used for data collection followed a standardized guideline.[402]

External validity refers to the extent to which the case study findings are generalizable, or rather transferable. Importantly, case studies rely on "analytical generalization" whereas large-scale deductive studies rely on "statistical generalization". The former is not generalization of some defined population that has been sampled, but of a broader theory of the researched phenomenon. The applicability of such a theory may be wider than the particular case(s) studied.[403] In this dissertation, the case selection process and the cases' content are openly described, which sets a frame of reference for the findings' further replication and testing.[404]

Reliability is concerned with the quality and documentation of the research procedures.[405] A case study is reliable if a later investigator yields similar results by following the research procedures as described by the earlier investigator. Thereby, "the emphasis is on doing the same case over again, not on replicating the results of one case by doing another case study".[406] In general, readers should be able to follow the research process.[407] Tactics used in this dissertation to ensure reliability include working with a case study database, developing a coding scheme, employing computer software for qualitative data analysis, and disclosing the research process.

---

401 See ibidem, pp. 136-141.
402 See Schnell et al. (2005), p. 387.
403 See ibidem, pp. 43-44; Miles / Huberman (1994), p. 279; Yin (2009), p. 43.
404 See Eisenhardt (1989), p. 537.
Section 7.4 discusses possible limitations to the external validity of this research.
405 See Miles / Huberman (1994), p. 278; Yin (2009), p. 45.
406 Source: Yin (2009), p. 45.
407 See Gummesson (2008), p. 40.

4 Case Descriptions: BMI Outcome and Process

This chapter aims to provide an in-depth understanding of the five single case studies, whereby each case is presented individually. Each case description begins with a portrayal of the traditional and the new business model by means of the business model canvas.[408] Secondly, the classification of the new business model as successful or failed BMI according to the BMI-identification tool developed in chapter 2 is illustrated. Thirdly, the process of the new business model is described from the idea to the final integration. As for the two non-successful BMIs, the process description spans across to the dissolution or divestment of the business unit. Fourthly, process phases are identified from the business unit manager's point of view, and their chronological order is visualized. Notably, all of the cases took place in different business units. The data underlying the case descriptions stems exclusively from the fieldwork. For simplicity and identity protection reasons, all mentioned persons involved in the cases are referred to as female. Non-English citations from interviewees have been translated into English by the scholar.

4.1 Case 1: "New-Tech Domain"

The case "New-Tech Domain" comprises of the BMI in an *ElectricCorp* business unit. It covers the innovation process – from the idea to the integration – of a new business model that, ever since, has performed successfully in financial terms. The business unit manager succeeded in developing a new business model around an emergent, new-to-the-firm technology. The BMI process started in 2005 and took about five years overall. Currently, both business models coexist in the focal business unit.

4.1.1 Portrayal of the Traditional and the New Business Model

The business model canvas shall be employed to juxtapose the traditional business model with the new one. The new business model refers to the one resulting from the BMI and the traditional one to the business model that was established before the BMI started. As mentioned in section 2.1.3.1, the business model canvas describes a business model through nine basic building blocks: value proposition, customer segments, channels, customer relationships, revenue streams, key activities, key resources, key partnerships and cost structure. Subsequently, the two business models are juxtaposed along these nine building blocks. Figure 12 summarizes the portrayal.

---

[408] The business model canvas by Osterwalder / Pigneur has been developed to facilitate the description and discussion of business models without oversimplifying the complexities inherent in business models; see section 2.1.3.1.

CASE "NEW-TECH DOMAIN": PORTRAYAL OF THE TRADITIONAL AND THE NEW BUSINESS MODEL IN THE BUSINESS MODEL CANVAS

"Traditional": established business model before BMI
"New": business model resulting from BMI

KP	KA / KR	VP	CR / CH	CS
Traditional: • Buyer-supplier relationships for input material (e.g., copper, insulation material) **New:** • Additional buyer-supplier relationships for new input material (e.g., optical fibers) • Contractor for molding of in-house designed connectors • Network of sales representatives (see CH)	**KA** **Traditional:** • Design, manufacture and sale of cables **New:** • Design of integrated multi-component, electrical systems • Production processes • Convincing customers **KR** **New:** New physical resources • Machinery • Quality test equipment New human resources • Product engineers ("scientific knowledge") • Machine designers and operators • Sales force (Existing employees did not have the skills for new value proposition.)	**Traditional:** • Design & manufacture of standard diameter round and flat cables resistant to mechanical stress, chemicals, fire, or radioactivity • Focus on quality and price **New:** 1) Design & manufacture of micro-miniaturized cables with state-of-the-art product characteristics, plus 2) Design & assembly of integrated electrical systems comprising additionally of optical fibers, connectors, and/or sensors • Strong quality focus	**CR** **Traditional and New:** • Personal assistance • Dedicated personal assistance • Customer events **CH** **Traditional:** • Direct sales force • Trade fairs **New:** • Direct sales force • Network of sales representatives outside of Europe (e.g., USA, Israel, South Korea)	**Traditional:** Manufacturers and system integrators in: • Factory automation • Process automation • Marine, Defense **New:** Manufacturers in: • Test and measurement technology • Electronics (e.g., semi-conductors) • Medical technology (e.g., surgery robots, micro-endoscopy, heart implantation, brain pressure) Business unit manager: "It is a different clientele."

C$	R$
Traditional: More cost-driven, high degree of capacity utilization for economies of scale **New:** More value-driven, relatively more fabrication than material cost compared to the traditional business model, overhead activities shared with traditional business model	**Traditional and New:** • Asset sale • List prices for standard products • Product feature dependent prices for customized products

VP=Value Proposition, CS=Customer Segments, CH=Channels, CR=Customer Relationships, R$=Revenue Streams
KA=Key Activities, KR=Key Resources, KP=Key Partnerships, C$=Cost Structure

Figure 12: Case "New-Tech Domain": traditional and new business model[409]

Traditional Business Model

Traditionally, the business unit offers round and flat cables in standard diameter ranges primarily for industrial applications. In terms of product features, the cables comply with what is required from above-average cable industry players. Hereby, the business unit's main competencies lie in the cable extrusion that enables it to sell cables that are particularly resistant to mechanical stress, chemicals, fire, or radioactivity. It serves manufacturers and system integrators in the product area of factory and process automation. To a smaller extent, producers of marine and defense applications are also addressed. Usually, the cables are sold by the meter, either from the warehouse or directly from the production line. Within the range of its technological competencies, the business unit can also customize cables to specifications given by the client. However, despite providing above-average quality, the cables still must be priced competitively. Customers are reached through a direct sales force. Each customer communicates with one of the business unit's sales staff or sales representatives, either by on-site visits, by email, or by telephone. The sales staff is structured based upon regions, customer types and some other criteria. Trade fairs help in the contacting of new customers. Revenues are generated through the sale of physical products. There are list prices for standard products or even

409 Source: own Figure adapted from Osterwalder / Pigneur (2010), p. 44.

framework agreements with big customers. As for customized products, quotes are calculated individually upon request.

Machinery and product managers constitute the key resources in the traditional business model. If customers demand specification changes, product managers have to adapt the bills of material and labor and, eventually, they also initiate alterations to the existing machinery. Buyer-supplier relationships are maintained for the sourcing of input material such as copper and insulation material. In general, the traditional business model is gradually becoming more cost- than value-driven. Despite providing good quality, the business unit is sensing the competitive pressure and therefore tries to maximize the capacity utilization in order to reach an acceptable price and margin level.

New Business Model

The value proposition in the new business model encompasses micro-miniaturized electrical systems for very demanding high-tech customers, and consists of micro-miniaturized copper cables, optical fibers, connectors, and/or sensors. In terms of product features, these electrical systems are completely state-of-the-art and, essentially, turn the business unit into a first mover. The value proposition includes, firstly, the design and manufacture of micro-miniaturized cables and, secondly, the design and assembly of the entire system, which solves the technical problems initially described by customers. Importantly, the business unit does not physically manufacture all the parts ultimately needed to build such an electrical system, but it has the sole design authority and performs the final assembly and quality control. This new value proposition is offered to manufacturers of test and measurement equipment, electronics, and medical technology. The electrical systems are used, for example, in the production of semiconductor chips, in surgery robots, or in micro-endoscopy. These customers represent a completely different clientele. They are addressed through a direct sales force, differing from the traditional one, and a carefully selected network of sales representatives. In order to increase revenues, the business unit has established partnerships with independent sales representatives, especially outside of Europe.

In terms of key activities, the business unit must have the scientific engineering know-how and it must conduct the entire cable production and assembly process because these areas are at present difficult to master and, therefore, offer great differentiation potential. Moreover, getting access to this completely new clientele is crucial. The new business model can only succeed if new customers, one by one, can be convinced of the quality and reliability of the innovative value proposition. The traditional business model does not address the new business model's target customers. Hence, there are no grown customer relationships the business unit could have built on.

The key resources in the new business model are the product engineers, the machinery, the machine operators, and the sales force. Without skilled product engineers it would be impossible to claim the design authority for this state-of-the-art electrical system.

> *"Developers must have the electrotechnical skills, they must carry out many different calculations, and they must have extensive application experience. We are moving towards science."*[410]

Moreover, the micro-miniaturized cables are produced in a completely new manufacturing cell. Thereby, each purchased machine has been modified by process engineers specifically hired for this project. The same holds true for the micro assembly machinery. In this context, the operators also constitute a key resource because they must bring with them a particular skill set and additionally receive special training. Furthermore, the sales force is a critical resource because each sales person must be capable of conveying the engineering knowledge to high-tech customers. With regard to external partnerships the new business model requires additional buyer-supplier relationships for the electrical system's other components. For instance, the business unit partners with a contractor concerning the molding of in-house designed connectors.

Consequently, the new business model's cost structure is value-driven. Technical experts and state-of-the-art machinery are necessary to deliver the value proposition. Moreover, within the total production cost, the relative share of fabrication compared to material is higher than in the traditional business model. Cost reduction is achieved by sharing the overhead structure with the traditional business model, particularly for G&A and indirect COGS functions.

4.1.2 Classification as BMI

Criteria for classifying a business model as BMI in the multi-business firm		**Business Model: "New-Tech Domain"**	
		Assessment (Yes/No)	**Reasoning**
1	New or changed-to-become-new value proposition	Yes	- Design and manufacture of multi-component electrical systems - New clientele of very demanding high-tech customers
2	Innovative value constellation: New, and/or changed, and/or suppressed working practices to fulfill the value proposition	Yes	New working practices in - product design - product manufacturing and assembly - reaching and convincing customers (Hiring of new employees for these activities and establishment of new partnerships)

[410] Source: business unit manager in interviews "New-Tech Domain".

3	New-to-the-firm (corporation)	Yes	No other *ElectricCorp* business unit is capable of offering multi-component electrical systems featuring micro-miniaturized cables or of catering to this clientele.
4	Integrated into the firm	Yes	*Option 3:* The new business model is integrated within an existing business unit where it adds to the unit's traditional business model. (see Figure 4: "Generic Options of BMI integration")
5	Created without M&A	Yes	No M&A activities throughout the BMI
6	Financial success	Yes	- Continuous revenue growth - Margins far above the firm's and above the business unit's average

Table 20: Case "New-Tech Domain": reasons for classification as BMI[411]

Table 20 illustrates the reasoning why the business model "New-Tech Domain" meets all of the criteria postulated in the BMI-identification tool and why it therefore classifies as BMI success. The previous subsection clearly shows that the new business model contains a new value proposition. Both the customer needs addressed by the business unit, as well as the final product, are novel and different. The new business model is new-to-the-firm and its realization did not involve any mergers or acquisitions. Subsequently, more details are provided for the criteria 2, 4, and 6.

Innovative Value Constellation

Innovativeness of the value constellation is visible through different working practices and originates from the creation or suppression of several activities in the value chain, from changes to several activities, and/or from changes in the order of activities.[412] In the case "New-Tech Domain", the business unit created new activities in the below three major areas.

- Firstly, in the area of product design, the engineers had to master the micro-miniaturization of cables as well as the design of multi-component electrical systems entailing those cables. These activities required scientific know-how that is not present in the traditional business model and hence led to the recruiting of new product engineers as well as to further qualification of existing engineers. Besides, in the new business model the engineers partner with a contractor for the molding of in-house designed connectors.
- Secondly, in the area of product manufacturing and assembly, the new business model involves different working practices for the machine operators. The machinery is newly built and differs from the equipment in the traditional business model. Initially, the business unit tried to assign existing operators to the new

[411] Source: own Table.
[412] See section 2.1.3.1.

machines, but scrap and quality complaints revealed that a specific skill set was necessary to operate them. Consequently, the business unit selected very few existing operators, the "best ones"[413], and recruited additional operators who were specifically trained on the new machines.

- Thirdly, the sales process in the new business model implicates new working practices. In order to convince the targeted high-tech customers, a sales person must be able to communicate with them on an almost scientific level. The entire existing sales force from the old business model failed at selling the new value proposition. For this reason, all of them had to tolerate cuts in their bonuses. While some sales people did not possess the basic qualifications necessary for acquiring the know-how, others lacked the motivation. In response, the business unit turned to individual product engineers and assigned them the task of selling the new offering. In addition, the business unit sells through independent sales representatives. These partnerships were established over the course of the BMI.

Integrated into the Firm

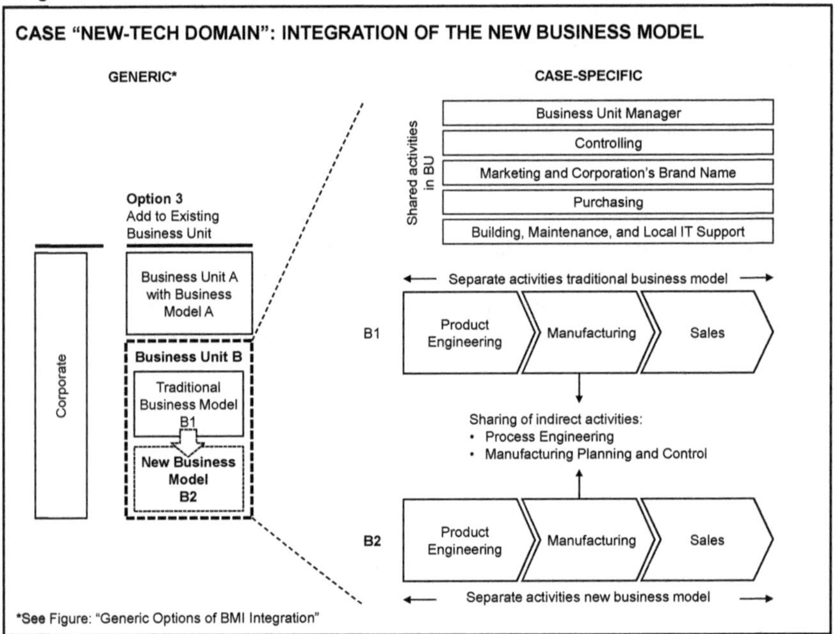

Figure 13: Case "New-Tech Domain": integration of the new business model[414]

The new business model is fully integrated into the firm. It is no longer labeled a "special" or "trial status". Revenues and costs are allocated to it. With regard to the

413 Source: senior sales manager in interviews "New-Tech Domain".
414 Source: own Figure.

three generic BMI integration options introduced in chapter 2, the new business model is integrated along the lines of option 3: "add to existing business unit".[415] In fact, the business unit currently operates two business models, whereby many direct activities are separated and numerous indirect activities are shared. MARKIDES / OYON stress that every company has to find a company-specific answer concerning how to integrate a new business model into the organization. The answer should enable the company to keep conflicting activities separate while simultaneously exploiting synergies wherever possible.[416] Figure 13 visualizes that both the traditional and the new business model are located in the same building and are headed by the same business unit manager. Multiple indirect activities are shared. Nevertheless, the activities of product engineering, manufacturing and sales are business model-specific and therefore remain separate.

Financial Success

Chapter 2 clarifies that a new business model must be value enhancing to qualify as BMI. However, the way of measuring the success of a new business model is not specified in the extant BMI literature.[417] Ideally, a combination of different measures can be shown to convey an impression of the new business model's performance and the shareholders' evaluation thereof.[418]

		2007	**2008**	**2009**	**2010**	**2011**	**2012 FC**	**2013 FC**	**2014 FC**
Sales Revenues in kEUR **New BM**	As Is	107	476	612	1,050	1,489	2,500	3,500	5,000
	Plan	540	1,480	2,200	2010: Year of official integration				
Operating Margin in % **New BM**					between 25 and 30	between 25 and 30	between 25 and 30		
Operating Margin in % **Business Unit**			16	15	24	27	22		
Operating Margin in % ***ElectricCorp***		5	2	-5	4	6	6		
Additional remarks by the business unit manager		- *"[...] reached single-year break-even in year 3 [after first investment in BMI], one year behind the initial [business] plan"* - *"[...] payback time over total investment was 5 years, two years behind the [initial business] plan."*							

Table 21: Case "New-Tech Domain": indicators of financial success[419]

415 See section 2.1.3.4.
416 See Markides / Oyon (2010), p. 30.
417 See section 2.1.3.5.
418 See ibidem.
419 Sources: own Table with data from interviews "New-Tech Domain" and the firm's website.

Table 21 displays the information gathered throughout the fieldwork on the financial performance of the integrated new business model. In recent years, sales revenues have constantly increased and, for the near future, significant growth is expected. Such a development indicates solid customer acceptance of the new value proposition. The exact operating margin of the new business model cannot be drawn from the business unit's ERP system.[420] However, from the identifiable contribution margin, it is estimated to reach between 25% and 30%. On average, this margin is higher than the business unit's overall operating margin. Furthermore, the new business model's operating margin is considerably higher than the corporation's operating margin. In consequence, the new business model enhances the firm's value and, assumedly, is perceived as "successful" by the corporation and its shareholders. Moreover, the initial total investment in the new business model has been paid back despite the severe global recession in 2009. Nonetheless, the repayment took two years longer than initially planned.

4.1.3 Description of the BMI Process

In 2005, one of *ElectricCorp's* central departments held an innovation workshop for the larger management circle during which, among other subjects, the trend towards micro-miniaturization was presented. The manager of the focal business unit became aware of this trend for the first time at this workshop. However, the idea was originally brought up by the product engineers and sales personnel of the focal business unit, who had already received sporadic customer requests for micro-miniaturized products before the workshop took place.

> *"Well, I consciously became aware of this idea in the context of this workshop. [...] The first structured discussion about the idea started afterwards."*[421]

Throughout the following months, the business unit manager and her co-management team engaged in market research on micro-miniaturization. An external market researcher was hired for information on products, customer segments, market sizes and growth. Furthermore, the internal sales force was involved in "structured discussions" about this topic. Eventually, the business unit manager gained trust in the opportunity's chances of success. Of particular importance for her were the clear signs of market growth.

> *"The entry into a market that is growing is always easier. It mitigates the predatory competitive behavior of established players."*[422]

Beyond having trust, the business unit manager also had some form of motivation to pursue this new opportunity. Firstly, approximately one fourth of the business unit's

---

[420] Operating margin is calculated by dividing the operating income or EBIT by sales revenues.
[421] Source: business unit manager in interviews "New-Tech Domain".
[422] Source: ibidem.

current products were being substituted or commoditized each year. Hence, there was a constant innovation pressure. Secondly, in 2005 the corporation decided for political reasons to reorganize; it removed existing business volume from the focal business unit and transferred it internally to another business unit. Therefore, the focal business unit manager at that time felt an inherent need to replace the lost business for her unit.

In 2006, the business unit manager initiated the elaboration of a business plan for embracing the opportunity of micro-miniaturization. The business plan expressed that the final goal was to become a first mover by offering multi-component, micro-miniaturized electrical systems. The first step, though, was to become coherently familiar with the design and manufacture of micro-miniaturized cables and their assembly.

> *"We first needed to ensure that we would master the processes for manufacturing micro-miniaturized cables. Then, we could move on to producing integrated electrical systems; [...] transforming ourselves from a follower into a first mover."*[423]

Furthermore, the business plan contained the sales development goals for each identified target segment, the required investments, and the expected profits. The findings from the market research were incorporated into the business plan. When compiling the business plan, the unit, by coincidence, received a new product engineer. This experienced engineer had successfully applied to the corporation and was subsequently referred to the focal unit. This engineer had worked in related product areas before and, with her market knowledge, largely contributed to the business plan. Importantly, she was also assigned many tasks mentioned in the business plan regarding the plan's realization, such as defining the equipment, contacting potential first customers and identifying suitable suppliers. However, the business unit manager emphasized in the interview that this opportunity would have been pursued even if the new engineer had not joined the unit's workforce:

> *"We would have moved forward even if [she] had not been available by assigning [her] tasks to another manager either from sales or product engineering. Probably, the project might not have developed in exactly the same way but the unit would have definitely moved forward."*[424]

The final business plan was presented to corporate headquarters with the aim of being granted the necessary financial resources, especially for the new machinery. The corporation approved it.

[423] Source: senior sales manager in interviews "New-Tech Domain".
[424] Source: business unit manager in interviews "New-Tech Domain".

Thereafter, the first realization step comprised of engineering state-of-the-art micro-miniaturized cables. For example, the new product engineer succeeded in optimizing the electro-magnetic shielding characteristics of such cables. The subsequent steps were to communicate the business unit's entry into this market and to produce very simple prototypes, mostly with existing machinery. The prototypes' main purpose was to support discussions with potential customers. However, very soon after engaging in the realization, it became obvious that parts of the existing organization resisted the project.

> *"There was the perception that the current business model delivered good-enough financial results and that current processes were well defined and stable. Thus, the question arose: 'Why should we even engage in something so new?' Others opposed the chosen mode of entry. [...] colleagues worried about me 'trying to sell products we did not even have yet'."*[425]

Above all, the manufacturing managers were unwilling to release their best operators for the prototype production. In reaction, the business unit manager built a three-person project team, which she took out of the established (line) organization and which subsequently reported directly to her. Through this empowerment, the project team gained status within the business unit and was given the chance to move more freely. Besides, compensation packages linked to the project's success served as another incentive for the project team. It was headed by the new product engineer and completed by another product engineer and one process engineer. The latter was recruited externally for this project. Other measures for overcoming the initial resistance by employees included the active promotion of this opportunity by the business unit manager with the remark of securing today's jobs for the future.

One of the project team's important tasks was to attract customers. By showing prototypes, potential customers were informed that the firm produced micro-miniaturized cables and that it planned on extending the offer to multi-component electrical systems. In response, the project team actually received many requests for quotation. However, it took much longer than planned to receive real orders.

> *"Gaining the trust of customers took about two years, much longer than anticipated. [One customer] confirmed that our system is technically superior to the one currently in use. But [this customer] did not order from us, probably because they did not sufficiently trust us yet to be a supplier for their sensitive products."*[426]

Nonetheless, due to the fact that the product quality was partly confirmed, the business unit manager did not lose confidence in the project's success. Indeed, the project team reapplied for new bid invitations with the same customers who had

---

425 Source: senior sales manager in interviews "New-Tech Domain".
426 Source: business unit manager in interviews "New-Tech Domain".

previously confirmed the product quality. Eventually, the team won some of those bids and thus achieved considerable order income. The first orders solely entailed micro-miniaturized cables, but over time, the business unit expanded its value proposition to the multi-component electrical systems. The head of the project team emphasized:

> *"It is crucial to stay in close contact with customers in order to learn about their upcoming new product lines or product replacements. [...] Attempting to squeeze other suppliers out of ongoing projects only destroys prices."*[427]

Retrospectively, the business unit did not manage to access every target segment listed in the business plan. By contrast, in successfully entered target segments, the generated revenues have been higher than originally planned, without taking the time delay into account. Literally, all of the large customers were acquired through the project team or those independent sales representatives identified and trained by both the project team and the business unit manager. The business unit's regular sales force did not succeed in selling the new value proposition, as an increased technical know-how was required to do so. In an attempt to stimulate the regular sales force to engage more with the new value proposition, the business unit manager directly linked their compensation packages with it. This measure did not turn out as hoped. In fact, the sales staff did not have the intrinsic motivation or the basic qualification to acquire the necessary technical knowledge, even though:

> *"[...] some of them lost a considerable part of their total annual salary."*[428]

Once the first large orders were won, the project team started to invest heavily in the new manufacturing cell. The team did not want to invest in new machinery before they knew exactly with which kinds of products they could attract customers. Remarkably, each machine was built or modified under guidance of the project team. In order to reduce costs while simultaneously keeping a high degree of secrecy, external and internal process engineers were given individual sub-projects. With regard to the machine operators, the project team first intended to train existing operators from the traditional business model on the new machinery. However, as evidenced through high scrap rates and occasional customer complaints, the project team discovered that most of those operators lacked the basic necessary skills. In consequence, new operators were recruited externally and assigned specifically to the new manufacturing cell.

> *"The operators of the machines for micro-miniaturized products must have a certain type of character. [...] For such projects of future importance the best people must be assigned."*[429]

---

[427] Source: senior sales manager in interviews "New-Tech Domain".
[428] Source: business unit manager in interviews "New-Tech Domain".
[429] Source: senior sales manager in interviews "New-Tech Domain".

In 2010, the project team was reintegrated into the established organization and micro-miniaturization officially stopped being considered as merely a project. At that point in time, the new manufacturing cell had reached a solid degree of capacity utilization; the new production processes were proven effective and an initial customer base for multi-component electrical systems was acquired. With the reintegration, the business unit manager wanted to avoid the duplication of overhead structures. Such duplication would have increased personnel costs and in addition, could have led to incongruous indirect processes within the business unit. However, resistance occurred especially in the area of manufacturing planning and control.

> *"The main reason for their reluctance – besides the fact that the new production processes differed from the established ones and hence unpleasantly required learning something new – is attributable to the 'not-invented-here' syndrome."*[430]

For overcoming the resistance, the business unit manager repeatedly emphasized the new business model's importance for the transition of the entire business unit towards a defendable technology position over the long term. Reflecting upon this strategy, the business unit recently started to merge the two separate product engineering departments in order to accelerate the diffusion of the technical knowledge related to the new value proposition.[431]

4.1.4 Visualization of the BMI Process

Figure 14 visualizes the BMI process in the case "New-Tech Domain", from the business unit manager's point of view. This visualization is based upon the process description in the previous subsection.

For the business unit manager, the BMI process retrospectively started when she became aware of this "New-Tech Domain" opportunity. Subsequently, she undertook measures aimed at gaining trust in it. With trust in this particular opportunity and the general motivation to pursue new initiatives, she resolved to move forward and engage in the opportunity's realization. The latter began by the elaboration of a business plan. Without a business plan, corporate headquarters would not have approved the necessary financial resources. Triggered by the apparent resistance of the established organization, the business unit manager then built a project team whose members were taken out of the established organization and who reported directly to her. She empowered the team to move relatively freely within the business unit. Notably, the dedicated team first figured out a viable value proposition and, only afterwards, invested considerable money in the value constellation required to deliver the value proposition. Once a certain degree of capacity utilization was reached and

---

430 Source: business unit manager in interviews "New-Tech Domain".
Katz / Allen (2007), p. 7, define the "not-invented here" syndrome as "the tendency of a project group of stable composition to believe it possesses a monopoly of knowledge of its field, which leads it to reject new ideas from outsiders to the likely detriment of its performance.

431 See Figure 13.

the new resources and processes had been set up and proven effective, the business unit manager officially integrated the new business model into the established organization.

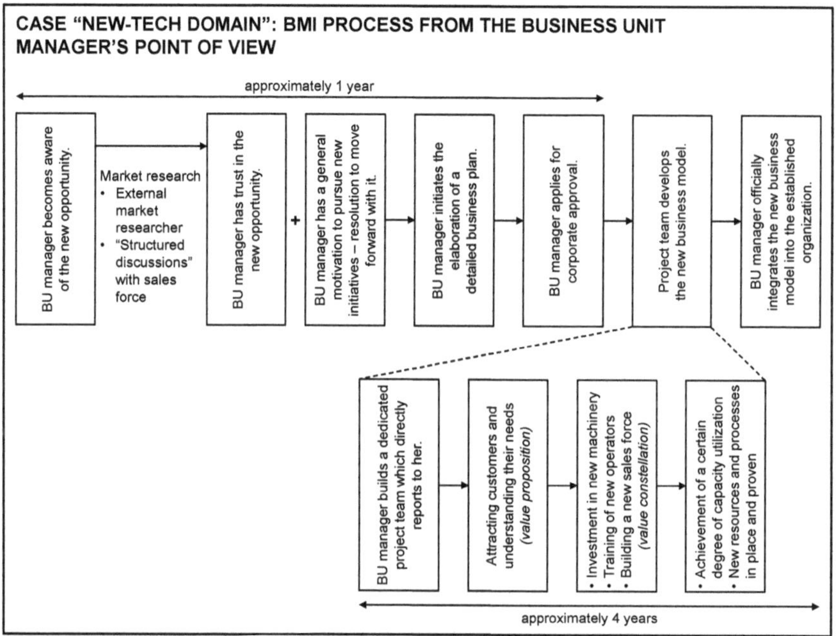

Figure 14: Case "New-Tech Domain": BMI process[432]

4.2 Case 2: "One-Stop Solution"

The case "One-Stop Solution" contains the successful BMI in another *ElectricCorp* business unit. This case covers the innovation process towards the integration of a new solution- and project-based business model that currently adds to the unit's established product-based business model. The time span from the BMI idea in 2004 until the official integration into the established organization amounts to approximately five years.

4.2.1 Portrayal of the Traditional and the New Business Model

Figure 15 juxtaposes the traditional business model with the new one. Both business models currently coexist in the focal business unit.

432 Source: own Figure.

CASE "ONE-STOP SOLUTION": PORTRAYAL OF THE TRADITIONAL AND THE NEW BUSINESS MODEL IN THE BUSINESS MODEL CANVAS

"**Traditional**": established business model before BMI
"**New**": business model resulting from BMI

KP	KA / KR	VP	CR / CH	CS
Traditional: • Buyer-supplier relationships for input material (e.g., copper, insulation material) **New:** • Corporation-internal and external buyer-supplier relationships for all cables, pipes and other electro-mechanical components • For some projects, partnerships or subcontracting agreements with well-respected providers of electrical installation services and/or civil engineering	**KA** **Traditional:** • Design and manufacture of state-of-the-art power cables **New:** • Engineering of holistic cabling solutions • Installation of cables and of all electro-mechanical equipment in infrastructure facilities • Project and risk management **KR** **Traditional:** • Machinery • Chemical engineers **New:** • No manufacturing • Project managers • Construction supervisors • Legal experts	**Traditional:** Design and manufacture of power cables sold by the meter – product business **New:** Cabling solutions for entire infrastructure projects including 1) planning, engineering, logistics, installation, as-built documentation 2) turn-key and/or general contracting The share of cables is only around 15-30% of the project volume. The major part is for services and other material, e.g., cable trays, pipes, cabinets, electro-mechanical components.	**CR** **Traditional:** • Personal assistance through internal sales force **New:** • Project managers • On-site presence during project realization **CH** **Traditional:** • Marketing activities • Internal sales force ("wait for call") **New:** • Contacting customers proactively • New sub-brand and marketing material	**Traditional:** • Providers of electrical installation services **New:** Solutions are sold to • investors in infrastructure construction projects, • System integrators, or • Engineering firms. Customers value receiving a turn-key solution from one source, i.e. "one-stop solution", instead of having to compare, choose and coordinate a plethora of different suppliers.

C$	R$
Traditional: More cost-driven **New:** Elements of both value- and cost-driven cost structures; relatively high share of variable costs from trading goods; G&A activities shared with the traditional business model	**Traditional:** Asset sale, (negotiable) list prices for standard products, benefits from orders generated by the new business model **New:** Fee for realizing the customer-specific solution

VP=Value Proposition, CS=Customer Segments, CH=Channels, CR=Customer Relationships, R$=Revenue Streams
KA=Key Activities, KR=Key Resources, KP=Key Partnerships, C$=Cost Structure

Figure 15: Case "One-Stop Solution": traditional and new business model[433]

Traditional Business Model

Traditionally, the business unit designs and produces power cables mainly for infrastructure facilities and energy distribution. Some power cables comply with the highest official technical standards concerning performance and security. Therefore, these products allow for a price premium. However, many customers do not require these high technical standards, which only a few cable producers can offer. Instead, the business unit is forced to additionally manufacture power cables of lower technical standards in order to guarantee a certain degree of capacity utilization. Globally, numerous producers achieve these lower technical standards. In consequence, the business unit experiences relatively high price pressure for many of its products.

Typically, the power cables are made-to-stock. They are stored in the business unit's own warehouse. When ordered by customers, they can be delivered to the construction site at short notice. Traditional customers are the providers of electrical installation services. The sales staff generates customer awareness by attending trade fairs or by advertising in the relevant trade journals. Orders are created once customers call the business unit's internal sales force for the supply of power cables. Usually, the sales process involves requests for quotation and subsequent price

433 Source: own Figure adapted from Osterwalder / Pigneur (2010), p. 44.

negotiations. For all products, there are list prices that are negotiable to a certain extent. Importantly, the traditional business model now benefits from orders won by the new business model.

Machinery and chemical engineers constitute the key resources in the traditional business model. Chemical engineers advance the performance and security characteristics inherent to the cables' insulation, which at present represents the main differentiator. Together with electrical engineers, they also determine the machinery. Buyer-supplier relationships are required for the sourcing of input material such as copper and insulation material. Overall, the traditional business model turned out to be more cost- than value-driven. Of course, the business unit still puts considerable effort into research and development activities in order to offer state-of-the-art power cables. On the other hand, it must pay close attention to cost in order to remain competitive in the lower quality segment.

New Business Model

In the new business model, the business unit offers turn-key cabling solutions for most types of newly built or reconstructed infrastructure facilities. Such a solution encompasses the planning, engineering, logistics, installation and documentation of all cable-related topics. Customers are specifically addressed on a project-by-project basis. To clarify in detail, the planning and engineering refers to determining the cable types, the cable and pipe lengths, the routing, the cable and piping ways, as well as the cable trays, based upon the principle guidelines given by the architect or customer. The planning is software-based and usually involves an on-site phase. Importantly, the solutions comprise of the customers' entire cable requirements, i.e. both power and communication cables. After the planning, the business unit organizes the solution's physical installation, which it also supervises on-site. Next to cables, pipes, trays, or gaskets, it also equips facilities with other electro-mechanical parts such as switches, transformers and switch cabinets. Hereby, the business unit ensures that all parts are at the right place at the right time, which requires, for example, effective supplier management, elaborated logistics and on-site material storage. After inspection and approval by the customer, the business unit completes and submits the "as-built documentation". Remarkably, the cables only constitute around 15%-30% of the typical project volume. Moreover, the business unit acts as a general contractor in most projects. For this reason, it promises customers not only the right cables, but also risk and cost reductions. These reductions are achieved through better coordinated logistics and installation services based upon the internally developed construction plans. In short, the new business model offers a cabling solution from one source, i.e. a "one-stop solution".

The new business model enables the business unit to move closer to the original commissioning authority; in other words, the business unit positions itself nearer to the project initiator. The new value proposition enables the business unit with the possibility to directly address the investors in infrastructure construction projects, i.e., the original commissioning authorities. Alternatively, the business unit has the possibility to provide its services to system integrators, who are assigned by the original commissioning authority for the duration of the construction project, and who then award turn-key and/or general contracts for sub-projects. Besides this, the business unit provides consulting services to engineering firms. Project managers directly contact potential customers once they learn about a new infrastructure construction project. For the communication with customers in the context of the new business model, a separate sub-brand plus dedicated marketing material are available. In some areas, the new sub-brand has already earned such a good reputation that customers approach the business unit and not vice versa. Typically, one project manager is assigned to one project. The project manager is often at the construction site and serves as the customer's main contact. After realizing the customer-specific solution, the business unit receives the predetermined fee.

The key activities in the new business model include the engineering of holistic cabling solutions for infrastructure facilities, as well as the planning and realization of a timely, cost-optimized installation of all cables and electro-mechanical equipment. Another key activity consists of the project and risk management, which are indispensable for firms offering turn-key and general contracting services. Consequently, the key resources in the new business model comprise of the project managers, civil engineers, construction supervisors and legal experts. Put differently, human resources are decisive for the new business model's success. The project managers design the cabling solution. They usually have an engineering background. The civil engineers and construction supervisors ensure the solutions' correct physical installation. Beyond that, the business unit must seek the advice of legal experts when drawing up turn-key and/or general contracts.

Further manufacturing facilities were not added for the new business model. Hence, buyer-supplier relationships are required for all components designed into the cabling solution, with the exception of those power cables supplied by the traditional business model. All other cables have to be procured either internally from the corporation's other business units, or externally from other cable producers. Similarly, it must turn to external suppliers for nearly all non-cable components. Moreover, the business unit engages in partnerships with civil engineering and electrical installation firms. Alternatively, it awards subcontracts to such service providers.

The new business model's cost structure embraces both value- and cost-driven elements. On the one hand, customers hire the business unit's services for "non-routine" construction projects. Therefore, the business unit needs experienced experts as project managers. On the other hand, the business unit must offer a better price-value ratio compared to customers doing the project by themselves, or rather "as before". Thus, the purchasing of components and services must also be managed with attention to cost. Of course, the relative share of variable costs per project is high. Sharing G&A activities with the traditional business model allows for fixed cost reductions.

4.2.2 Classification as BMI

Table 22 provides an overview of the reasons to classify the business model "One-Stop Solution" as a BMI success. All the criteria postulated in the BMI-identification tool are met. The previous subsection broadly illustrates that the new business model comprises of a new value proposition, i.e. criterion 1. In reference to criteria 3 and 5, the new business model is new-to-the-firm and was developed without any mergers or acquisitions. Further explanation is given below to show the ways in which criteria 2, 4, and 6 are fulfilled.

Criteria for classifying a business model as BMI in the multi-business firm		Business Model: "One-Stop Solution"	
		Assessment (Yes/No)	**Reasoning**
1	New or changed-to-become-new value proposition	Yes	- Holistic cabling solution for infrastructure facilities - Customers are investors or system integrators; i.e. higher position in the contract award process
2	Innovative value constellation: New, and/or changed, and/or suppressed working practices to fulfill the value proposition	Yes	New working practices concerning - planning and engineering - logistics and installation - "as-built documentation" - project and risk management Hiring of new and training of existing employees, new suppliers and partnerships
3	New-to-the-firm (corporation)	Yes	No other *ElectricCorp* business unit - caters to those customers, or - offers general contracting and turn-key services.
4	Integrated into the firm	Yes	*Option 3:* The new business model is integrated within an existing business unit where it adds to the unit's traditional business model. (see Figure 4: "Generic Options of BMI Integration")
5	Created without M&A	Yes	No M&A activities throughout the BMI
6	Financial success	Yes	- Continuous revenue growth - Margins are far above the firm's and the business unit's average

Table 22: Case "One-Stop Solution": reasons for classification as BMI[434]

[434] Source: own Table.

Innovative Value Constellation

In contrast to the traditional one, the new business model does not entail any internal manufacturing activities. This is not a requirement for delivering the value proposition.[435] Below is a description of the new working practices.

- Planning and engineering activities form the decisive part of the new value constellation. For these new working practices, the business unit at first relied on internal senior product managers who had gathered experience in this field mostly from former jobs outside of the business unit or firm. Later, additional project managers were recruited externally.
- Another set of new working practices relates to the logistics and physical installation of the cabling solution. In the traditional business model, the business unit only supplies but does not install power cables.
- If necessitated by the project, the business unit cooperates with other electrical installation and civil engineering companies, which also represents a new working practice.
- Other cable producers and suppliers of complementary components are approached for material procurement. Such a working practice does not exist in the traditional business model either.
- Eventually, the business unit had to learn about the legal and risk issues inherent to general contracting and turn-key services. This learning process involved an intense dialogue with firm-internal and firm-external legal experts.

Integrated into the Firm

Since 2009, the new business model is officially integrated into the firm with revenues and costs allocated to it. The business unit manager decided to keep the new business model within the boundaries of her business unit. Therefore, the focal business unit presently operates two different business models. This form of integration corresponds with the generic BMI integration option 3: "add to existing business unit", as presented in chapter 2. However, the number of activities shared between both business models is relatively limited; only the corporation's brand name, as well as the unit's G&A and marketing capacities are shared. The new value proposition is offered under an additional sub-brand and the employees working for the new business model are located in a different building. Figure 16 shows that the activities in the traditional business model aim at manufacturing components, whereas the activities in the new business model aim at delivering solution-oriented services.

---

[435] Nonetheless, many customers value the fact that the business unit is also a cable manufacturer; see section 4.2.3.

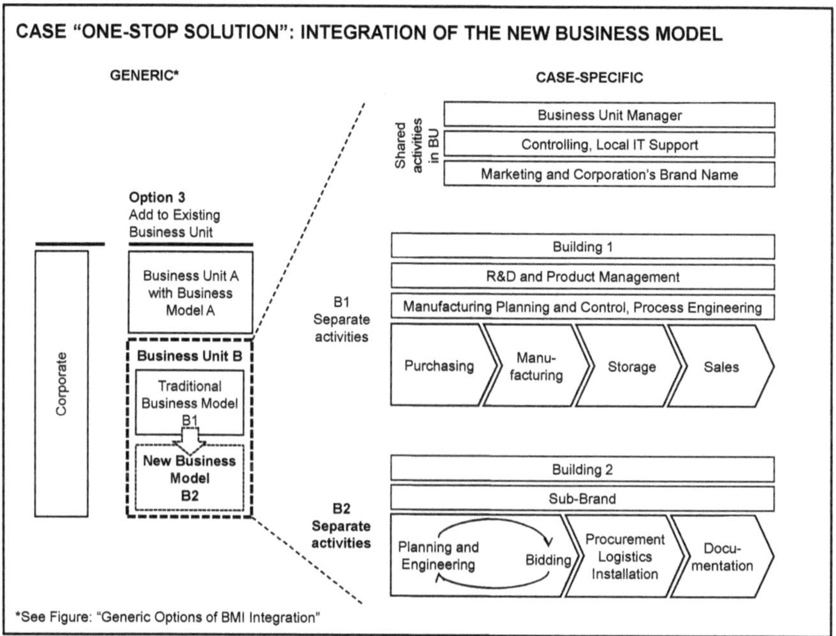

Figure 16: Case "One-Stop Solution": integration of the new business model[436]

Financial Success

	2009	2010	2011	2012
Sales Revenues in kEUR **New BM**	1,571 (2009: Year of official integration)	6,449	11,538	14,733
Additional remark by the business unit manager	*"The order backlog until 2014 is exceeding 50 million Euros."*			
Contribution Margin in % **New BM**	~60	~30	~30	~30
Operating Margin in % **Business Unit**	9	10	7	8
Operating Margin in % ***ElectricCorp***	-5	4	6	6
Additional remark by the business unit manager	*"[Projects won through the new business model] generate the highest contribution margin within the business unit."*			

Table 23: Case "One-Stop Solution": indicators of financial success[437]

436 Source: own Figure.
437 Sources: own Table with data from interviews "One-Stop Solution" and the firm's website.

The data in Table 23 indicates that the new business model enhances the value of both the business unit and the corporation. Since 2009, the year of official integration, annual sales revenues have continuously increased and the high order backlog points to further growth. Undoubtedly, customers accept the new value proposition. Overall, the business unit has a low three-digit million Euros sales figure. With regard to profit, the exact operating margin of the new business model cannot be drawn from the business unit's ERP system. However, the computable contribution margins are very high. According to the business unit manager, the projects won through the new business model generate the highest margins within her unit. Moreover, the business unit's operating margins are consistently higher than those of the corporation. Hence, there are reasons to believe that the corporation and its shareholders perceive the new business model as "successful".

4.2.3 Description of the BMI Process

In the early 2000s, the business unit manager noticed that customers increasingly requested quotations for power cables without knowing which kind of cables they actually needed.

> *"Together with those potential customers, our product management first had to work out an adequate cable specification. Hereby, we provided know-how to customers free of charge, which was only motivated by the hope that these customers would then place an order with us."*[438]

Besides this development, a key moment took place in 2004, when the business unit manager first experienced that in certain circumstances additional services beyond mere cables are possible to sell. Back then, the business unit had won a seemingly normal order to supply power cables for a certain construction project. The responsible product manager attended the construction site and engaged in a talk with the general contractor about the project's inherent difficulties and possible solutions for them. Triggered by this talk, the business unit then received additional small orders.

> *"At the beginning, we were only supposed to deliver cables. But throughout the order's execution, we received additional small orders for linking cables with connectors and elaborating a cable laying concept for the emergency exit."*[439]

During the same period, the business unit manager realized that many of the unit's products were beginning to face increasing price pressure. The business unit's customers were predominantly providers of electrical installation services who themselves were bidding for a construction project. Thus, in order to win a project, they often had to underbid their competitors in price. For this reason, they required a

438 Source: business unit manager in interviews "One-Stop Solution".
439 Source: business unit manager in interviews "One-Stop Solution".

low price quote from cable producers. The winning provider then tried to further lower the cable prices by requesting and comparing quotes from multiple cable producers. Such behavior was possible because investors, especially public investors, would often require the power cables' technical standard to be at the lower end of what is legally compulsory. Globally, more and more cable producers have been achieving these lower technical standards.

> *"Our typical product business is close to becoming commoditized."*[440]

Simultaneously, the business unit manager understood that, in the short- to medium-term, the demand for power cables of higher technical standards, which allow for differentiation, would not grow as strongly as necessary for the business unit to operate at full capacity and generate further growth. During a regular meeting with top management in 2004, the business unit manager presented her worries about the increasing price pressure. Based upon her personal observations described above, she suggested the repositioning of the business unit towards areas where differentiation and growth would still be possible. As a promising example, she referred to this one project in 2004, in which the business unit exceptionally sold connectors as trading goods and additionally provided a cable laying concept. She expressed her sentiment that the original commissioning authority of infrastructure construction projects would appreciate seeing all of their cabling needs responded to by just one partner.

> *"I argued that 'System' has to become one of our future success factors meaning that we have to sell something around the cable. [...] 'Services' should become another success factor. Customers wish to deal with only one contact for the entire project [...]"*[441]

However, corporate managers reacted skeptically. Since the financial performance of the business unit at the time fully met the objectives, they were less enthusiastic about new business models. As a result, this top-management presentation did not lead to any decisions to be followed by immediate action. It was more of an exchange of strategy ideas. Nevertheless, corporate managers stressed that they did not wish to engage in M&A in this context.

In 2005, the business unit recruited an experienced electrical engineer and deployed her in the existing product management team. Before joining the business unit, she worked in the field of electrical installation and had gathered experience from involvement in numerous construction projects. Soon after her start in the new position, she approached the business unit manager with her own product ideas beyond the actual cable. At that time, the business unit manager of course was open-minded for those ideas.

---

440 Source: ibidem.
441 Source: ibidem.

"Before [she] arrived, I did not have a sparring partner for discussing possible new products and services."[442]

From her experience, the new product manager knew, for example, that especially smaller operators of infrastructure facilities had only limited cabling knowledge.

"In my former function outside [ElectricCorp], I had already noticed that many energy utility companies only had a little in-house know-how about cable application, engineering or construction."[443]

She also knew that architects of big infrastructure construction projects frequently only integrate principle guidelines into the overall design, rather than a precise and detailed cabling solution. This task was then left to other parties, e.g. the providers of electrical installation services, who often do not have that competence. Moreover, she confirmed that the original commissioning authorities, and particularly public investors, would appreciate complete solutions from one source. The product manager furthermore believed that it was possible to improve the efficiency of electrical installation services.

"I have always tried to industrialize the electrical installation. In contrast with manufacturing companies that use bills of material and labor, the providers of electrical installation services often operate without an exact installation and time plan."[444]

The business unit manager and the new product manager discussed their product ideas openly and developed possible directions for the business unit to follow.

"A pioneering spirit evolved, urging us to test our ideas in reality."[445]

In 2006, the business unit manager decided to take action. She initiated the preparation of a "cabling solution offer" for a power plant reconstruction project. By approaching the original commissioning authority directly, the business unit positioned itself nearer to the project initiator. It eventually won the bid and executed the project in 2007, in which, for the first time, it operated in the form of a general contractor.

"The cable engineering and installation requirements were relatively small in this first project. The major tasks consisted of the removal of old cables, their replacement and connection, and the physical construction works."[446]

---

[442] Source: ibidem.
[443] Source: head of new business model in interviews "One-Stop Solution".
[444] Source: ibidem.
[445] Source: business unit manager in interviews "One-Stop Solution".
[446] Source: ibidem.

For the latter task, the business unit manager employed the plant's maintenance "blue collar team", which superbly mastered this new-for-them working practice. Another simplification factor for the business unit manager in this first project was that no cables other than those internally produced by the business unit were necessary. Nonetheless, the investor clearly valued the simplification and risk reduction brought to her by the business unit.

> *"If this offer had not existed, the investor would have had to find service providers and component suppliers for each subtask."*[447]

Notably, the execution of this first project was very much driven by the business unit manager herself, by the new product manager, and by an additional experienced product manager from another business unit who had been contacted about it by the focal business unit manager.

> *"Retrospectively, this first project was very hard work. [...] Failure could have led to negative personal consequences for us, despite the project's relative small scope."*[448]

Afterwards, the business unit manager had precise knowledge about what customers find appealing. Moreover, she figured out which internal processes and resources were necessary to replicate such a performance, independent of the managers involved in the first project. With the help of internal lawyers and external consultants, legal topics were also clarified; these included the terms and conditions of sale in general contracting, as well as liability and cost escalation clauses. Subsequently, the business unit manager bid for further similar projects in 2007 and 2008. For the execution of the won projects, she arranged for training courses for the members of the "blue collar team".

> *"Meanwhile, all team members have been trained to become construction managers and supervisors."*[449]

When necessary, she organized partnerships with electrical installation providers, who had been customers of the unit's traditional business model. In 2008, she first recruited new employees exclusively for the new business model. Until then, only existing staff resources were used.

The resistance of the established organization to the new business model was clearly perceptible by the business manager.

---

[447] Source: head of new business model in interviews "One-Stop Solution".
[448] Source: business unit manager in interviews "One-Stop Solution".
[449] Source: head of new business model in interviews "One-Stop Solution".

"Across all hierarchy levels, people mainly thought of it as 'too big for us'. However, this resistance simply further motivated me to demonstrate the viability of the new business model." [450]

However, she took constructive criticism very seriously, especially with regard to project and risk management, and acted accordingly. In fact, in the beginning of 2008, the business unit intended to enter into a construction joint venture with other companies for a rather big project. Corporate managers explicitly worried about the potential risk attached to the firm upon involvement in such a joint venture. For the first time in the BMI process, corporate managers actively intervened. Eventually, after intense consultation with legal experts and several talks with corporate managers, the parties involved ultimately came to a mutual understanding that the risk was controllable.

In 2008, without further SWOT, or any other formal market analysis, the business unit manager was sure that the new business model would become a sustainable success. A new sub-brand and specific marketing material had been created during the year. Eventually, the existing order backlog triggered the business unit manager to officially integrate the new business model into the established organization.

"In 2008, I had to decide if I wanted to integrate [the new business model] by founding a new legal entity [adding to the corporation] or by keeping it within the existing legal structures." [451]

The first option would have catered to public investors. Regulation often requires them to request offers for each single order. With the first option, public investors would legally be allowed to place a mandate for planning and engineering with the new legal entity, and simultaneously to award an order for cable delivery with the existing legal entity. However, at that time, the business unit already had a workaround for such a problem. Besides, the business unit manager feared the complexity inherent to inter-company business and decided to integrate the new business model into the existing business unit. A new department dedicated to delivering the new offering was set up and moved into a separate building. Moreover, a separate budget reflecting the new business model was compiled.

The business unit manager perceived a number of advantages linked to this form of integration.

"In retrospect, it was the right decision. Now, I can position the business unit as both a service provider and component supplier. No other direct competitor has achieved a similar positioning. Customers can be welcomed either in the new or in the old building, depending on the situation. Furthermore, many investors value

450 Source: business unit manager in interviews "One-Stop Solution".
451 Source: ibidem.

that the business unit belongs to a solvent corporation; especially when awarding a general contract. Some customers complain that, when engineering the cabling solution, the new business model team would not be neutral vis-à-vis cable suppliers. These customers argue that the cables produced by [ElectricCorp] would automatically always be designed into the solution. Although this is not the case, solving this argument would require a corporate spin-off, which, due to the new business model's success, is not an option."[452]

4.2.4 Visualization of the BMI Process

Based upon the process description above, Figure 17 visualizes the BMI process in the case "One-Stop Solution" from the business unit manager's point of view.

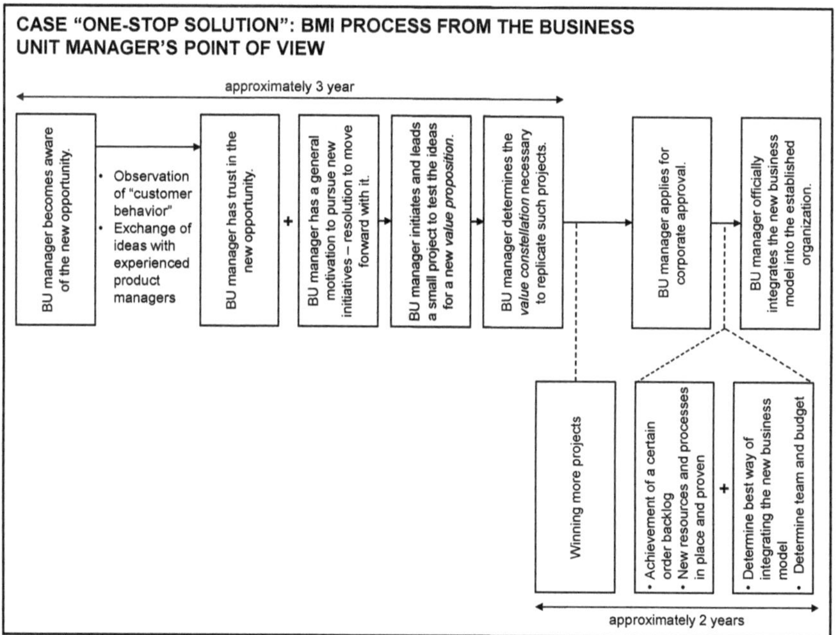

Figure 17: Case "One-Stop Solution": BMI process[453]

The business unit manager became aware of the basic outlines of what would eventually become the "One-Stop Solution" business model when one customer ordered services in addition to the supply of power cables. The business unit manager then gained trust in this opportunity. She observed that more and more customers approached the business unit without precise knowledge of the required cable types. Experienced product managers also confirmed her observation as well

---

[452] Source: ibidem.
[453] Source: own Figure.

as the potential for her new business model idea. Moreover, she was motivated to pursue new initiatives because the margin situation in the traditional business model was expected to deteriorate.

With the aim of testing the new idea, the business unit manager initiated a rather small project, in which the business unit delivered a cabling solution as a general contractor for the first time. Subsequently, she determined the value constellation, i.e. the resources and processes necessary to replicate such projects. Parts of the established organization opposed the development towards the new business model. However, instead of building a separate team, the business unit manager herself, together with convinced product managers, advanced the opportunity within the established structures. After winning more similar projects, it was proven that the new value proposition was sustainable and new staff were recruited specifically for the new business model. About this time, the business unit manager officially integrated the new business model into the established organization. Before the official integration, the business unit manager succeeded in persuading corporate headquarters that the risk from acting as a general contractor was controllable, even in bigger projects or construction joint ventures.

4.3 Case 3: "Integrate for Control"

The case "Integrate for Control" encompasses the successful BMI in a *ChemCorp* business unit. Initially a supplier of coatings to carmakers, the business unit evolved to become integrated into its customers' paint shops. This move now enables the business unit to control the quality of the coated car bodies, in addition to the material consumption. The idea for this new business model was first raised in 1992, and fully realized and integrated into the firm approximately three years later.

4.3.1 Portrayal of the Traditional and the New Business Model

Figure 18 illustrates the main characteristics of the traditional and the new business models. Alongside the new value proposition, the focal business unit still offers the traditional value proposition to the same customer group. Correspondingly, the BMI resulted in a redesign of the unit's traditional business model.

Traditional Business Model

Traditionally, the business unit produces paints and coatings for the automotive industry. In car manufacturing, coatings are usually applied to the car bodies for protection and decoration purposes before the final car assembly. The coatings are processed in designated paint shops typically with the help of paint and application robots. A car's paint system consists of four different layers. The e-coat protects the car from rust. The subsequent primer smooths out uneven surface irregularities and offers stone-chip protection. Thereafter, the basecoat colors the car body and finally, the clearcoat seals all of the paint layers. Drying may be required after each layer. Global key account managers are assigned to each major carmaker. Together with their sales team, they try to sell as much coating material to their respective key account as possible. Importantly, carmakers do not only purchase entire paint systems from the business unit, but also individual layers or even individual colors. For that reason, the business unit designs customized colors for car manufacturers. Moreover, it engages in research and development activities to improve the coatings' appearance characteristics, their durability, and their environmental sustainability. Production facilities and chemical engineers constitute the business model's key resources. Input chemicals are sourced mainly from other *ChemCorp* business units. Customers put considerable cost pressure on the business unit, which therefore tries to achieve maximum capacity utilization.

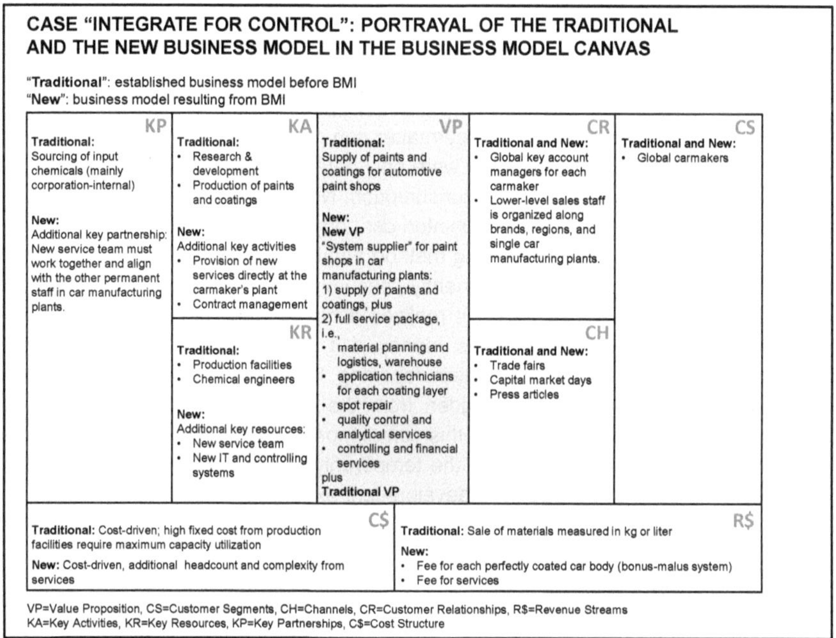

Figure 18: Case "Integrate for Control": traditional and new business model[454]

New Business Model

With the new business model, the business unit addresses the same customers, but offers the service of perfectly coating the car bodies instead of just providing the coatings. This offering is linked to a full service package for the carmakers' paint shops which essentially enables the business unit to control the coatings' processing.

> *"Service packages comprise of application technicians who operate the paint shop's robots, the supply systems and other equipment; of specialists for material*

[454] Source: own Figure adapted from Osterwalder / Pigneur (2010), p. 44.

planning, logistics, and the paint shop's consignment warehouse; of spot repair and quality management experts; and of a financial team for performance controlling and correct invoicing."[455]

Moreover, since carmakers typically steer towards avoiding single sourcing, the business unit offers to qualify a second supplier for the same coatings it delivers. The technicians and other specialists are employed and trained by the business unit, but permanently based at one car manufacturing plant. The size of one service team can reach up to 70 employees, depending on the plant's dimension. The new business model involves new IT and controlling systems. The material planning for the paint shop is electronically connected with the business unit's production planning.

The revenue of the coatings depends upon the performance of the paint application. To clarify, the business unit is paid for each perfectly coated car body. In fact, coatings are semi-finished goods that turn into finished goods after their application. With this new invoicing method, the carmaker can plan the exact painting costs per car upfront. Traditionally, these costs were only determinable after painting, because there can be fluctuations in material consumption. Now, a certain price is assigned to each layer. Hence, the price for one painted car body results from the sum of all layer prices. Beyond that, the new invoicing method entails a bonus-malus system. When the business unit succeeds in permanently consuming less kilograms of material per car body than originally calculated, it realizes a higher price per kilogram. On the other hand, the business unit loses money if it consumes more material – for instance, when a painted car body needs repairing. Successful permanent reductions of material consumption are not hidden from the customer. In contrast, they are equally shared with the customer. In this context, price adaption rounds usually take place every three months. However, the temporarily higher kilogram-prices help the business unit to cover its research & development expenses.[456]

"Yes, the absolute contribution margin for the same amount of cars declines. However, nobody can stop that. This is technological progress."[457]

Further revenue streams stem from the business unit's paint-shop-related services. Importantly, the business unit does not operate the paint shop on its own behalf since it considers such an operator model as too risky. Instead, it invoices the rendered services to the carmaker. The business unit's main selling argument constitutes its superior process knowledge. By using its own application technicians, it is able to improve the paint shop's "first car okay rate"[458] and hence the productivity of the

---

455 Source: account manager in interviews "Integrate for Control".

456 Sample calculation in four steps: 1. Start: 3kg per car with € 5 per 1kg = € 15 income for business unit per car. 2. Reduce consumption to 2kg per car. 3. Material reduction is shared equally between carmaker and business unit. 4. New income for business unit per car = € 12.50; i.e. € 6.25 per 1kg.

457 Source: account manager in interviews "Integrate for Control".

458 Source: ibidem.

entire car manufacturing plant. This rate refers to the amount of coated car bodies that do not have to return to the paint shop for repair, but can directly move forward into the final assembly. The higher this rate, the more cars can be manufactured within a given amount of time (ceteris paribus). In summary, the integration into the customer's value chain enables the business unit to control the processing, which, in turn, generates advantages for both the customer and the business unit.

4.3.2 Classification as BMI

Table 24 summarizes the reasons for classifying the business model "Integrate for Control" as BMI. In regard to criteria 3, the new business model was completely new-to-the-firm upon integration. As for criteria 5, the BMI process did not entail any mergers or acquisitions. The previous subsection presents the new value proposition. Subsequently, further explanation is given in reference to criteria 2, 4, and 6.

Criteria for classifying a business model as BMI in the multi-business firm		Business Model: "Integrate for Control"	
		Assessment (Yes/No)	**Reasoning**
1	New or changed-to-become-new value proposition	Yes	- Perfectly coated car bodies instead of the coatings that have semi-finished goods characteristics ⇨ *new-to-the-world offering at the time of introduction* - Paint-shop related services
2	Innovative value constellation: New, and/or changed, and/or suppressed working practices to fulfill the value proposition	Yes	- New working practices for providing the new services (hiring and training of new employees) - New working practices in controlling, IT, and contract management
3	New-to-the-firm (corporation)	Yes	- No other *ChemCorp* business unit produces paints and coatings. - No other *ChemCorp* business unit has ever before integrated itself so deeply into a customer's value chain.
4	Integrated into the firm	Yes	*Option 2:* The new business model is integrated by the redesign of the focal unit's traditional business model. (see Figure 4: "Generic Options of BMI Integration")
5	Created without M&A	Yes	No M&A activities throughout the BMI
6	Financial success	Yes	- Positive margins for business unit - Many carmakers changed to the new offering - Significant market share gains

Table 24: Case "Integrate for Control": reasons for classification as BMI[459]

[459] Source: own Table.

Innovative Value Constellation

Delivering the new value proposition requires new working practices in at least three main areas, as detailed below.

- Firstly, the business unit must employ a team capable of rendering the new services. Initially, new employees were hired. They underwent intensive training by experts from the focal business unit, as well as by firm-external experts, e.g., from a manufacturer of automotive paint shop equipment. For example, they had to learn how to control the paint shop's equipment and supply systems, how to program and operate the application robots and how to identify and repair quality problems. Moreover, for each car, the service team has to ensure that no more than the calculated quantity of coatings is consumed. Overall, the service team must have the audacity and know-how to directly interfere at the shop floor when incidents thwart the business unit's contractual obligations.

- Secondly, the sales and controlling staff faced new working practices. In fact, the value proposition "perfectly coated car bodies" implies a more complex type of sales contract, typically with a longer-term duration. In this regard, the business unit had to ensure that the "counting" of the perfectly coated car bodies on the shop floor reflected the reality. Plus, the internal bookkeeping systems had to be adapted to the new accounting unit.

- Thirdly, new IT interfaces and the corresponding software had to be established between the car manufacturing plants and the sites of the business unit; their purpose is to optimize production planning, logistics, or the knowledge exchange among technical experts along the entire value chain. Besides, the new business model adds significantly to the headcount, which needs to be managed internally.

Integrated into the Firm

The new business model was officially integrated in 1995 along the lines of option 2: "redesign of existing business unit".[460] Choosing this option aimed at offering both the new and the traditional value propositions to the same customer group. In other words, the global key account managers are able to offer to carmakers either the delivery of material only or the delivery of "perfectly coated car bodies" in combination with a service package. Nowadays, numerous car manufacturing plants have already adopted the second option, but there are still plants that employ their own paint shop operators. If carmakers perceive their own knowledge of the processing of coatings as sufficient, they most probably only order the material. Additionally, through the new business model integration, the R&D department can now access important data directly from those paint shops that are operated by the business unit. Figure 19 depicts this form of integration.

[460] See section 2.1.3.4.

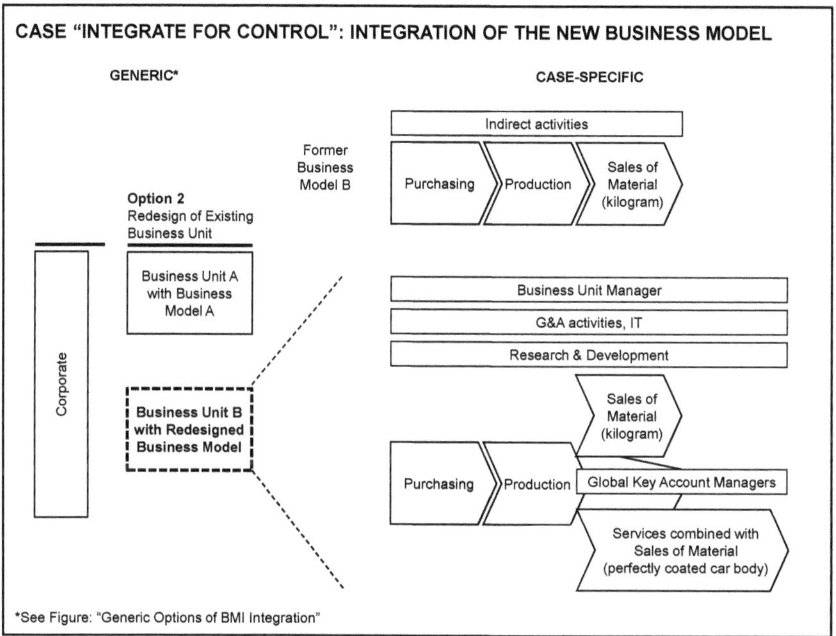

Figure 19: Case "Integrate for Control": integration of the new business model[461]

Financial Success

	1991	1992	1993	1994	1995	1996	1997	1998	1999
Sales Revenues in bn EUR **Division**	10,7	10,3	10,2	10,8	10,8	11,3	12,8	12,1	12,5
					1995: Year of official integration				
Operating Margin in % **Division**	3%	3%	2%	3%	3%	5%	7%	10%	10%
Operating Margin in % ***ChemCorp***	5%	3%	3%	5%	9%	9%	10%	9%	7%
Additional remarks by the interviewees	- *"Pretty fast after we successfully finished the first project, [other carmakers] changed to the new business model."* - *"Competitors introduced services only many years later. They did not come up with any additional service ideas."* - *"We significantly increased our market share."* - *"By the way, we won the [ChemCorp] innovation award, the [local region] innovation award, and the [European Business Award] by the EU."* - *"We started an industry revolution."*								

Table 25: Case "Integrate for Control": indicators of financial success[462]

[461] Source: own Figure.
[462] Sources: own Table with data from interviews "Integrate for Control" and the firm's website.

It would be inadequate to determine the new business model's success from an increase in total revenue, because this figure ultimately depends on the number of cars produced by the carmakers. Moreover, only division financials were made available (Table 25). The division comprises of the focal unit in addition to several other business units. Therefore, these financials are of limited value. However, the interviewees emphasized that after the business unit successfully introduced the new business model at the first carmaker, other carmakers quickly adopted the new offering too. Consequently, the unit's main competitors were forced to introduce such a business model as well, but they did not manage to do so for several years. As a result, the business unit won considerable market share. Notably, the competitors then more or less just copied the focal business unit. They did not introduce essentially new services or other business model ideas. Considering that today numerous car manufacturing plants pay the paint suppliers for the perfect coating of car bodies plus the service package, the new business model can be perceived as sustainably successful.

4.3.3 Description of the BMI Process

In 1992, the business unit manager initiated a workshop that was aimed at finding ideas for how the unit could improve its position within the automotive industry. She invited participants from all major functions, i.e. sales managers, R&D engineers, financial controllers, as well as the managers of various production sites. The workshop took place outside of the usual working hours on six consecutive Saturdays and was professionally led by an external moderator. In fact, the business unit did not suffer in financial terms at that time. By contrast, it was doing well. However, the business unit manager felt that her unit did not properly exploit its competencies. She argued that, firstly, the existing competencies should facilitate a better differentiation from competitors; and secondly, they should be better recognized and valued by the carmakers.

> *"We asked ourselves: How can we strengthen our position in the automotive industry? How can we convert our services into money – at that time, the carmakers did neither see nor pay for them? How can we realize higher prices per kg? Until then, the carmakers had not adequately rewarded our efforts to reduce the material consumption."*[463]

Moreover, the business unit manager expected carmakers to put more pressure on automotive suppliers in the future. Hence, the workshop's core question was:

> *"How can we effectively [maintain as well as] increase our profits?"*[464]

[463] Source: department head in interviews "Integrate for Control".
[464] Source: ibidem.

The subsequent discussions brought about two major findings: Firstly, profits can be increased when the amount of kilograms used per car is lower than the amount of kilograms paid by the carmaker. Secondly, such a scenario can only be achieved if the business unit controls the processing of the coatings.

Afterwards, the workshop participants discussed what the business unit could offer carmakers in order to be granted control over the paint shops. In this regard, three important ideas emerged: Firstly, if carmakers only had to pay a predetermined price per perfectly coated car body, they would no longer bear the cost of excess material consumption. Secondly, a better "first car okay rate" would improve the productivity of the entire car manufacturing plant.[465] Thirdly, product innovations could lead the way to lower investment costs for paint shop equipment, as well as to a reduced energy input for the painting procedure. In detail, R&D engineers thought about a primer that does not require oven-drying. The global key account managers presented these new ideas to selected customers.

> *"At first, after we had developed the idea, we actively approached several carmakers. We discussed our idea with them and incorporated their feedback"*[466]

Relatively soon thereafter, in 1993, the business unit was approached by a carmaker who planned to build a new manufacturing plant for a new car model. With reference to the plant's new paint shop, the carmaker addressed three different paint shop equipment manufacturers and three different coatings suppliers, among them the focal business unit. The carmaker asked the six companies to form "couples" and to submit as a couple joint quotations comprising of the new paint shop's investment and operating costs, as well as of the material costs for coatings. Not surprisingly, the business unit manager was eager to use this project to turn the workshop's ideas into reality. She set up a dedicated project team to engage in talks with all three equipment manufacturers.

> *"We talked to all three of them to explore their possibilities. One of them mentioned the possibility of additional product innovations for improving the paint shop's environmental sustainability and was therefore chosen as a partner."*[467]

Conversely, this partner also appreciated the business unit's new ideas which the other two coatings suppliers did not have. In order to win the contract, the couple's offering had to stand out from what was then market standard. The business unit knew that the carmaker's best "first car okay rate" in its existing manufacturing plants was 58%. In consequence, it offered a rate of 75% if it could control the processing of the coatings. The carmaker would only have to pay a fixed price for each perfectly coated car body, which would be reduced if the 75% were not reached. Besides,

---

465 See section 4.3.1 for an explanation of the "first car okay rate".
466 Source: department head in interviews "Integrate for Control".
467 Source: ibidem.

repair costs would remain with the business unit. Price calculations were based upon the thickness of the respective layers, the area of the car body's surface and other factors. Hence, when preparing this quotation, the business unit was forced for the first time to determine how exactly it wanted to achieve the ideas from the workshop.

> *"At that time, we had to start calculating. Before, it was all just theory: m², thickness of layers, assumption of a first car okay rate; our offer had to outstrip common market standards all together."*[468]

Above all, the equipment manufacturer guaranteed that investment costs for the paint shop would not exceed a certain amount. If so, the equipment manufacturer would pay for the difference. Moreover, above mentioned product innovations were incorporated into the quotation. Eventually, the carmaker awarded the contract to the business unit and its partner. Nonetheless, the business unit almost did not receive corporate headquarters' approval. The first project application was refused. Only after a second, better prepared presentation was corporate management convinced and thus approved the project. The target date for opening the new car manufacturing plant was in 1995. Thus, all parties were only given two years to implement the offering. This tight schedule forced the equipment manufacturer to start immediately with the planning of the work shop. Likewise, the focal unit's R&D project team immediately began to develop the coatings. However, at that time the car was not yet fully designed which constituted an additional problem for the business unit.

> *"Realizing such a concept usually takes ten years. Thanks to an intensive period of simultaneous engineering we did it in two years. Engineers from all three parties continuously visited one another [...]."*[469]

The new paint shop was supposed to comprise of three parallel lines. Importantly, when negotiating the contract with the carmaker, the business unit had insisted on the prior completion of one paint shop line. The first line was already completed in 1994 for the business unit to test the processing of the new coatings and their appearance on the new car. Very often, the R&D engineers went directly to this line to examine in practice how the single layers act upon each other and to find out what still needed to be improved. Only after the quality of the first line's paint system was approved by all parties, were the other two lines installed accordingly.

> *"We experimented much with the first test line. Our engineers continuously went to the site and conducted test runs. In contrast to finished products, such as pharmaceuticals, paint only becomes a finished product when it is applied on the car. The paint shop equipment must be adjusted accurately."*[470]

---

[468] Source: ibidem.
[469] Source: R&D manager in interviews "Integrate for Control".
[470] Source: ibidem.

Furthermore, the project team wanted this first line to be a means for practicing the new working practices. For the paint shop's operation, predominantly young staff were recruited. They were then trained not only by the business unit, but also by the paint shop manufacturer. For the generation of profits, it was crucial that the paint shop team would be capable of meeting the calculated layer thickness exactly, and of intervening before any quality problems could occur. In 1995, the car manufacturing plant was officially opened and put into operation. As agreed in the contract, the carmaker revised the paint shop's performance three months after the start of production.

> *"[The customer] found that all contractual terms were fully met. What is more, the carmaker recognized that the ongoing continuous improvement projects offered an enormous potential both to further increase the 'first car okay rate' and to lower the material consumption per coated car body. Hereupon, we negotiated with the carmaker that profits from these projects should be shared 50/50 between both parties. Such a deal had never before existed in the industry. This was incredible."*[471]

The business unit eventually improved the "first car okay rate" in this plant to 90%. Another interesting fact is that the business unit was contractually obliged to qualify a second coatings supplier two years after the start of production. Until then, it was the exclusive supplier. However, none of the competitors were qualified at that time because their coatings still lacked the required specification. Put differently, the integration into the customer's value chain in combination with product innovations generated a substantial competitive advantage for the business unit. Nevertheless, achieving this success was hard work. The internal resistance was enormous. For instance, the controlling managers worried about making losses from supplying material without being able to invoice it upon delivery:

> *"How would a perfectly coated car body be determined? How can we ensure that the customer does not take advantage of us? How can we possibly adapt our IT systems so fast?"*[472]

Furthermore, the project team's R&D engineers were concerned about the short time frame in which the product innovations had to be realized. Also, the sales staff complained. They argued that selling perfectly coated car bodies would be impossible. They would only be able to sell coatings measured in kilograms. In response, the business unit manager constantly motivated her project team and helped them to overcome the obstacles. Besides, despite the initial resistance, the project's progress was present in daily conversation.

---

[471] Source: department head in interviews "Integrate for Control".
[472] Source: ibidem.

"The global key account managers especially wanted to know about the project's status, the problems and solutions."[473]

In 1996, another carmaker adopted the new offering, followed by another in 1997. They each used it for one of their existing manufacturing plants. There, too, the service teams succeeded in significantly augmenting the "first car okay rate". Hence, the new business model proved operable without the need to build a new paint shop or to partner with a paint shop equipment manufacturer. At that time, the entire global car industry showed great interest in the focal unit's new business model. Back then, carmakers intensively sought ways to reduce their costs and to improve their efficiency. The new business model constituted an opportunity to achieve such goals.

4.3.4 Visualization of the BMI Process

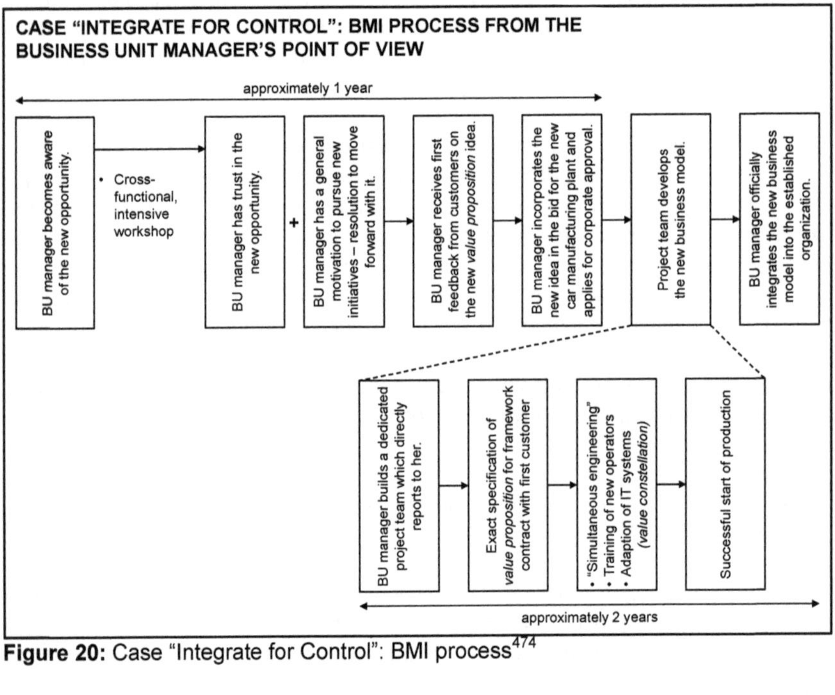

Figure 20: Case "Integrate for Control": BMI process[474]

Figure 20 displays the BMI process in the case "Integrate for Control" from the business unit manager's point of view. The business unit manager was aware that her unit had the competencies for achieving a better position in the automotive industry. After holding a cross-functional, intensive workshop, she saw her notion confirmed and gained trust in the workshop's new business model idea. Even though

---

[473] Source: ibidem.
[474] Source: own Figure.

her unit did not struggle financially, she was motivated to pursue the idea in order to gain market share, as well as to maintain and increase profits. Subsequently, the business unit presented its idea to selected carmakers and received initial positive feedback. Shortly after, the chance arose for executing the new idea in a new car manufacturing plant. The business unit manager insisted on trying it out. She set up a dedicated project team and, after corporate approval, charged it with realizing the idea at the first customer. Within the following two years of hard work, resistance and constant trial-and-error, the team successfully finished the project. Thereupon, the business unit manager officially integrated the new business model and additional customers adopted the new offering.

4.4 Case 4: "Special-to-Standard"

The case "Special-to-Standard" encompasses a failed BMI in *ElectricCorp*. In 2010, about three years after the official integration, the new business model was dissolved because of the projected high financial losses from providing standard cable harnesses to the aviation industry. The development towards the new business model was driven by a business unit manager, whose unit traditionally manufactures special cables and special cable assemblies for non-aviation industries. The case description reconstructs the main events within the five years from the idea to the final dissolution of the new business model. The titles of the cited interviewees are not mentioned in the source details for identity protection.

4.4.1 Portrayal of the Traditional and the Failed New Business Model

Figure 21 depicts the traditional and the failed new business model in the business model canvas. The traditional model is still in operation, whereas the failed business model no longer exists.

Traditional Business Model

Traditionally, the business unit offers copper cables and cable assemblies for special purpose applications in the following three main target industries: telecommunication, industrial automation and medical technology. Nearly all products fulfill very high performance requirements and can be considered state-of-the-art. Thanks to strong design competences, the business unit is also capable of supporting customers with special cable requests from other industries. The connectors necessary for the cable assemblies are not molded in-house and are only partially designed by the business unit. The direct sales force regularly visits existing and potential new customers in order to find out about their needs and to win orders. Besides, customer awareness of the business unit's products is generated via trade fairs or by advertising in the relevant trade journals. Customers experience personal assistance by the business unit's product management and/or internal sales staff. Moreover, regular customer events aim at further strengthening customer relationships. Since most products have been designed specifically for the customer, the volume per order is often relatively small, whereas the negotiated higher prices reflect upon the unit's special engineering competences.

The traditional key activities include customized design and the precise manufacture of special cables and assemblies that fulfill very high performance criteria. Hence, electrical and chemical engineers, as well as the accessible machinery constitute the key resources in the traditional business model. Buyer-supplier relationships are maintained for the sourcing of input material such as copper, insulation material, or connectors. Clearly, the traditional business model is value-driven because delivering the value proposition requires employing experienced engineers at a high cost, as well as state-of-the-art machinery.

CASE "SPECIAL-TO-STANDARD": PORTRAYAL OF THE TRADITIONAL AND THE FAILED NEW BUSINESS MODEL IN THE BUSINESS MODEL CANVAS

"**Traditional**": established business model before BMI
"**Failed**": failed new business model

KP

Traditional:
- Buyer-supplier relationships for input material (e.g., copper, insulation material, connectors)

Failed:
- All components including cables were sourced externally.
- The component suppliers had to be approved by the OEM.
- Due to the relatively small volume, the business unit suffered from long lead times and high costs when procuring the components, specified by the customer, on its own behalf.

KA

Traditional:
- Design + manufacture of special solutions

Failed:
Stable overall process chain including:
- order taking
- product management (BoM and BoL changes)
- batch tracing
- procurement

KR

Traditional:
- Engineers
- Machinery

Failed:
- New building
- New machinery (too expensive)
- New IT (too expensive)
- No new engineers experienced in aviation
- No low wages

VP

Traditional:
Design and manufacture of special copper cables and special cable assemblies

Failed:
- Assembly of standard cable harnesses according to the exact but frequently changing specification given by one aviation OEM customer

(Future ambition was to offer to OEMs own design and engineering services for electrical systems used in aircrafts.)

CR

Traditional:
- Personal assistance
- Customer events

Failed:
- Business unit management
- Dedicated personal assistance on lower levels was set up only very late.

CH

Traditional:
- Direct sales force
- Trade fairs

Failed:
- OEM customer was approached and won by BU management.
- BU management intended to win more aviation OEMs in the future.

CS

Traditional:
- Telecommunication
- Industrial Automation
- Medical technology
- Other customers requiring special solutions

Failed:
- Aviation (OEM)

C$

Traditional: Value-driven

New: Cost-driven; Profits could have been achieved through economies of scale. But fixed assets plus wages were too expensive in relation to volume and unit prices in the framework contract.

R$

Traditional: Asset sale; product feature dependent prices for customized (special) products, smaller volume orders

Failed: Asset sale; Long-term framework contract with OEM; Specified annual volumes and unit prices

VP=Value Proposition, CS=Customer Segments, CH=Channels, CR=Customer Relationships, R$=Revenue Streams
KA=Key Activities, KR=Key Resources, KP=Key Partnerships, C$=Cost Structure

Figure 21: Case "Special-to-Standard": traditional and failed business model[475]

Failed New Business Model

The dissolved business unit offered cable harnesses for one OEM aircraft manufacturer. From a technical point of view, the components of these harnesses could be characterized as standard. None of the assembly's components were state-of-the-art. Instead, these goods were sold in high volumes at low cost. Specifications for the harnesses were given by the customer and dependent upon the type and configuration of the aircrafts to be built. The business unit complied with the official

[475] Source: own Figure adapted from Osterwalder / Pigneur (2010), p. 44.

aerospace quality management standards as well as with the additional requirements set by the customer, for instance, with regard to batch tracing. The business unit management saw this value proposition as an entry into the aviation industry that had previously not been addressed by the corporation. For the future, the business unit management intended to become a design and engineering partner for all major OEMs. The unit's only customer was initially approached directly by the management of the traditional business unit, which further planned to approach more aircraft OEMs. Likewise, the relationship with the customer was maintained by the business unit management. However, the customer also wanted direct contacts on lower hierarchy levels for operational and quality management-related issues.

> *"They did not communicate dedicated contact persons to [the customer]. [The customer] randomly talked with whomever [it] could get a hold of."*[476]

The revenue streams in the failed business model originated from a framework contract with the OEM. This contract was negotiated by the management of the traditional business unit. It specified unit prices and annual volumes for several consecutive years. Compared to the unit's typical orders, the overall volume specified in this contract can be seen as very large. However, other suppliers of cable harnesses to the aviation industry usually deal with much bigger volumes.

In the failed business model, no single activity was per se more crucial than others for realizing the value proposition. Rather, it was important to have a stable process chain in place – from the order reception to the shipment of the final product - that fulfills the OEM's quality and lead time requirements. The business unit management underestimated the challenge of setting up such a process chain. For instance, it took a very long time until the electronic data interchange with the customer functioned error-free. Furthermore,

> *"[...] product engineers often needed more time than expected to translate the frequently changing assembly specifications into the correct bills of material and labor."*[477]

Another serious challenge was the installation of batch tracing, which is very important in the aviation industry. Moreover, the procurement of some of the parts regularly took too long. Nonetheless, the process chain in place at the moment of the business unit's dissolution was considered stable by the customer. The management of the traditional business unit knew upfront that to a certain degree new tangible and human resources would be necessary to deliver the value proposition. But only after the framework contract was signed did it gradually realize what exactly it had to invest in. An additional building was constructed at the same site as the traditional business model. Investments included new state-of-the-art machinery for the

---

[476] Source: interviews "Special-to-Standard".
[477] Source: ibidem.

automatic assembly as well as new IT systems for the electronic data interchange and for batch tracing. Furthermore, new operators were hired. By contrast, the business unit management did not recruit new process or product engineers with experience in the aviation industry. Instead, it entrusted the engineers from the traditional business model. All components including cables were sourced externally on behalf of the business unit and then assembled in-house. However, it was the OEM who specified the components and chose their suppliers.

> *"We did not have the permission to qualify additional component suppliers that could have bridged supply shortages or offered lower prices."*[478]

In fact, this business model was completely cost-driven. For standard cable harnesses, aircraft OEMs would choose suppliers solely by the lowest price offered. But retrospectively, the fixed assets installed by the business unit management, e.g., the new machinery or the IT systems, were far too expensive to reach the cost per unit fixed in the framework contract.

4.4.2 Classification as Failed BMI

Table 26 provides an overview of the reasons to classify the business model "Special-to-Standard" as BMI failure. The BMI process did not entail any mergers or acquisitions. Further explanation for all other criteria is explicated below.

Criteria for classifying a business model as BMI in the multi-business firm		**Business Model: "Special-to-Standard"**	
		Assessment (Yes/No)	**Reasoning**
1	New or changed-to-become-new value proposition	Yes	- First tier supplier to aviation industry (industry-specific quality management standards) - Standard cable harnesses instead of special cables or special assemblies - High volume / low cost instead of low volume / high cost
2	Innovative value constellation: New, and/or changed, and/or suppressed working practices to fulfill the value proposition	Yes	New working practices in - electronic data interchange with OEM - product engineering - assembly (new machinery and new operators) - batch tracing
3	New-to-the-firm (corporation)	Yes	No other *ElectricCorp* business unit had ever before supplied components to the aviation industry.

[478] Source: ibidem.

4	Integrated into the firm	Yes	*Option 1:* The new business model was integrated through a new additional business unit. (see Figure 4: "Generic Options of BMI Integration")
5	Created without M&A	Yes	No M&A activities throughout the BMI
6	Financial success	No	- High financial losses - Dissolution of framework contract despite penalty to prevent further losses - Closure of business unit and exit from aviation industry

Table 26: Case "Special-to-Standard": reasons for classification as failed BMI[479]

New Value Proposition

The physical product – an assembled cable harness – appears similar in both business models. However, the product features and the application are fundamentally different. In the failed business model, the firm clearly addressed a new customer need.

Innovative Value Constellation

The below new working practices had to be adopted in order to fulfill the value proposition.

- The business unit had to understand how to set up the electronic data interchange system with the OEM, which was essential for order reception. Eight to nine IT-interfaces with the OEM had to be simultaneously maintained, whereas in the traditional business model one IT-interface has been sufficient if at all necessary.

- Furthermore, the product engineers from the traditional business model had to learn how to read the harness specifications given by the OEM and how to translate them into the correct bills of material and labor.

- New machinery for automatic assembly was bought that had not previously existed in the traditional business model. New operators were hired for running these machines and also for manual assembly.

- Moreover, the new business unit had to install an industry-specific batch tracing system. Previously, no business unit in the entire corporation had gathered experience of such a system.

New-to-the-Firm (Corporation)

The failed business model was not new-to-the-world. There is at least one well-established competitor delivering a similar product to the same aircraft OEM.

479 Source: own Table.

However, the business model was new to *ElectricCorp* as it had never before delivered components to the aviation industry.

Integrated into the Firm

The framework contract with the OEM was signed in 2007. Thereafter, a new additional business unit was officially integrated into the firm by corporate management (Figure 22). It was intended to execute the framework contract and further develop the firm's footprint in the aviation industry. Investments into a new building and new machinery were made. Moreover, new operators were recruited by the new business unit. As for the product management, process engineering, IT and G&A activities; the new business unit worked with the staff available in the traditional business model.

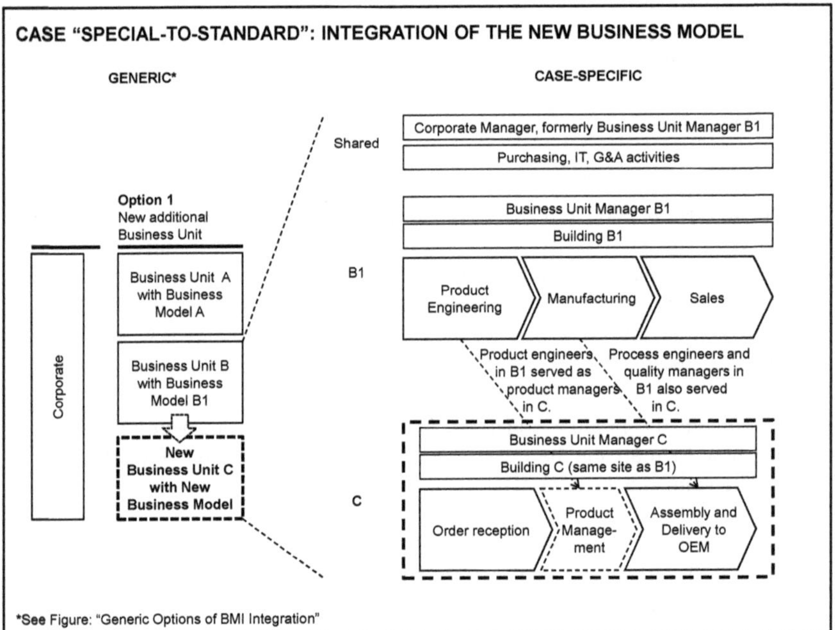

Figure 22: Case "Special-to-Standard": integration of the new business model[480]

Financial Failure

The delivery of products to the OEM started at the end of 2008. Throughout 2009, it became obvious that the investments had been too high to generate profits within the boundaries of the framework contract. After unsuccessful negotiations with the OEM, corporate management decided in the beginning of 2010 to cancel the framework contract and to exit from the aviation industry entirely. A penalty had to be paid to the

[480] Source: own Figure.

OEM for dissolving the contract; furthermore the internal expenses such as severance payments and depreciation were less costly than the business's continuation (Table 27).

Indicators of financial failure
- Interviewee: *"If we had continued, the negative EBIT would have accumulated to [mid-range two digit] million Euros until the end of the framework contract. Such a loss would have endangered the entire site."*
- Press article in 2010: *"[ElectricCorp's] annual result contains a negative effect of [low-range two digit] million Euros from giving up the project with [the aircraft OEM]."*

Table 27: Case "Special-to-Standard": indicators of financial failure[481]

4.4.3 Description of the Failed BMI Process

One of the product managers, who had previously worked in aerospace, approached the business unit manager with the idea of supplying cable products to the aviation industry; an industry in which the business unit had no prior exposure. The business unit manager approved of the idea because it potentially meant additional revenues and a broader customer base. Nevertheless, the overall financial situation of the business unit was good at that time. In 2005, both managers contacted a major aircraft OEM that eventually became their customer.

> *"During the negotiations, they promised a lot to the customer. They strongly emphasized the firm's existing skill set."*[482]

They convinced the OEM to close a framework contract with them for the delivery of standard cable harnesses – designed by the OEM – to be embedded in aircraft. In contrast to special cable harnesses, the standard ones are typically delivered in large volumes. Consequently, the cumulative order volume specified in the contract foresaw a high two-digit million Euros amount. Hence, with only one contract, the business unit became a first tier supplier in the aviation industry and also immediately visible to all other industry players due to the relatively large order volume. On the other hand, the competition for standard cable harnesses is much more intensified than for special ones. Thus, prices are decisive. Moreover, the OEM only assigned a relatively small share of its total demand for those products to the business unit.

The framework contract was signed in 2007. It specified market level unit prices. Before the signature, both managers elaborated a business and resource plan in order to show that the given unit price could be reached while still generating profits. The business plan was presented to corporate management who approved of it since it promised positive margins and since entry into this industry broadened the entire firm's customer base. Notably, both managers envisioned the business unit eventually designing own cable products for aircrafts.

481 Sources: own Table with data from interviews "Special-to-Standard" and from a press article.
482 Source: interviews "Special-to-Standard".

"In the framework contract we did not position ourselves as a subcontractor or as an 'extended work bench' like most competitors, but as an autonomous production company."[483]

After the signature, a new business unit was founded, dedicated to the aerospace industry, with the former product manager becoming the business unit manager. The manager of the traditional business unit was promoted to corporate management level overseeing the managers of both her former and the new business unit. Notably, before and during the contract negotiations with the customer, both managers avoided involving other industry experts or visiting companies that manufacture similar components.

According to the original schedule, the delivery of the harnesses to the OEM should have started at the beginning of 2008. However, delivery only started at the end of 2008. In fact, it took much longer than anticipated to build up the new production line and to have it running according to the customer's requirements. New machinery had to be purchased and new operators had to be hired and trained. One of the major problems was to install a functioning batch tracing system, which also involved new IT solutions. Hereby, the new business unit gave complete trust to the existing process engineering team, which was never before confronted with such a task. Establishing the IT-interfaces with the OEM turned out to be another major problem. Further delay was caused by the fact that until the end of 2008, messages from the OEM relating to operations often did not reach the right person within the new business unit on time. Partly with the help of engineers from the OEM and external IT experts, the business unit eventually fixed the operational problems, achieved the quality standards, and could start delivery.

"At some points, we even surpassed the quality requirements."[484]

In mid-2008, a new corporate level manager was sent to the site to oversee both business units there, together with the promoted former business unit manager. The new manager was skeptical about the profitability of the aerospace business and, during 2009, she recalculated the business plan that had been presented to corporate management together with the framework contract in 2007. She found that the cost for one delivered unit was indeed much higher than the mutually agreed unit price. The actual costs for the new production line including the IT solution far exceeded the assumed costs. Furthermore:

"The frequency and extent of the OEM's change requests to the standard product specification was perceived as very demanding."[485]

483 Source: ibidem.
484 Source: ibidem.
485 Source: ibidem.

Concerning the additional costs, when it was only necessary to purchase limited quantities of certain components, the components' procurement from the approved vendors was too expensive, and also took too long. Until the arrival of those components, other harnesses were produced that the OEM only bought for a reduced price, if at all. The recalculation by the new corporate level manager predicted very high cumulative losses for the new business unit if the framework contract was continued in its original form. Consequently, she entered into negotiations with the OEM with the goal of improving conditions. Even though the OEM acknowledged the problems, it was not willing to change the framework contract because other suppliers managed to deliver similar products for an even lower unit price. Moreover, the business unit could not have managed to relocate the production line to a low cost country soon enough. Corporate management then decided in the beginning of 2010 to dissolve the framework contract and to exit the aviation industry entirely. Thereafter, the new machinery was sold to competitors who confirmed its very high technical standard. The two managers who had initiated and built the new business model, along with the newly hired operators, were required to leave the firm.

4.4.4 Visualization of the Failed BMI Process

Figure 23 visualizes the BMI process in the case "Special-to-Standard" from the point of view of the former manager of the traditional business unit.

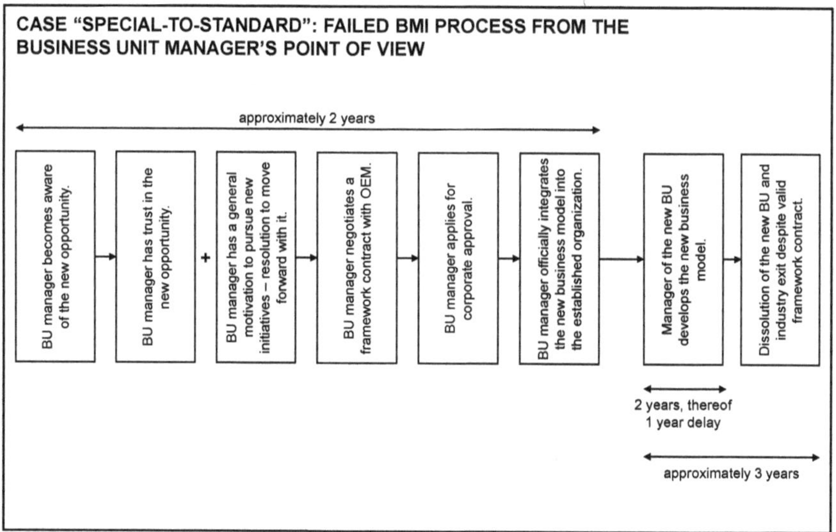

Figure 23: Case "Special-to-Standard": BMI process[486]

[486] Source: own Figure.

She was made aware of the aerospace opportunity by a proposal from a product manager, who had previously gathered experience in this industry. Due to the unavailability of the business unit manager for this research, the fieldwork did not reveal how exactly she gained the confidence, firstly, to enter the aviation industry and, secondly, to focus on standard cable harnesses in the first place. However, the interviewees confirmed her confidence in the opportunity. Her motivation to pursue this opportunity can be explained by the prospect of increased revenues and a more diversified customer base. Both the business unit manager and the product manager contacted the OEM and negotiated the framework contract. This was then translated into a business plan and then successfully presented to corporate management. Immediately following, a new additional business unit was officially integrated into the organization with the task of executing the framework contract. With a delay of approximately one year over the business plan, the new production line was established and the delivery of the standard cable harnesses to the OEM began. One year later, corporate management decided to withdraw from the framework contract and to completely dissolve the new business unit because of the projected high losses associated with continuing the contract's execution.

4.5 Case 5: "System House"

The case "System House" entails the blocked attempt for a BMI in a financially struggling business unit of *ElectricCorp*. Corporate management was confronted with two different new business model proposals. If successfully realized, the first option would have constituted a BMI, whereas the second option would have eliminated elements of the traditional business model. But neither of the proposals was attempted. Instead, corporate management eventually decided to sell the business unit. The case covers a time span of two years; it begins with the understanding that the traditional business model was no longer sustainable, and it ends with the divestment in 2010.

4.5.1 Portrayal of the Traditional and Two Proposed Business Models

Figure 24 portrays the business unit's traditional business model and indicates how the two new business model proposals differentiate therefrom. In the first proposal, both the value proposition and the value constellation would have been new-to-the-firm. Given its integration, this new business model could have classified as BMI. The second proposal foresaw the narrowing down of the traditional business model to those activities that in the past had proven profitable. Consequently, this new business model proposal did not contain new-to-the-firm elements and would not have qualified as BMI. However, it shall still be presented as it is an integral part of this case.

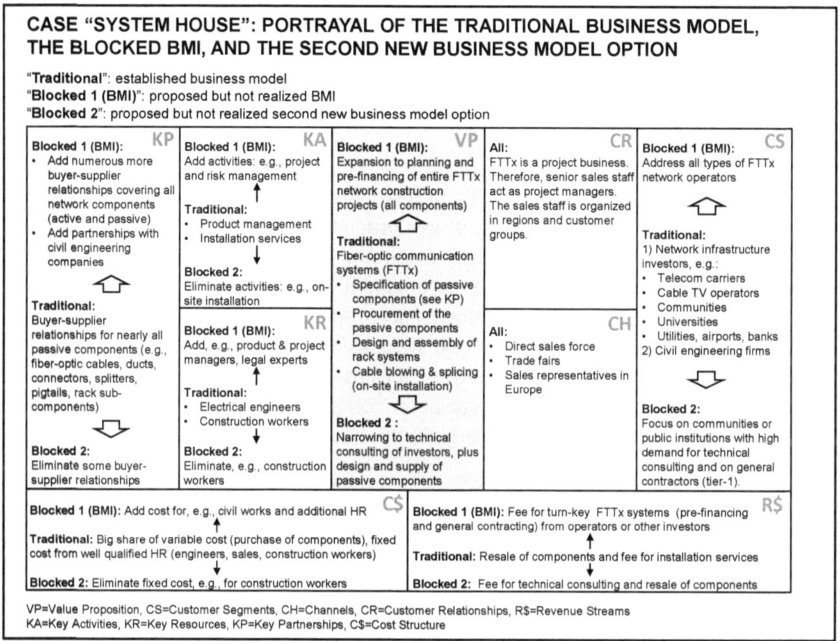

Figure 24: Case "System House": traditional and proposed business models[487]

Traditional Business Model

The business unit offered passive components for broadband fiber-optic telecommunication systems that connect the operator's switching equipment in a region's "wire center" or "central office" to final internet or cable television consumers. These systems replace existing copper infrastructure based on telephone wires or coaxial cables and are often referred to as "Fiber to the x" (FTTx) networks, whereby x can stand for, e.g., home (H), node (N), or building (B). Based on the customer-provided network topology, the business unit specified the best suited passive components and delivered them to the construction site. Passive components include fiber-optic cables, ducts for cable protection, connectors, splitters, and racks. Nearly all components were specified by the business unit but procured from outside the corporation. Consequently, numerous buyer-supplier relationships had to be maintained. In-house, the business unit focused on the assembly of rack systems. It furthermore mastered the blowing and splicing of the fibers and was thus capable of supporting the on-site installation of those components. Customers for passive components were the investors in such infrastructure types; they include, for instance, telecom carriers, cable TV operators, communities, utilities, universities, airports, banks and hospitals. By contrast, the on-site installation services were offered to civil engineering companies, which physically build the network. The

487 Source: own Figure adapted from Osterwalder / Pigneur (2010), p. 44.

business unit employed supervisors and workers who performed installation services directly at the construction site. Customers were addressed either by the business unit's direct sales force or by one of its sales representatives throughout Europe. Press articles, trade fairs or speeches at FTTx events were intended to draw attention and interest.

Table 28 illustrates that the business unit generated losses over the four years prior to its divestment. Over those years, it was gradually winning fewer and fewer new projects. Moreover, many of those externally procured components became commodities, which increased the price pressure. Beyond that, the business unit's rack systems had not been substantially improved by its engineers since the early 2000s. In the meantime, competitors had successfully copied them and were offering them at a cheaper price. The main reason for customers choosing the business unit was increasingly based upon its installation competencies, rather than its product competencies. Due to decreasing margins, the business unit failed to cover its fixed costs.

Performance of business unit with the traditional BM	**2006**	**2007**	**2008**	**2009**	**2010** (Divestment at year-end)
Sales Revenues in kEUR	~14,500	~16,000	~17,000	~14,500	~10,500
Operating Margin in %	2,9%	-2,5%	-4,1%	-11,5%	-12,5%

Table 28: Case "System House": the business unit's financial performance[488]

Notably, in 2009, the business unit provided consulting services for the first time to a community encompassing the definition of an appropriate FTTx network topography and the corresponding passive architecture. However, it was only a pilot project. The business unit did not make the community pay for this service.

Proposed BMI: "System House"

The first new business model proposal consisted of an offering expansion. Accordingly, the business unit would become a "System House" capable of realizing entire FTTx networks, even on its own behalf. Eventually, the business unit would have turned into an investor in FTTx infrastructure who sells or leases turn-key systems to other investors or operators. For such a business model, the below new resources and processes would have to be added.

- FTTx networks would also comprise of active components, approximately to the same extent as the passive ones. Active components include, for example, converters, switches, routers and servers. Therefore, additional product management competencies, non-existent in the entire corporation, would have

[488] Source: own Table with data from interviews "System House".

been needed as well as additional buyer-supplier relationships. The product management of active components would have represented a new-to-the-firm activity.

- The business unit would have had to engage civil engineering companies for the networks' installation. Moreover, it would have had to partner with such firms when providing after-sales maintenance services.
- Similar to the "One-Stop-Solution" business model, the business unit would have had to act as general contractor. For this task, additional project managers would have been needed with general contracting experience. Furthermore, legal experts would have had to be consulted, for example, on risk management issues.
- The business unit would have had to pre-finance entire projects. Pre-financing would have represented another new-to-the-firm aspect. In general, the corporation aims at preserving its cash flows.

In the form of an FTTx "System House", the business unit could have marketed the entire value chain. Promoters of this proposal assumed that customers found such a value proposition more appealing. They argued that, with increasingly augmented project volume, the business unit would have improved its position vis-à-vis the component manufacturers, resulting in higher profit margins.

Second New Business Model Proposal

The second new business model proposal emphasized narrowing down the offering and combining it with consulting. Accordingly, the business unit would have focused on customers with a high demand for technical consulting, such as communities.

> *"These customers would have been charged for being provided with the appropriate FTTx network topography and passive architecture. Simultaneously, the business unit could have offered the same customers all the passive components needed to realize the proposed network architecture."*[489]

The gratis pilot project in 2009, mentioned above, proved that this customer group, which rarely employs its own FTTx experts, has the need for technical consulting. Furthermore, overall accepted technical standards for FTTx networks, which would render a customer-specific network planning obsolete, have not yet evolved. Paradoxically, many passive components have commoditized but there is still much variety in each component's exact technical specification. The latter depends on a network's architecture and is thus customer-specific. The business unit could have won new projects by delivering the added value of network planning. Moreover, the proposal foresaw the elimination of all on-site installation services offered by the business unit.

---

[489] Source: senior project manager in interviews "System House".

> *"Cost analyses revealed that the construction-related services were generating losses on a stand-alone basis."*[490]

In contrast with the first new business model proposal, general contracting was not seen as necessary to win new projects. Instead, general contractors could have been approached as potential customers for the passive components.

4.5.2 The Business Unit's Divestment Process

In the beginning of 2009, corporate management decided to send one of its project managers from the central strategy department to the focal business unit.

> *"My task was to analyze all available financials in order to identify the reasons for the unit's unexpectedly bad financial performance over the last two years. [...] Since the local controller was simultaneously the chief purchasing manager, collecting data was not always easy."*[491]

The business unit manager agreed to this measure because she was not satisfied with the local controller's performance. The latter had been hired by the former director of the unit's main plant. This director had worked at that plant since its foundation in the 1990s, whereas the business unit manager had joined only in mid-2008. Understandably, this director's influence within the business unit was substantial. However, from a formal point of view, the business unit manager possessed superior decision-making power. After her arrival, the project manager recalculated the profitability of single product and service segments, customers, countries and finished projects.

> *"It took me more than three months to fully understand the unit's complex business model. [...] I also developed several cost-cutting measures aimed at quickly improving the unit's bottom line. However, their effect was limited due to the unit's relatively small size."*[492]

The project manager's report to corporate management in mid-2009 revealed that the unit's current business model was not sustainable and that strategic measures were necessary to achieve the turnaround. Thereupon, corporate management assigned the project manager to develop a new business model proposal from her office in the central strategy department. Moreover, corporate management dismissed the plant director because she was held responsible for the unit's difficult situation. Subsequently, the business unit manager was given this position on an interim basis until end-2009, when a new plant director was appointed from within the company by corporate management.

---

[490] Source: ibidem.
[491] Source: ibidem.
[492] Source: ibidem.

Also at the end of 2009, the project manager finished her new business model proposal and distributed it to both corporate management and business unit management. It contained the idea of narrowing down the offering, as described above.[493] Corporate management took the existence of this proposal as the reason to meet with business unit management for mutually determining the future direction of the unit's business model. The meeting took place in the beginning of 2010, and both the business unit manager and the new plant director attended. In the meeting, the proposal was put up for open discussion and quickly objected to by the new plant director, who made the below remark.

> *"I considered construction-related services such as the blowing of fiber-optic cables or the splicing of fibers as essential for winning projects. Having those services in-house would allow the business unit to react quickly to such demands. [The project manager] did not have enough time to thoroughly understand the [traditional] business model and therefore applied inappropriate methods when calculating those services' profitability."*[494]

Beyond that, the new plant director pled for an overall "System House" business model entailing the planning, realizing, and pre-financing of entire FTTx network construction projects.[495] Basic features of this alternative proposal were already brought up by the former plant director in 2008 but were only discussed unit-internally. In this discussion, the business unit manager was undecided. She neither positioned herself for nor against one of the two new business model proposals. On the one hand, she acknowledged that pre-financing and general contracting could help differentiate the business unit from other component manufacturers. On the other hand, she stated that she did not find it necessary to enter into each project as a general contractor. With reference to the pilot project in 2009, she argued that the technical planning of FTTx networks could be sufficient to win a project.

Eventually, corporate management concluded the meeting without a new business model decision. Instead, it expected the business unit within the next months to clarify how it should best offer added value to its customers in the future. However, corporate management did not receive such feedback. The new plant director was busy with carrying out operational-level changes at her plant.

> *"I did not see it as my task to identify strategic recommendations. The business unit manager, who is positioned above me, exists to fulfill this task."*[496]

However, the business unit manager apparently did not arrive at a conclusion within those months. During mid-2010, in the face of repeated and considerable financial

---

493 See section 4.5.1 "Second New Business Model Proposal".
494 Source: new plant director in interviews "System House".
495 See section 4.5.1 "Proposed BMI: 'System House'".
496 Source: new plant director in interviews "System House".

losses and without the desired feedback, corporate management lost patience and decided to sell the business unit. Strategic investors were approached and the business unit was sold to one of them at the end of 2010.

> *"I sensed that from the summer of 2010 [corporate management] did no longer want to be bothered with it."*[497]

4.5.3 Visualization of the Business Unit's Divestment Process

CASE "SYSTEM HOUSE": THE BUSINESS UNIT'S DIVESTMENT PROCESS

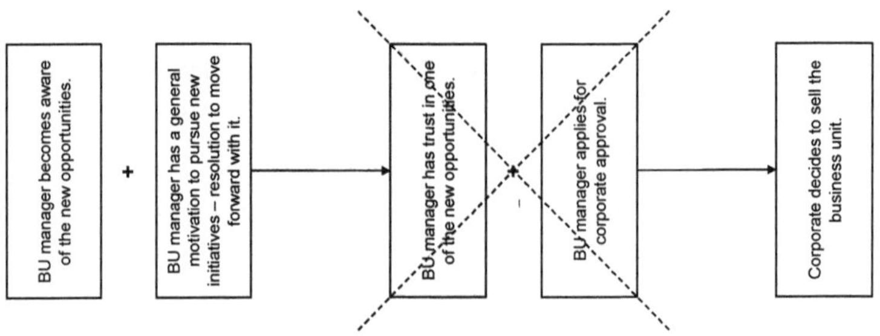

Figure 25: Case "System House": business unit's divestment process[498]

Figure 25 visualizes the process of the divestment from the business unit manager's point of view. She was aware of two new alternative opportunities and, due to the persistently poor financial situation, was also generally motivated to engage in new initiatives. Nonetheless, she did not develop trust in any of those opportunities. Even though it was expected of her, she did not confront corporate management with her own new business model proposal. Subsequently, corporate management decided to sell the business unit.

4.6 Summary of the Case Descriptions

This chapter's purpose is to create familiarity with each of the five cases that together represent the empirical basis for discovering answers to the research question. This carefully selected, "polar type" sample comprises of three positive and two negative BMI cases. For each case, it is shown how the new business model differs from the traditional one, and in which way the BMI identification criteria are met. Moreover, the BMI process is described and visualized from the business unit manager's point of view.

---

[497] Source: ibidem.
[498] Source: own Figure.

Summarizing the positive cases (“BMI Success”):

- The case 1 “New-Tech Domain” elucidates how a business unit manager succeeded at developing and integrating a new business model for the commercialization of an emergent, new-to-the-firm technology.
- The case 2 “One-Stop Solution” depicts how another business unit manager succeeded in realizing a new solution- and project-based business model that can theoretically function independently of the unit’s traditional product-based business model.
- The case 3 “Integrate for Control” illustrates how another business unit manager succeeded at incorporating the unit into the customers’ value chain, thereby redesigning the traditional business model.

Summarizing the negative cases (“BMI Failure”):

- The case 4 “Special-to-Standard” describes how another business unit manager, whose unit traditionally manufactures special products to non-aviation industries, failed in realizing a new business model dedicated to providing standard products to the aircraft manufacturers.
- The case 5 “System House” presents the blocked attempt for a BMI in another business unit that was financially struggling and eventually sold by corporate management.

The findings presented in the subsequent chapters are induced from these cases.

5 A Conceptual BMI Process Model

Visualized in Figure 26, this chapter presents a conceptual BMI process model. It integrates all five case-specific process models, and includes the illustration of the point at which the two negative BMI cases failed. It is derived from merging the single-case process models into one broader process model.[499] It abstracts from the concrete course of action in each BMI and, therefore, is of a more general character.

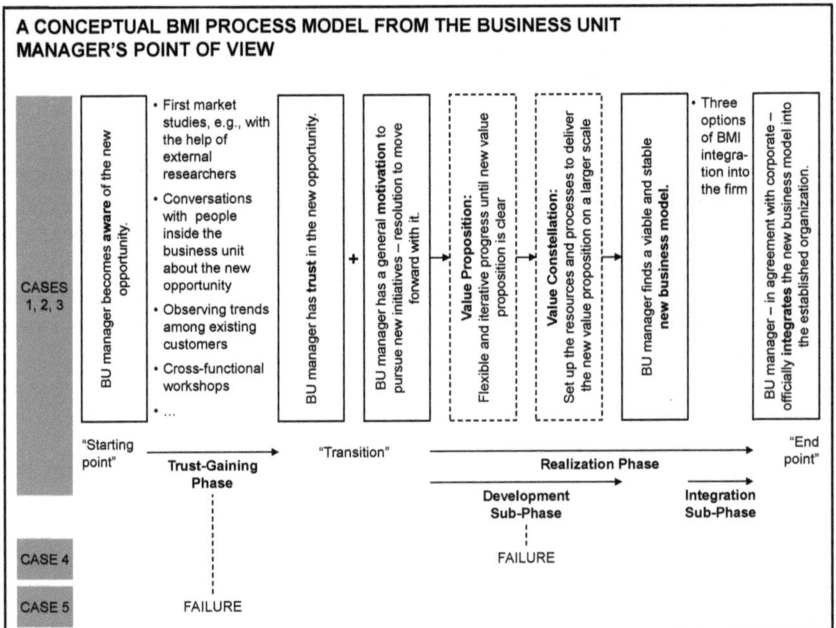

Figure 26: Conceptual BMI process model[500]

This model reflects the business unit manager's perspective on the BMI process. It contains a starting and end point, the two major phases of trust-gaining and realization, as well as a point of transition between these two phases. The second major phase, realization, is separated into two sub-phases, development and integration. The solid rectangles throughout the model denote, on the one hand, preconditions to engage in the phases and, on the other hand, effects from the phases. Within the development phase, the dotted rectangular blocks "value proposition" and "value constellation" reveal the sequence of management priorities within a phase. Henceforth, distinct management practices can be attributed to phases, sub-phases, or blocks.

[499] See section 3.4 for the technique used to arrive at the conceptual BMI process model.
[500] Source: own Figure.

Starting Point

From the business unit manager's point of view, the BMI process begins when she becomes aware of the new opportunity. Hereby, the term new opportunity does not necessarily mean a clearly laid-out new business model. Rather, it refers to an indication of the direction in which the firm or the business unit could develop. The five cases show that ideas can originate from the following:

- observing technology trends,
- observing customer behavior,
- unusual customer requests,
- observing competitors, or
- newly hired staff with experience in other companies or industries.

If the idea does not stem directly from the business unit manager, other employees can make their idea known to her through, for example, workshops or direct conversations.

Trust and Motivation

Case	General motivations to pursue new opportunities	
	From the case descriptions	**Motivational factor**
1	- Need to replace lost business (lost due to political reasons) for the business unit - Constant product innovation pressure in the traditional business model because of relatively quick commoditization or substitution	- Desire to grow - Latent threat in current market
2	- Demand for power cables of higher technical standards too low to generate further growth for the business unit - Convert existing know-how into additional profits - Current products at the edge of becoming commoditized, leading to increased margin pressure	- Desire to grow - Use of internal competencies - Latent threat in current market
3	- Better exploitation of existing competencies to allow for a better differentiation - Customers expected to increase price pressure	- Use of internal competencies - Latent threat in current market
4	- Broaden the customer base - Generate additional growth through existing competencies	- Desire to grow - Use of internal competencies
5	- Sustained financial losses	- Direct threat of extinction

Table 29: Overview of motivational factors[501]

The business unit manager then enters into a trust-gaining phase. If, in the end, she has developed trust in the new opportunity so that it seems worth pursuing; plus if she has some form of motivation to generally pursue new opportunities, the BMI

[501] Source: own Table.

process continues with the realization phase. Notably, trust and motivation of the business unit manager appear to be two preconditions for engaging in the physical realization of the new (business model) idea. Case 5 demonstrates that if trust is missing, the transition from the trust-gaining into the realization phase might not take place. As for the motivation to generally pursue new opportunities, the cases 1 to 4 reveal that such motivation can result from combinations of the following factors: the desire to grow, the desire to make use of internal competencies and a latent threat on the margins in the traditional business model. Case 5 discloses that the immediate threat of extinction due to sustained financial losses represents another motivational factor. Table 29 illustrates how these four motivational factors occur in the cases.

Realization

The subsequent realization phase is divided into the development and the integration sub-phases. In fact, the development sub-phase can span several years. Within this phase, the first management priority should be the determination of the new value proposition. Visions and ideas must be transformed into a concrete and tangible plan of action. The three successful BMI cases illustrate that this task requires flexibility and room for iterations, as well as resources dedicated for testing. Only after the new value proposition is clear should the new value constellation be set up, i.e. those resources and processes necessary to deliver the new value proposition on a larger scale. Once the new business model is developed and its viability proven, the business unit manager – in agreement with corporate management – may officially integrate it into the established organization, whereby it transitions into daily routine. Thereby, the BMI process ends.[502] Case 4 reveals that the official integration of a new business model (through signing the framework contract) can lead to failure, if performed before it is proven that the new value proposition is deliverable at a profit. In fact, in that case the business unit manager disregarded the importance of the development sub-phase.

Chapter 6 provides deeper insights into the phases, sub-phases and blocks.

[502] See section 2.1.3.4.

6 BMI Management Practices for Business Unit Managers

This chapter presents the management practices supporting business unit managers in successfully realizing BMI in multi-business firms; they are induced from the five cases.[503] BMI literature asserts that, throughout the BMI process, managers may face organizational rigidities, risk and uncertainty.[504] Indeed, not only the two failed but also the three positive cases confirm that BMI entails some form of risk taking, pointed out specifically by these three citations:

- *"Setting up the [new-tech domain] was risky [...]."*[505]
- *"Failure could have led to negative personal consequences for us [...]."*[506]
- *"Courage is needed [...] to engage in such a project."*[507]

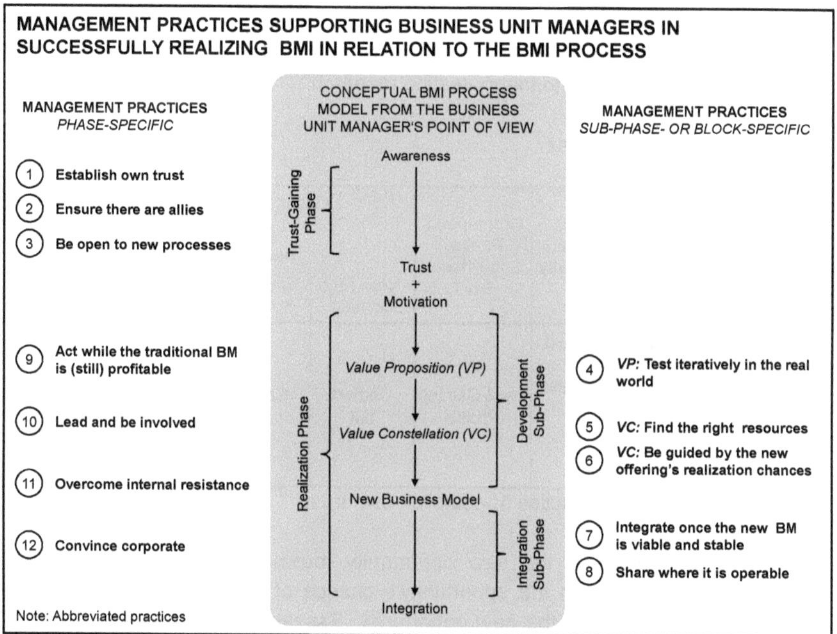

Figure 27: Management practices in relation to the BMI process[508]

The here-presented twelve management practices offer ways for business unit managers to mitigate the risk, to overcome organizational rigidities and to eventually

503 See section 3.4 for a description of the technique used to arrive at the management practices.
504 See (e.g.) Davidson / Leavy (2008), p. 27; McGrath (2010), p. 258; Sosna et al. (2010), p. 384; Taran (2012), p. 48.
505 Source: business unit manager in interviews "New-Tech Domain".
506 Source: business unit manager in interviews "One-Stop Solution".
507 Source: R&D manager in interviews "Integrate for Control".
508 Source: own Figure.

bring the BMI process to a successful conclusion. Together, they build a strategic approach for realizing BMI. Business unit managers applied them in all of the studied BMI success cases, whereas, in the failure cases, many of these management practices were ignored.

Figure 27 displays the abbreviated wording of the twelve induced management practices. Furthermore, the figure illustrates how they relate to the phases, sub-phases and blocks of the conceptual BMI process model explicated in chapter 5. The encircled numbers to the left of each management practice correspond to the section within this chapter that explains the respective management practice in detail. Each section illustrates how the management practices were carried out in the successful BMI cases and in which negative BMI case they were not carried out. Since the research question addresses business unit managers, the wording of each management practice begins by "Business unit managers should [...]." Moreover, it shall be noted that they have the character of propositions since they result from theory-building as opposed to theory-testing research.[509]

6.1 Establish Own Trust

#	Proposition as to which practices support business unit managers in successfully realizing BMI.	Correspond. Phase / Sub-Phase / Block	Cases Supporting Proposition			
			BMI Success			BMI Failure
			"New-Tech Domain	"One-Stop Solution"	"Integrate for Control"	"System House"
1	Business unit managers should establish trust in the new opportunity's chance of success before engaging in its realization. *Establish own trust*	Trust-Gaining Phase	Carried out	Carried out	Carried out	Not carried out

Table 30: Management practice 1: establish own trust[510]

After becoming aware of the new opportunity, business unit managers should establish their own trust in the opportunity's chance of success before taking any action to physically realize the new opportunity. Essentially, trust enables business unit managers to later internally promote the new opportunity's realization efforts and to endure possible setbacks. Without trust, it seems that business unit managers are not capable of transitioning the BMI into the realization phase. As evidenced by the three success cases, the variety of measures to build trust is manifold. They can include combinations of the following:

- engaging or hiring of external market experts or researchers;
- conversations with

509 See Eisenhardt (1989), p. 545; Dul / Hak (2008), pp. 176-177.
510 Source: own Table.

  - internal sales force,
  - internal product managers,
  - other employees;
- cross-functional workshops; or
- observing trends among existing customers.

In the case "New-Tech Domain", the business unit manager hired external market researchers to deliver information on products, customer segments, market sizes and projected growth. In addition to assigning such external service providers, business unit managers can engage in conversations with their sales force, with internal product managers or with other employees, in order to hear about their opinions on the new opportunity. These conversations can have the form of normal one-on-one talks, of more structured discussions or of official workshops.

> *"From our market research, a clear trend towards micro-miniaturization became evident. [...] I gained trust in this opportunity."*[511]

In the case "Integrate for Control", the business unit manager initiated a workshop held over several weekends. She invited representatives from each of the business unit's internal departments to this workshop. After intensive discussions, she could confirm her notion that a new business model would allow the business unit to make better use of its existing competencies.

As in the case "One-Stop Solution", business unit managers may furthermore establish trust in a new opportunity by observing trends among their existing customers.

> *"I noticed that during the beginning of the last decade, more and more customers first had to be told by us which products they should order before they were capable of actually placing an order."*[512]

What is more, the same business unit manager experienced how her unit, seemingly by chance, received an order not only to supply cables, but also to install them. Through these two occurrences, which were observed in the context of the traditional business model, as well as through subsequent internal conversations, she built trust in a new business model opportunity that would allow the firm to fully benefit from such trends.

In the case "System House", the business unit manager did not establish trust in any new business model proposal. She neither promoted one of the two already proclaimed new business model proposals nor did she come up with a third idea. Even though her unit made losses over several consecutive years, and even though

---

[511] Source: business unit manager in interviews "New-Tech Domain".
[512] Source: business unit manager in interviews "One-Stop Solution".

corporate management clearly expected it from her, she did not position herself as supporting any business model changes. Archival documents clearly disclose her indecisiveness in this matter. In fact, she had joined the business unit already in mid-2008. The initial meeting with corporate management first took place in the beginning of 2010. The time in between should have been sufficient for her to thoroughly understand the complex traditional business model and why it was generating losses. On the other hand, the two existing new business model proposals were relatively concrete and more or less developed without the involvement of the business unit manager. The proposed BMI "System House" originally stemmed from the former director of the unit's main plant, and the second new business model proposal was developed by the project manager from the central strategy department. Such an idea origin distinctly differs from the three BMI success cases; the ideas in these cases either originated from the business unit manager or were at an early, pre-developed stage when the business unit manager heard of them for the first time. After the corporate management meeting in the beginning of 2010, the business unit manager of the "System House" case presumably wanted to take enough time to thoroughly understand and compare both options in order to gain trust in one of them. However, without any feedback from her until mid-2010, corporate management decided to divest this unit.

6.2 Ensure There Are Allies

#	Proposition as to which practices support business unit managers in successfully realizing BMI.	Correspond. Phase / Sub-Phase / Block	Cases Supporting Proposition			
			BMI Success			BMI Failure
			"New-Tech Domain	"One-Stop Solution"	"Integrate for Control"	"System House"
2	Business unit managers should ensure that they are not the only ones in their unit who have trust in the new opportunity before engaging in it. *Ensure there are allies*	Trust-Gaining Phase	Carried out	Carried out	Carried out	n/a (not carried out but related to practice 1)

Table 31: Management practice 2: ensure there are allies[513]

In all of the success cases, the business unit managers were not the only ones within their units who had trust in the new opportunity's chance of success before any action was taken to physically realize it. In each of these cases, other employees also believed in the chance of success and could provide further sensibility checks. Hence, each business unit manager could rely on at least a small team of "allies" that later helped her to move the new opportunity forward and to overcome internal resistance.

513 Source: own Table.

"I did the first market studies together with [the co-plant manager] and later we involved [a newly recruited, experienced product manager]. [Her] market insights were particularly valuable. [...] [She later] headed the project team."[514]

In the case "One-Stop Solution", the business unit manager only decided to move forward with her novel idea after a new product engineer, who had just joined the business unit, approached her with a similar idea. Both became "sparring partners" and together they personally executed the first small "One-Stop Solution" project. In the case "Integrate for Control", the business unit manager invited her most important department managers to a cross-functional workshop. Eventually, participants from this workshop contributed significantly to the realization of the new business model.

"I was already a participant in the 1992 workshop. I was involved in this project for the whole time from the very beginning to the end."[515]

With regard to the negative BMI cases, this management practice was not carried out in the case "System House". However, such a statement is not entirely applicable concerning the circumstances of the case. Since the business unit manager did not establish trust in any of the new opportunities proposed, she did not reach the stage of ensuring that she would have allies.

6.3 Be Open to New Processes

#	**Proposition as to which practices support business unit managers in successfully realizing BMI.**	Correspond. Phase / Sub-Phase / Block	Cases Supporting Proposition			
			BMI Success			**BMI Failure**
			"New-Tech Domain	"One-Stop Solution"	"Integrate for Control"	"Special-to-Standard"
3	Business unit managers should consider ex-ante that, in order to realize the new opportunity, bringing in new processes may become necessary. *Be open to new processes*	Trust-Gaining Phase	Carried out	Carried out	Carried out	Not carried out

Table 32: Management practice 3: be open to new processes[516]

A business model qualifies as BMI in a multi-business firm if it contains an innovative value constellation, characterized by new-to-the-firm working practices. In other words, new processes are a constitutive characteristic of BMI. According to the studied BMI cases, in the trust-gaining phase business unit managers do not yet know the exact final design of the new business model. It could be that during the trust-gaining phase, they did not even think of the final business model as a BMI.

514 Source: business unit manager in interviews "New-Tech Domain".
515 Source: department head in interviews "Integrate for Control".

516 Source: own Table.

However, in all success cases, the business unit managers were aware that they probably would have had to bring in new processes if they had wanted to realize the new opportunity; this was not so in the failure case "Special-to-Standard". Hence, being open to new processes upfront seems to increase the likelihood that, during the development sub-phase, the design of processes and the choice of resources are guided by what is necessary to deliver the new value proposition, instead of what is already existent in the traditional business model.

In the case "New-Tech Domain", the business unit manager considered upfront that at least the following three new processes would have to be brought in: (1) a new process engineer with a better suitable skill set would have to be recruited to design an appropriate manufacturing cell; (2) the existing sales force would have to be trained on the new products; and (3) the business unit would have to partner with third parties somewhere along the chain of production. Later in the development sub-phase, she then quickly supported the project team when it additionally asked for new operators or new sales channels. In the case "One-Stop Solution", the business unit manager was clearly aware that new processes would have to be established in order to transition from a product-based into a solution-based business model. In the 2004 management meeting, she argued,

> *"'Services' should become another success factor."*[517]

In the case "Integrate for Control", all participants of the initial workshop in 1992 knew that the traditional set of working practices would have to be heavily expanded in order to realize the vision of being integrated in the carmakers' production line.

> *"We already knew in the initial workshop [...] that we would have to bring in [...] new processes."*[518]

By contrast, in the case "Special-to-Standard", business unit management did not consider upfront that supplying standard cable harnesses to a major OEM in the aviation industry would require new-to-the-firm processes. It knew that it had to invest in new resources such as a new building or new machinery. However, it did not think it would have to establish major new working practices that would differ significantly from the ones necessary to supply special cable assemblies for other industries. In the trust-gaining phase, the business unit management did not talk to, e.g., independent industry experts and it did not further investigate the reasons behind the fact that major competitors in this market more or less act as an "extended work bench" and not as an autonomous production company. Ultimately, setting up the new production system took much longer than anticipated. Plus, the standard cable harnesses were produced at an unsustainable cost.

---

[517] Source: business unit manager in interviews "One-Stop Solution".
[518] Source: department head in interviews in "Integrate for Control".

"The attitude of the former management can be summarized with: 'We are good at assembling for healthcare, as well as automation and drives applications. Thus, we can also do it in aviation'."[519]

6.4 Test Iteratively in the Real World

After the transition from the trust-gaining into the realization phase, business unit managers' first priority should be determining the new value proposition. The three BMI success cases show that hereby, business unit managers should support flexibility and iterative testing directly with customers when developing the most promising new value proposition. Sections 6.5 and 6.6 additionally explain the parallel effects on the value constellation from such testing.

#	Proposition as to which practices support business unit managers in successfully realizing BMI.	Correspond. Phase / Sub-Phase / Block	Cases Supporting Proposition			
			BMI Success			BMI Failure
			"New-Tech Domain"	"One-Stop Solution"	"Integrate for Control"	"Special-to-Standard"
4	Business unit managers should support flexibility and iterative testing directly with customers when developing the most promising new value proposition. *Test iteratively in the real world*	Realization Phase ------ Development Sub-Phase ------ Value Proposition	Carried out	Carried out	Carried out	Not carried out

Table 33: Management practice 4: test iteratively in the real world[520]

In the case "New-Tech Domain", the initial business plan for the new integrated electrical systems foresaw market entry into five different customer segments. Ultimately, only two segments could be entered. In the three missed segments, either the demand for those electrical systems did not exist as initially assumed or the market entry barriers were too high, such as in the defense segment. However, the missing of three segments was compensated by much higher than initially planned revenues in the other two segments. Put differently, the business plan's financial targets were fulfilled but in another way. Crucial to entering the two segments was maintaining close contact with potential customers.

"At first, rather simple prototypes were presented to customers in order to create awareness of the business unit and to discover the current and future needs of those high-tech customers."[521]

Subsequently, tailored bids could be prepared for each customer individually. Often, the very first bid was rejected. However, the business unit learned from the reasons

519 Source: interviews "Special-to-Standard".
520 Source: own Table.
521 Source: senior sales manager in interviews "New-Tech Domain".

for rejection, improved their bids, and eventually won the follow-up or other projects of the same customer. As for the new business model's current largest single customer, the business unit first supplied only micro-miniaturized cables. At the subsequent iteration, it moved on to supplying more complex, multi-component electrical systems.

In the case "One-Stop Solution", the ideas around a new value proposition were at first tested within the scope of a relatively small project. The customer received cable engineering and installation services which the business unit manager considered as rather easy and that were deliverable while utilizing existing employees. Nevertheless, the involved employees had to execute new working practices because the business unit had never before offered these kinds of services.

> *"This project can be seen as a test with customers. It determined the core service package of [the new business model]."*[522]

The package of services provided in this first successful project built a nucleus that was transferred to subsequent projects and, little by little, was enlarged by additional services requiring new employees. After approximately two years of iterative real-world testing, a catalogue of services evolved that today represents the new business model's value proposition.

Likewise, in the case "Integrate for Control" the business unit manager supported a flexible and iterative approach, which consisted of involving customers throughout the development of the new value proposition. As a very first step, the idea was presented to customers of the traditional business model for the purpose of testing their reaction. As a second step, the idea was realized for one single customer through a two-year development project. The emerging new value proposition was then integrated into a new business model that customers found increasingly appealing. Besides, during the two-year development project, the business unit insisted on maintaining enough freedom for experimentation and testing in order to reach the outcome desired by both the customer and the business unit.

> *"We actively insisted on a much earlier installation of the first line for experimentation and training purposes."*[523]

In the failed BMI case "Special-to-Standard", the business unit manager supported neither flexibility nor iterative testing directly with its customers while developing the new value proposition. On the contrary, she signed a framework contract valid for several years that specified the products, quantities and unit prices before the firm had attempted to manufacture anything for this or any other aircraft OEM. In negotiations, she promised the customer that the business unit would be able to fulfill

[522] Source: head of new business model in interviews "One-Stop Solution".
[523] Source: department head in interviews "Integrate for Control".

all of the customer's requirements and finally convinced the customer to enter into this kind of framework contract. Afterwards, she recognized that fulfilling the customer's requirements was in fact very difficult for the newly founded business unit. Difficulties arose from the customer's frequent, small product changes; the required IT-interfaces and the strict quality criteria. After huge problems in the beginning, the business unit ultimately overachieved customer requirements, thereby far exceeding the target costs per unit. In short, the business unit only really understood the new value proposition once it was too late.

> *"[...] we even surpassed the quality requirements. If there was a quality problem, we were able to find out exactly if it had been caused by an operator, by the raw material or by a tool, and we could identify which other parts might have been affected by the source of error."*[524]

6.5 Find the Right Resources

#	**Proposition as to which practices support business unit managers in successfully realizing BMI.**	Correspond. Phase / Sub-Phase / Block	Cases Supporting Proposition			
			BMI Success			**BMI Failure**
			"New-Tech Domain	"One-Stop Solution"	"Integrate for Control"	"Special-to-Standard"
5	Business unit managers should find those human and non-human resources, as well as external partners that enable the delivery of the value proposition at a profit. If those resources are not available in the traditional business model, they must be built up. *Find the right resources*	Realization Phase ------ Development Sub-Phase ------ Value Constellation	Carried out	Carried out	Carried out	Not carried out

Table 34: Management practice 5: find the right resources[525]

Once business unit managers understand the new value proposition, they should find those human and non-human resources, as well as external partners that enable the delivery of the value proposition at a profit. In fact, running real-world tests of the new value proposition requires certain processes to be executed while utilizing certain resources. Consequently, the processes to replicate such a test and deliver the new value proposition on a larger scale are generally determinable. Therefore, the resources essential to running those processes are generally determinable. If those resources are not available in the traditional business model, they must be built up. Above all, the processes and resources must be configured and chosen in a way that facilitates the generation of profits for the focal business unit. This implies that within

---

524 Source: interviews "Special-to-Standard".
525 Source: own Table.

the new value proposition an indication for obtainable prices has already been identified.

The cases exemplify that the teams developing the new business model can easily make use of buildings or G&A structures from the established organization. However, for enabling the more critical, business-related processes to run as desired, in all three BMI success cases, either new employees were hired or existing ones were trained. In the case "New-Tech Domain", new operators were hired.

> *"The operators from the established business model were not capable of operating the new machines. Many of them acted clumsily. What is more, they were not willing to relearn. We had to recruit new operators and then trained them to work only at the new machines."*[526]

Similarly, a new sales network had to be established, since the existing sales force lacked the basic technical knowledge or the motivation to learn something so fundamentally new. Furthermore, the business unit manager recruited new product and process engineers, and engaged into an external partnership with a manufacturing service provider. Likewise, during the initial project, the business unit manager in the case "Integrate for Control" supported the hiring and training of new personnel for providing the envisioned services at the carmaker's paint shop.

> *"They were trained to notice quality defects, to act correctly and to intervene. They had to learn how to operate and program the robots for an optimized paint application. [...] [The equipment manufacturer] strongly supported the training."*[527]

Additionally, some of the sales and controlling staff had to undergo training. In the case "One-Stop Solution", the first project was driven by the business unit manager in person, as well as by two experienced product managers. Afterwards, the business unit manager was aware of the core processes required to replicate such a project without having to involve the same project managers. Job profiles for those rendering such projects in the future were determined. Based upon those job profiles, the plant's maintenance team was re-trained to perform as construction supervisors, and the staff was recruited either from the traditional business model or from outside the firm.

In the BMI failure case "Special-to-Standard", the business unit manager made the following false assumptions:

- the existing employees would know which processes were required for providing the new value proposition, and

[526] Source: business unit manager in interviews "New-Tech Domain".
[527] Source: department head in interviews "Integrate for Control".

- those processes could be carried out with employees already working in the traditional business model.

In line with the initial business plan, as corresponding to the framework contract, investments into a new building and new machinery were made. Moreover, new operators were hired and shown how to assemble the rather simple cable harnesses. However, for the critical processes such as product management, IT, process engineering, or quality management, the business unit manager did not recruit additional staff with experience in the aviation industry. Neither did she organize specific training for the existing staff. New resources were not even built up after the conclusion of the framework contract, when it was evident that a new value proposition had to be delivered. During the first year of the contract's duration, huge problems with regard to providing the value proposition became obvious. Solving those problems required external help.

> *"[The OEM] sent its field engineers to help us solve our production problems. [...] We had to engage several external IT consultancies [...]. We were overstrained."*[528]

However, all those measures, additional investments and the time delay had not been priced into the framework contract. Finally, it was impossible to deliver the value proposition at a profit.

6.6 Be Guided by the New Offering's Realization Chances

#	**Proposition as to which practices support business unit managers in successfully realizing BMI.**	Correspond. Phase / Sub-Phase / Block	Cases Supporting Proposition **BMI Success**		
			"New-Tech Domain	"One-Stop Solution"	"Integrate for Control"
6	Business unit managers should let their (major) decisions on new resources be guided solely by the extent to which the new value proposition is realizable. *Be guided by the new offering's realization chances*	Realization Phase ------ Development Sub-Phase ------ Value Constellation	Carried out	Carried out	Carried out

Table 35: Management practice 6: be guided by the realization chances[529]

Once business unit managers understand the new value proposition, their decisions on major investments into new resources dedicated to delivering this value proposition should be guided solely by the extent to which this value proposition is in fact realizable. Undoubtedly, business unit managers must provide the resources to

[528] Source: interviews "Special-to-Standard".
[529] Source: own Table.

enable the iterative real-world testing of the new idea until eventually the outline of the most promising new value proposition emerges. For example, in the case New-Tech Domain, a new process engineer with special knowledge was recruited right at the beginning of the realization phase; also, money was invested to produce the first prototypes. Indeed, opportunity costs arise when business unit managers or other employees commit time to such testing; as done, for instance, in the first "One-Stop Solution" project. Likewise, in the case "Integrate for Control", business unit staff spent much time preparing the first actual quote entailing the new value proposition ideas. However, as depicted by all three BMI success cases, major investments into new resources should only be made once it has been proven that the new offering is possible to be sold.

To exemplify, in the case "New-Tech Domain", machinery for the new manufacturing cell was only purchased after the business unit manager knew which specific products in which segments would have the highest chance of being ordered by customers. Over time, further machinery was added based on won orders.

> *"In the beginning, it is not necessary to determine exactly which machinery is to be put up. It is dependent on identifying the most interesting directions and the most potential sales volume, and on the orders won."*[530]

For realizing the first smaller "One-Stop Solution" projects, the business unit manager mainly deployed internal resources and partnered with external firms. New employees necessary for delivering the new value proposition were only recruited after the bid for a larger project was won.

> *"For the purpose of planning and execution of the [first smaller] projects, we called in other internal resources from [our site], as well as external companies and consultants. [...] Only during the course of the [first larger] project did we begin to hire new personnel dedicated to the future new business model."*[531]

In the case "Integrate for Control", those new employees needed to carry out the services for the first time at the carmaker's paint shop were only hired and trained after the business unit concluded a contract with the carmaker. The same holds true for the necessary upgrades in the business unit's IT and controlling systems.

> *"We won the contract. We had to recruit a new team that would do the job."*[532]

---

530 Source: senior sales manager in interviews "New-Tech Domain".
531 Source: business unit manager in interviews "One-Stop Solution".
532 Source: department head in interviews "Integrate for Control".

6.7 Integrate Once the New BM is Viable and Stable

#	Proposition as to which practices support business unit managers in successfully realizing BMI.	Correspond. Phase / Sub-Phase / Block	Cases Supporting Proposition			
			BMI Success			BMI Failure
			"New-Tech Domain	"One-Stop Solution"	"Integrate for Control"	"Special-to-Standard"
7	Business unit managers should integrate the new business model into the established organization once a clearly-outlined, tested and promising new value proposition can be delivered from a stable value constellation. *Integrate once the new BM is viable and stable*	Realization Phase ------ Integration Sub-Phase	Carried out	Carried out	Carried out	Not carried out

Table 36: Management practice 7: integrate once the BM is viable and stable[533]

In all three BMI success cases, the new business models were physically developed, to some extent, outside of the established organization that executes the daily routine processes of the traditional business model. Only once a clearly-outlined, tested and promising new value proposition can be delivered from a stable value constellation, should business unit managers integrate the new business model. In other words, if a functioning new business model has been developed, it should officially become a part of the established organization. Consequently, the new processes and their underlying working practices become daily routine, too; this helps the new business model to grow further. On the other hand, a new business model that has not proven profitable should not become an official part of the established organization. It happened in the case "Special-to-Standard". Here, a new business model was integrated into the firm as an additional business unit before it was physically developed and before there was any proof that the planned value constellation would deliver the new offering at a profit.

"The old management believed that it would eventually make a profit."[534]

The opposite holds true for the three BMI success cases. In the case "New-Tech Domain", the new business model was developed by a dedicated project team that was taken out of the line organization specifically for this task. It determined the most promising value proposition; and it installed the machinery, the operators and the sales network to deliver this value proposition. Once several profitable high runners (i.e. products produced in larger numbers) had guaranteed a solid degree of capacity utilization in the new manufacturing cell, the business unit manager decided to officially integrate the new business model and to perceptibly remove the special

[533] Source: own Table.
[534] Source: interviews "Special-to-Standard".

project characterization of this venture. Members of the project team were transferred to functional departments. The former departments of product engineering and sales were each split into two sub-departments; whereas the departments for manufacturing planning and control and for process engineering had to manage both business models.

> *"The trigger [for integration] was surely the size of this area and the reached capacity usage from high runners. This decision was driven by the will to not duplicate overhead functions, to guarantee somehow unified processes within the organization and to terminate the special project characterization [...]"*[535]

Likewise, in the case "One-Stop Solution", the business unit manager only decided to officially turn the new business model into a regular part of the established organization after the following occurred: after it was proven that the new value proposition could be delivered at a profit; after the core processes were determined; and after a certain order backlog was secured. This decision entailed, for example, informing the public about the new solution offering via the firm's website and other marketing material. Moreover, this decision resulted in setting up a new department, whose members were completely taken out of their former departments or newly recruited.

> *"Momentarily, there are two parallel business models existing in our unit: the product- and the solution-oriented one. [...] The solution-oriented business model is financially very successful [...]."*[536]

Similarly, in the case "Integrate for Control", the new offering was sold to other carmakers only after it was proven that the new business model could indeed be a financial success for the business unit. Essentially, official integration meant that the processes established in the first project could be copied when providing the new value proposition to other customers. From the first project, the business unit's global key account managers, as well as the involved staff in sales, controlling, IT, R&D and other functions, knew which working practices had to be carried out to repeat this success.

6.8 Share Where It is Operable

To exemplify, during the integration sub-phase in the case "New-Tech Domain", the business unit manager asked the manufacturing planning and control department to, for the future, take charge of the new manufacturing cell. Until then, these activities had been carried out by the project team. The business unit manager was convinced that, with the help of the project team, the department's employees would achieve the skills required for the new working practices. Her motivation was to avoid the

---

535 Source: business unit manager in interviews "New-Tech Domain".
536 Source: business unit manager in interviews "One-Stop Solution".

duplication of overhead structures resulting from a second official manufacturing planning and control department. By contrast, the sales department was split into two sub-departments because, when developing the new value constellation, it became obvious that the existing sales staff was unable to relearn the new skills. The business unit manager understood which aspects of the unit were operable to share and which were to remain distinct to the new value constellation.

#	Proposition as to which practices support business unit managers in successfully realizing BMI.	Correspond. Phase / Sub-Phase / Block	Cases Supporting Proposition			
			BMI Success			BMI Failure
			"New-Tech Domain"	"One-Stop Solution"	"Integrate for Control"	"Special-to-Standard"
8	Business unit managers should assess which resources from the established organization can rationally be shared with the new business model when integrating. *Share where it is operable*	Realization Phase ------ Integration Sub-Phase	Carried out	Carried out	Carried out	n/a (not carried out but related to practice 5)

Table 37: Management practice 8: share where it is operable[537]

In the case "One-Stop Solution", the business unit manager determined that the only resources from the established organization suitable for sharing with the new business model were the corporation's brand name, as well as the unit's G&A and marketing capacities. Consequently, during the integration sub-phase, she set up a new department and moved it to a different building. Thereby, she wanted to ensure that the interests from the traditional established organization would not influence the expansion of the new solution-based business model.

In the case "Integrate for Control", the business unit manager intended to offer both the traditional and the new value proposition to carmakers through the existing business unit. The first successful project proved that the staff from the established organization, who would be asked to perform additional new working practices, could be trained to do so. Such affected staff first included the global key account teams not participating in the initial project. In fact, the initial project brought about a transferable blueprint containing not only the new working practices but also the changes to be made in the IT and bookkeeping systems. Consequently, the business unit manager concluded that the resources from the established organization could rationally be shared to deliver both value propositions

"Within global key accounts, we run both 'business models'."[538]

---

[537] Source: own Table.
[538] Source: account manager in interviews "Integrate for Control".

In the case "Special-to-Standard", the business unit manager decided to share multiple resources from the established organization with the new business model, even though a new additional business unit was set up. However, sharing those resources did not prove to be operable for the new business model, as explained above in the context of management practice five. These explanations also apply in the context of management practice eight, since the new business model was developed after being officially integrated. The two management practices merge.

6.9 Act While the Traditional BM is (Still) Profitable

#	Proposition as to which practices support business unit managers in successfully realizing BMI.	Correspond. Phase / Sub-Phase / Block	Cases Supporting Proposition			
			BMI Success			BMI Failure
			"New-Tech Domain	"One-Stop Solution"	"Integrate for Control"	"System House"
9	Business unit managers should engage in BMI when profits from the traditional business model are (still) within the corporation's expectations. *Act while the traditional BM is (still) profitable*	Realization Phase	Carried out	Carried out	Carried out	Not carried out

Table 38: Management practice 9: act while the traditional BM is (...) profitable[539]

Once business unit managers have established trust in a new opportunity's chance of success, they should conduct the transition from the trust-gaining into the realization phase while the traditional business model is still profitable. The BMI success cases reveal these two important requirements for realizing BMI:

- financial resources, and above all
- time.

Waiting until the financial performance of the traditional business model turns negative increases the pressure for immediate action. Most likely, such pressure hinders business unit managers from performing all the necessary tests to find both the most promising new value proposition and the required value constellation. The blocked BMI case "System House" exemplifies that if a business unit generates financial losses over a longer period of time due to strategic reasons, and if the business unit manager does not take any action towards a new business model, corporate management may act in the place of the business unit manager.

In the case "New-Tech Domain", it took much longer than initially estimated to receive the first orders for the new products. Thanks to the financial resources provided by the (still) profitable traditional business model, the business unit had the

[539] Source: own Table.

financial strength to maintain the project team, the tests with customers, the manufacturing of prototypes, and the tests for finding the right value constellation. In the case "One-Stop Solution", the profit margins of the traditional business model were expected to deteriorate. However, when the BMI realization phase began, the business unit's financial performance still met the objectives of the corporation. This situation enabled the business unit manager to slowly develop the new business model by testing her ideas through several smaller cabling solution projects. Likewise, in the case "Integrate for Control", carmakers were expected to put increasingly more pressure on automotive suppliers. Nonetheless, the business unit did not struggle financially when it entered into the BMI realization phase.

6.10 Lead and Be Involved

Business unit managers should lead the BMI's realization phase and be closely involved in the activities aimed at developing and integrating the new business model.

#	**Proposition as to which practices support business unit managers in successfully realizing BMI.**	Correspond. Phase / Sub-Phase / Block	Cases Supporting Proposition **BMI Success**		
			"New-Tech Domain	"One-Stop Solution"	"Integrate for Control"
10	Business unit managers should lead and be closely involved in the realization of the new business model. *Lead and be involved*	Realization Phase	Carried out	Carried out	Carried out

Table 39: Management practice 10: lead and be involved[540]

Notably, in all three BMI success cases, the business unit managers took an active role and strongly supported the BMI realization efforts.

> *"I assigned two more of my best employees [...] to this task. The team was taken out of the line organization and reported directly to me."*[541]

In the case "New-Tech Domain", the project team charged with developing the new business model was set up and incentivized by the business unit manager. It reported directly to her as opposed to the heads of the functional departments. The business unit manager empowered this team to move freely within the unit, to use the BMI budget granted by corporate management, and to directly approach the functional departments with their requests.

[540] Source: own Table.
[541] Source: business unit manager in interviews "New-Tech Domain".

"For successfully concluding such a project, a little firm inside the firm is needed".[542]

Moreover, the business unit manager actively promoted the BMI efforts in her entire unit, not only to create awareness, but also to raise the project's significance. In the case "One-Stop Solution", the business unit manager herself executed the first cabling solution project with the help of two product managers.

"We went into this first project with such enthusiasm."[543]

What is more, the business unit manager performed the following: encouraged product managers to bid for similar projects, organized partnerships with electrical installation providers, arranged training for the "blue collar team", recruited new employees and triggered the creation of a new sub-brand and marketing material dedicated to the new value proposition.

The "Integrate for Control" BMI was led by two different business unit managers. Both persons actively supported the BMI's realization.

"The new business unit manager was as strongly motivated as [her] predecessor."[544]

The rotation took place at the end of 1994 when the BMI was already in an advanced stage. Such a rotation is a typical event in multi-business firms. The first business unit manager started the BMI. She organized the initial workshop in 1992 and she set up the project team. This team prepared the quote for the carmaker's new paint shop and subsequently realized it. Both business unit managers bolstered the project team in their strong effort to develop the new business model.

"They were the figureheads who constantly motivated and supported us."[545]

The second business unit manager fostered the BMI after the project team presented her with the objectives connected to the BMI. An auxiliary factor in this context was that, by that time, it was already foreseeable what exactly was capable of being achieved by this project. She could easily discern that the BMI would indeed be the pathway to a substantial competitive advantage. Overall, this case study demonstrates that BMI in multi-business firms can succeed even if corporate standards are such that the business unit managers are being rotated to another position every 2-3 years.[546]

542 Source: senior sales manager in interviews "New-Tech Domain".
543 Source: business unit manager in interviews "One-Stop Solution".
544 Source: department head in interviews "Integrate for Control".
545 Source: ibidem.
546 See section 2.3.6.

6.11 Overcome Internal Resistance

#	Proposition as to which practices support business unit managers in successfully realizing BMI.	Correspond. Phase / Sub-Phase / Block	Cases Supporting Proposition BMI Success "New-Tech Domain	"One-Stop Solution"	"Integrate for Control"
11	Business unit managers should overcome any form of unit-internal resistance to the realization of the new business model. *Overcome internal resistance*	Realization Phase	Carried out	Carried out	Carried out

Table 40: Management practice 11: overcome internal resistance[547]

During the BMI's realization phase, business unit managers should overcome any form of unit-internal resistance to realizing the BMI. Hereby, resistance does not refer to constructive debates aimed at diversifying perspectives or creative problem solving. For instance, in the case "One-Stop Solution", the business unit manager took employees' remarks on paying attention to appropriate risk management very seriously. Rather, resistance refers to employees who, driven by personal motives, argue and/or act against the BMI with the purpose of avoiding the changes it entails. In all BMI success cases, the business unit managers had to handle such resistance in order to prevent the BMI process from being blocked.

In the case "New-Tech Domain", some middle managers openly argued from the very beginning of the realization phase, that they did not see the necessity for the business unit to engage in something so fundamentally new. The traditional business model would be stable and generate acceptable financial results. Because of the fear that parts of the established organization could block the BMI, the business unit manager built a dedicated project team and took it out of the line organization. Throughout the realization phase, she intervened if necessary.

> *"The head of production objected to transfer his best people to the new machines. Only after the [business unit manager's] intervention did he do it."*[548]

In the case "One-Stop Solution", employees from all hierarchy levels also argued against the BMI efforts, since they thought it too ambitious. However, this resistance did not take effect, since the business unit manager herself, together with her allies, performed many of the activities to realize the new business model. In this regard, the management practice "overcome internal resistance" is intertwined with the practice "ensure there are allies".

---

[547] Source: own Table.

[548] Source: senior sales manager in interviews "New-Tech Domain".

In addition to using their formal power, the business unit managers tried communication and support mechanisms to convince reluctant employees of the BMI's potential advantages. For example, during the integration sub-phase in the case "New-Tech Domain", the manufacturing and control department was unwilling to carry out the new additional working practices. Consequently, the business unit manager repeatedly explained that the new business model would be important for moving the entire business unit into a defendable technology position over the long term. Likewise, in the case "Integrate for Control", the business unit manager constantly emphasized the project's importance. When employees objected the feasibility of certain topics, she offered to organize what would be necessary to make those topics accomplishable. In this sense, the management practice "overcome internal resistance" is closely related to the practice "lead and be involved".

6.12 Convince Corporate

#	Proposition as to which practices support business unit managers in successfully realizing BMI.	Correspond. Phase / Sub-Phase / Block	Cases Supporting Proposition			
			BMI Success			BMI Failure
			"New-Tech Domain	"One-Stop Solution"	"Integrate for Control"	"System House"
12	Business unit managers should convince corporate management of the new opportunity. *Convince corporate*	Realization Phase	Carried out	Carried out	Carried out	n/a (not carried out but related to practice 1)

Table 41: Management practice 12: convince corporate[549]

Business unit managers should convince corporate management of the new opportunity. Essentially, the events in all studied cases underline the imperative of having corporate headquarters' formal approval for realizing the BMI. Cross-case differences concern the following:

- the point within the realization phase when applying for corporate approval, and
- the way to persuade corporate management.

In the case "New-Tech Domain", the business unit manager applied early for corporate approval by presenting a business plan containing among other things a time schedule, essential investments, and financial targets. This early presentation was needed in order to be granted the financial resources for the new machinery. Throughout the entire realization phase, the business unit manager had to submit status reports to the corporate management.

> *"We credibly demonstrated that we had only executed the necessary investments. Thereby, we gained more room to maneuver."*[550]

[549] Source: own Table.
[550] Source: business unit manager in interviews "New-Tech Domain".

By contrast, in the case "One-Stop Solution", the business unit manager had to persuade corporate management of the new opportunity towards the end of the realization phase. Corporate management's main concern was not granting financial resources for investments into tangible assets, since those were hardly necessary.

> *"[Corporate management] was concerned about the legal risks inherent to the new business model."*[551]

Historically, the corporation tried to avoid bigger risk-exposure. However, acting as a general contractor in bigger construction projects potentially exposes the firm to considerable financial risks. For this reason, corporate headquarters wanted to be assured that the business unit had found the means to control those risks. In response, the business unit manager engaged in several talks with corporate management and, eventually, with the help of legal experts, could reach a mutual understanding with corporate management that the business unit could design contractual agreements in a way that would limit the risk exposure. The business unit manager further brought up the convincing argument to corporate management that she had already successfully conducted the first smaller solution projects.

In the case "Integrate for Control", the first contract containing the new value proposition had to be approved by corporate management. Achieving this approval was difficult.

> *"[Corporate management] initially rejected the project. [...] Then, the second time, we were better prepared and convinced them."*[552]

In fact, corporate management rejected the draft contract after it was initially presented to them. Corporate management considered of the services to be provided to the carmaker as too much of a revolution for the firm. However, the business unit manager did not give up and did not inform the carmaker, the soon-to-be contractual partner, about this rejection. Instead, the business unit manager put much effort into the preparation of a second presentation which was held in front of a slightly different circle of corporate managers. Finally, they approved it. Remarkably, over the course of the realization phase, corporate headquarters announced this project as one of the firm's flagship projects and openly supported it.

The blocked BMI case "System House" also indicates that corporate management must be persuaded of intended fundamental business model changes in one of their business units. After the business unit manager met with the corporation's executive board in the beginning of 2010, the board clearly expected the business unit manager to come up with both a proposal for the redesign of the unit's business model, and an explanation for why this proposal should be the one to approve of.

---

[551] Source: business unit manager in interviews "One-Stop Solution".
[552] Source: department head in interviews "Integrate for Control".

However, as the business unit manager never brought forward her own proposal to convince corporate of the new opportunity "System House", and anyway had not gained trust in this new business model proposal, the BMI could never enter the realization phase.

6.13 Summarizing List of the Management Practices

Table 42 lists the twelve management practices induced from the five cases that support business unit managers in successfully realizing BMI in multi-business firms. Their extended and abbreviated wording is shown, as well as their correspondence to the phases, sub-phases, or blocks of the conceptual BMI process model presented in chapter 5. Moreover, Table 42 displays from which cases each management practice is induced. Some management practices do not have a negative counterpart in any of the two BMI failure cases. Nevertheless, this condition does not mean that those management practices are of minor importance. Quite the contrary: business unit managers applied those, in all of the three BMI success cases; in other words, across business units and across corporations. Therefore, all twelve management practices are of high relevance in the context of BMI in multi-business firms and together they build a strategic approach to BMI.

#	Propositions as to which practices support business unit managers in successfully realizing BMI.	Correspondence to the phase / sub-phase / block of the BMI process model	Cases Yes: Carried out No: Not carried out				
			1	2	3	4	5
1	Business unit managers should establish trust in the new opportunity's chance of success before engaging in its realization. *[Establish own trust]*	Trust-Gaining	Yes	Yes	Yes		No
2	Business unit managers should ensure that they are not the only ones in their unit who have trust in the new opportunity before engaging in it. *[Ensure there are allies]*	Trust-Gaining	Yes	Yes	Yes		n/a
3	Business unit managers should consider ex-ante that, in order to realize the new opportunity, bringing in new processes may become necessary. *[Be open to new processes]*	Trust-Gaining	Yes	Yes	Yes	No	
4	Business unit managers should support flexibility and iterative testing directly with customers when developing the most promising new value proposition. *[Test iteratively in the real world]*	Realization / Development / Value Proposition	Yes	Yes	Yes	No	
5	Business unit managers should find those human and non-human resources, as well as external partners, that enable the delivery of the value proposition at a profit. If those resources are not available in the traditional business model, they must be built up. *[Find the right resources]*	Realization / Development / Value Constellation	Yes	Yes	Yes	No	
6	Business unit managers should let their (major) decisions on new resources be guided solely by the extent to which the new value proposition is realizable. *[Be guided by the new offering's realization chances]*	Realization / Development / Value Constellation	Yes	Yes	Yes		
7	Business unit managers should integrate the new business model into the established organization once a clearly-outlined, tested and promising new value proposition can be delivered from a stable value constellation. *[Integrate once the new BM is viable and stable]*	Realization / Integration	Yes	Yes	Yes	No	
8	Business unit managers should assess which resources from the established organization can rationally be shared with the new business model when integrating. *[Share where it is operable]*	Realization / Integration	Yes	Yes	Yes	n/a	
9	Business unit managers should engage in BMI when profits from the traditional business model are (still) within the corporation's expectations. *[Act while the traditional BM is (still) profitable]*	Realization	Yes	Yes	Yes		No
10	Business unit managers should lead and be closely involved in the realization of the new business model. *[Lead and be involved]*	Realization	Yes	Yes	Yes		
11	Business unit managers should overcome any form of unit-internal resistance to the realization of the new business model. *[Overcome internal resistance]*	Realization	Yes	Yes	Yes		
12	Business unit managers should convince corporate management of the new opportunity. *[Convince corporate]*	Realization	Yes	Yes	Yes		n/a

Table 42: List of management practices[553]

[553] Source: own Table.

7 Conclusion and Implications

Kindled by today's profound environmental dynamics, the ability of firms to sustain business models with returns above the industry average is steadily decreasing. BMI offers firms a path back to high returns and profitable growth. It aims at the seizure of new opportunities by crafting the right new business model and requires an "entrepreneurial drive" in the strategy design of established firms. However, organizational rigidities may immobilize established industry players, causing them to execute their existing business model for too long. Moreover, these rigidities may contribute to a new business model being initially conceived from or later adapted towards the traditional business model. Most likely, in such cases, the new opportunity's greater potential would remain unexploited. Therefore, scholars deem a deliberate approach to BMI necessary, which most firms currently do not employ. In fact, among a broad range of industries, top management is seeking guidance on how to innovate in their business models. So far, scientifically-derived recommendations supporting managers in realizing BMI are still lacking. This final chapter reviews how this dissertation contributes to closing such research gap. Section 7.1 first provides an overall conclusion of the dissertation. Sections 7.2 and 7.3 then illuminate the findings' managerial and theoretical implications. Finally, section 7.4 discusses limitations and avenues of further research.

7.1 Conclusion

Empirical evidence discloses that deliberate management decisions define or, after the occurrence of emerging and surprising events, redefine the direction a business model follows. Moreover, extant literature suggests that knowledge about business models and potentially value-creating BMI mainly resides within the business units as opposed to the corporate headquarters. Moreover, using the example of Nokia, ASPARA et al. demonstrate that corporate managers refer to internally existing elements when transforming the corporation's business model.[554] Therefore, the research portrayed in this dissertation seeks to advance the understanding of how business unit managers in multi-business firms successfully conduct the innovation of business models. The research question presented was:

> *Which management practices support business unit managers in successfully realizing business model innovation in multi-business firms?*

BMI research is still in its early stages and has not yet provided a consistent set of testable hypotheses relating to the role of business unit managers in BMI. For this reason, an explorative multiple-case study design was chosen as research method. Overall, five cases from five different business units were carefully selected and deeply analyzed. The "polar type" sample of cases, covering three successful and two failed BMIs, enabled the possibility to combine replication logic with failure

---

[554] See section 1.2.

analysis and, thus stimulated the consideration of otherwise probably unmentioned but important management practices.

In order to arrive at the case data, at first, a working definition of BMI in multi-business firms was developed by using a rich body of existing literature. Corresponding to this definition, a BMI-identification tool was compiled comprising easily understandable criteria and indicators that, together with practitioners, enabled the identification of suitable cases. The final set of five cases that was subject to in-depth study was selected out of nineteen cases initially proposed by the contacted managers. Moreover, extant literature containing the phrase "business model innovation" was reviewed. The goal was to discover managerial activities or behaviors that authors have mentioned as possibly relevant for performing BMI. These activities then served the scholar as an early orientation in the initial case interviews.

The collected case data was analyzed, firstly, with the aim of thoroughly understanding each BMI process from the business unit manager's point of view. The single-case processes begin with the initial idea and span, in the BMI success cases, to the final integration of the new business model; in the failure cases, they reach to the dissolution or divestment of the entire business unit. All five single-case processes were then merged into one conceptual BMI process model of a more general character. Secondly, the case data was analyzed with the aim of identifying those management practices carried out by business unit managers across the BMI success cases, but lacking in the BMI failure cases. Through pre-determining the conceptual BMI process model beforehand, the appropriate delineation of distinct management practices was facilitated, and their attribution to single phases, sub-phases or blocks within this model was enabled. As a result, this dissertation proposes to business unit managers a strategic approach to realizing BMI in multi-business firms.

The following two major constituents build this approach:

1. *A conceptual BMI process model from the business unit manager's point of view*
    - See chapter 5.
    - See Figure 26 for a summarizing depiction.

2. *Twelve management practices for business unit managers*
    - See chapter 6.
    - See Figure 27 and Table 42 for an overview of how each management practice corresponds to the conceptual BMI process model.
    - See Table 42 for an overview of how the management practices transpired in the cases.

As outlined in chapter 3, the usual measures for ensuring the validity and reliability of the findings were taken. In chapter 4, each case that was subject to within-case and cross-case analysis was systematically described.

7.2 Managerial Implications

The research presented in this dissertation focused on the role of business unit managers in the context of BMI in multi-business firms. It brought about propositions as to which management practices support the successful realization of such a challenging and inherently risky endeavor as BMI. The results are very tangible and their immediate usability for business unit managers is explicit. Moreover, this research disclosed points of contact during the BMI process between the business unit level and the corporate level. Corporate managers are typically required to grant or to refuse permission for integrating a new business model. Knowledge about a strategic approach to realizing BMI would enable corporate managers to assess the prospects of a proposed new business model, as well as to provide constructive advice to business unit managers. Hence, this dissertation's findings are also of high relevance for corporate managers, who wish to propel BMI. In addition to presenting the above mentioned strategic approach to BMI, the dissertation shed light on the origins of BMI ideas within corporations and illustrated possible ways of new business model integration. Furthermore, the final propositions are of high interest for owner-managers and top-executives of established single business entities, who consider BMI as an important means to profitable firm growth. Owner-managers are not reliant on the decision-making of corporate headquarters; thus not every proposition induced from this research is applicable in the context of single business entities, and particularly, not proposition 12: *"Convince corporate"*. However, the larger part of the results is evidently transferable to established single business entities.

7.3 Theoretical Implications

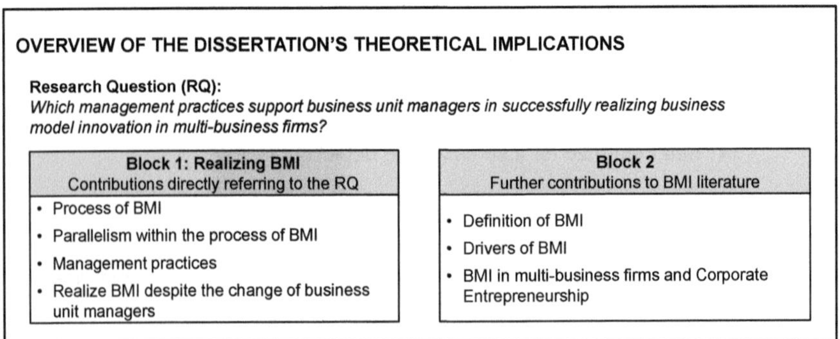

Figure 28: Overview of the theoretical implications[555]

[555] Source: own Figure.

This section elucidates how the research presented in this dissertation contributes to the emerging literature on BMI. To provide a clear visualization, the single contributions are separated into two blocks (Figure 28). The first block comprises the contributions that directly refer to the research question, and the second block contains the dissertation's further contributions to BMI literature. Below, each single contribution is further explicated according to its block.

Block 1: Realizing BMI – Contributions directly referring to the research question

- *Process of BMI.* An in-depth study of the process of realizing BMI is an integral part of the current research agenda on BMI.[556] The dissertation at hand contributes to this research agenda by introducing an empirically-derived process model of BMI in multi-business firms. It complements the BMI process models presented by SOSNA et al. and FRANKENBERGER et al.

  [SOSNA et al. proposed two BMI process phases, development and roll-out. They studied the different types of organizational learning in BMI through a single-case design.[557] Based upon innovation literature, FRANKENBERGER et al. derived four generic process phases: initiation, ideation, integration and implementation. From studying BMI via a multiple-case design, they gained confidence in the phases' applicability and integrated them into the so-called "4I-framework of BMI".[558]]

  Other BMI process models proposed in extant literature, such as the ones by TEECE[559] or ENKEL / MEZGER[560], appear to be theory-derived instead of empirically-derived suggestions.

- *Parallelism within the process of BMI.* Implicitly, the here-presented BMI process model contributes to the following current investigation: whether the BMI process is to be understood as a sequence of different stages or as stages happening in parallel.[561] GÜNZEL / HOLM raised this question specifically in regard to the

556 See Holm et al. (2013), p. 328; Schneider / Spieth (2013a), pp. 22-23.
557 See Sosna et al. (2010), p. 390. The authors structure the BMI process at Naturehouse into two main phases, each of which contains two stages: 1. development phase, 1.1 initial business model design and test stage, 1.2. business model development stage; 2. roll-out phase, 2.1 scale up with "suitable" business model stage, 2.2 sustained growth through organization-wide learning stage.
558 See Frankenberger et al. (2013), pp. 249-273.
559 See Teece (2010), p. 173. Teece suggests that a business model can be designed in the following five stages: 1. select technologies and features to be embedded in the product/service, 2. determine benefit to the customer from consuming/using the product/service, 3. identify market segments to be targeted, 4. confirm available revenue streams, and 5. design mechanisms to capture value. The empirical foundation of this five-stage business model design process is not specified.
560 See Enkel / Mezger (2013), p. 4. The authors use a multiple-case study to explore cross-industry imitation in the context of business models. For the purpose of displaying the overlap between the cross-industry imitation process and the BMI process, the authors suggest a generic BMI process, from a literature review, consisting of the two main phases "Design" and "Implementation". However, the study's empirical focus is on cross-industry imitation.
561 See Dmitriev et al. (2013), pp. 32-33; Günzel / Holm (2013), p. 21.

innovation at the front-end and back-end of the business model.[562] The research in the dissertation at hand found that the BMI process is sequential, entailing a starting and an end-point as well as consecutive phases. Within the development sub-phase, the priority should first focus on the value proposition. Nonetheless, the iterative testing of a new value proposition directly with customers already required certain new processes to be executed. These processes were then later incorporated into the new value constellation. Hence, innovating at the front-end had parallel effects on the back-end of the (new) business model.[563]

- *Management practices.* BUCHERER et al. assert that BMI literature lacks scientifically-based recommendations in terms of management frameworks and methods supporting BMI.[564] MASON / SPRING suggest a greater focus on practice-oriented studies that would help academics understand how managers develop and transform business models.[565] The dissertation at hand contributes to filling this research gap by providing data-driven insights into the management practices applied in successfully concluded BMIs. The induced management practices add to the conceptual BMI process model and, together, build a strategic approach to BMI. This approach lays down how business unit managers may succeed in realizing a new business model through trust-gaining, continuous testing and active leadership; thereby overcoming the rigidities in established organizations and mitigating the risk inherent to BMI. In short, this research delivers a set of testable hypotheses relating to the role of business unit managers in BMI.

- *Realize BMI despite the change of business unit managers.* CHESBROUGH observed that many organizations have a "business model innovation leadership gap".[566] He points out that the general managers of specific businesses in larger firms are typically rotated from one position to another one every 2-3 years. Even though these managers might have the authority, they lack the time to realize BMI.[567] Through the case "Integrate for Control", the research at hand contributes to this discussion. The case demonstrates that BMI can be realized despite a change in business unit managers. Although introduced and officially led by the initial business unit manager, the BMI was then materially advanced by a dedicated project team. After the change took place, the project team convinced the new business unit manager to continue this project by presenting the yet-proven, fact-based indicators on what would be achievable through the BMI.[568]

Block 2: Further contributions to BMI literature

---

[562] See ibidem.
[563] See sections 6.4, 6.5, 6.6.
[564] See Bucherer et al. (2012), p. 183.
[565] See Mason / Spring (2011), p. 1040.
[566] See Chesbrough (2007), p. 16.
[567] See Chesbrough (2010), p. 361.
[568] See section 6.10.

- *Definition of BMI.* Research on BMI has evolved from acknowledging the business model as a new unit of innovation that is distinct from products or processes. This new field of research lacks an established definition of BMI, mainly due to a vague understanding and missing theoretical grounding of the business model concept itself.[569] This dissertation contributes to greater definitional clarity by offering a holistic (working) definition of BMI that was developed from a rich body of literature. The definition contends that only system-wide changes, entailing both value proposition and value constellation, qualify as BMI. Thereby, the notion of BMI is distinguished from the notion business model development. Sole product or process innovations, when applied to an established business model, may rather represent forms of business model development. Moreover, the BMI working definition was operationalized through a corresponding BMI-identification tool that would facilitate not only the testing of the here-presented propositions but also other future empirical research on BMI.[570]

- *Drivers of BMI.* The dissertation shed light on the drivers that motivate business unit managers, who facilitate an already established business model, to engage in BMI. Indeed, gaining a deeper understanding of such drivers is another integral part of the research agenda on BMI.[571] This explorative multiple-case study found that combinations of the desire to grow, the desire to make use of internal competencies and a latent threat on the margins in the established business model motivate business unit managers to pursue new opportunities. Another motivational factor constitutes the immediate threat of extinction due to sustained financial losses.[572]

- *BMI in multi-business firms and Corporate Entrepreneurship.* The emerging literature on BMI in established firms has not conclusively determined which extant theoretical streams provide a suitable theoretical grounding for advancing this research. The dissertation contributes to this current discussion by providing links between BMI in multi-business firms, as defined in section 2.1, and the research arena of CE. Consequently, it is suggested that this dissertation's findings complement the research on CE.[573] Alternatively, existing literature relating to CE might provide further explanatory support for the proposed management practices supporting business unit managers in successfully realizing BMI.

7.4 Limitations and Avenues of Further Research

Limitations

As described in chapter 3, in case study research the precise *documentation of the research process* represents an important quality criterion. In this research, the

569 See section 2.1.
570 See ibidem.
571 See Schneider / Spieth (2013a), p. 21.
572 See chapter 5.
573 See section 2.2.

documentation remains limited with regard to names of the research objects, i.e. the names of the multi-business firms, business units, and informants. Many interviewees insisted on anonymity to prevent any unintentional disclosure of competitively relevant information. Nonetheless, the scholar aimed to describe both the research process and the studied events as comprehensively as possible.

In reference to *internal validity*, as with any study, more interviews and more internal secondary data could have revealed further details to test the causal effects proposed in this dissertation. However, the major tactics, commonly proposed to ensure both construct and internal empirical validity, were applied when collecting and analyzing this "polar type" sample of cases.[574]

In reference to *external validity*, as discussed in section 3.5, case study research relies on analytic as opposed to statistical generalization. It aims at contributing to a broader, more in-depth theory of the researched phenomenon. In this sense, the contributions of this dissertation might be limited for two reasons: Firstly, the structure of a multi-business firm – meaning its organization in different business units, headed by at least partially autonomous business unit managers – might be influenced by the industry it is in. The five in-depth studied cases cover business-to-business transactions in the industries of electrical engineering and chemicals. All five business units belong to corporations that fulfill the characteristics of a multi-business firm as typically described in management literature.[575] However, future research on management practices for realizing BMI in multi-business firms might bring about industry-related differences. Secondly, the five business units and corporations are all headquartered in Western Europe. Hence, further research might also reveal dissimilarities based upon managers' varying cultural values in other regions.[576]

Moreover, it must be considered that multi-business firms have the option of charging a central service department for realizing BMI. Daimler, for instance, set up a central "Business Innovation" department. This department collects internally existing business ideas. For the most promising ideas, it develops and pilots new business models that add to the existing ones.[577] However, this dissertation focused on the business unit as the scene of BMI.

Avenues of Further Research

The dissertation at hand delivered a consistent set of testable hypotheses relating to the role of business unit managers in BMI that had not existed before. Hence, an avenue of further research would be to replicate these findings either through additional case studies or through questionnaire-based, large-scale quantitative studies. Such research projects should consider the fact that managers might feel

---

574 See chapter 3, especially section 3.5.
575 See section 3.1.
576 See (e.g.) Hofstede (1993); Crossland / Hambrick (2007), pp. 784-785.
577 See Zollenkop (2011), pp. 207-208.

more secure in participating and providing information on a BMI's realization, if they are not directly asked about the specific outcome of the BMI.

Before engaging in further empirical studies to test the hypotheses, literature from related research fields could be examined with the goal of detecting explanatory support for the here-presented findings. BUCHERER et al., for example, started to investigate similarities and differences between BMI and product innovation.[578] Furthermore, this dissertation proposed to compare the findings with extant literature relating to the larger arena of Corporate Entrepreneurship.

Another avenue of further research would be to focus specifically on the role of corporate managers. This research already disclosed that interaction between the business unit and the corporate level occurs in the BMI process. Therefore, studies that explore the behavior of corporate managers in the context of realizing BMI in multi-business firms would complement such theory.

What is more, insights resulting from this dissertation – in particular the trust-gaining phase – might supplement research on the commercialization of innovations in start-ups. This research introduced the trust-gaining phase as an integral part of a successful BMI process. In reference to start-ups, DMITRIEV et al. found from studying the business model development process at four technology start-ups, that the back-end elements of the business model, i.e. the available key resources, complementary assets and the partners' network, have a filtering effect on business idea formulation. The authors stress that, after setting out to realize the initial concept, entrepreneurs may need to rework the entire business idea because of issues with the back-end elements.[579] The research at hand, although focused on established firms, similarly found that it may take time-consuming iterations and continuous testing with customers until the most promising new value proposition appears. However, as for the BMI success cases, each business unit manager went through a trust-gaining phase before entering the development sub-phase; and in fact, in none of the BMI success cases did the initial business idea later have to be changed entirely. Hence, further research on BMI at start-ups might explore whether trust-gaining among entrepreneurs – in other words answering the question: "What do I know before I start?" – has a moderating effect on the extent of a later business idea change.

---

[578] See Bucherer et al. (2012), p. 183.
[579] See Dmitriev et al. (2013), p. 29.

Appendix

Coding scheme with anchoring examples from interviews and internal secondary data

#	BMI Process: Phase	BMI Process: Sub-phase and Block	Definition of Management Practice	Anchoring examples from successful cases	Coding rule	Anchoring examples from failed cases	Coding rule
1	Trust-Gaining Phase	n/a	Business unit managers should establish trust in the new opportunity's chance of success before engaging into its realization. *Establish own trust*	"[...] a clear trend towards micro-miniaturization became evident. [...] I gained trust [...]." "In the beginning of the last decade, our product management received more and more customer requests without any specification." "Back then, we were originally supposed to only deliver cables. But out of conversations with the customer at their site, we were asked to develop a concept about how to fit the cables into the building." "The idea arose out of intense discussions about how possibly we can better benefit from our competencies."	Code if it indicates trust in the new opportunity before the BMI's realization started.	"At the board meeting, I [new plant director] argued against his [central strategy department] new business model proposal. [He] did not have enough time to thoroughly understand the [traditional] business model and therefore applied inappropriate methods [...]. From the minutes of a board meeting: [Corporate manager:] "Should the unit focus on being a general contractor in the future?" [Business unit manager:] "Yes" [Business unit manager later in the same meeting:] "We should not enter into every project as a general contractor."	Opposite to coding rule for successful cases
2			Business unit managers should ensure that in their unit they are not the only ones who have trust in the new opportunity before engaging into it. *Ensure there are allies*	"In my former function outside [ElectricCorp], I had already noticed that many energy utility companies only had a little in-house know-how about cable application, engineering or construction." "The workshop was initiated by our business unit manager. The participants represented all different functions such as production, sales, controlling, and R&D." "With strong involvement of [other managers within the unit] we conducted a first market research."	Code if it indicates that other managers within the unit trust the new opportunity.		
3			Business unit managers should consider ex-ante that, in order to realize the new opportunity, bringing in new processes may become necessary. *Be open to new processes*	"We compiled a business plan which also entailed the business model design." "Already in 2004, I argued that 'System' has to become one of our future success factors meaning that we have to sell something around the cable. [...] 'Services' should become another success factor. Customers wish to deal with only one contact for the entire project [...]" "We already knew in the initial workshop [...] that we would have to bring in [...] new processes."	Code if it indicates ex-ante thoughts on a new business model.	"The attitude of the former management can be summarized with: 'We are good at assembling for healthcare, as well as automation and drives applications. Thus, we can also do it in aviation'."	

(Continued)

4	Realization Phase	*Sub-Phase:* Development *Block:* Value Proposition	Business unit managers should support flexibility and iterative testing directly with customers when developing the most promising new value proposition. *Test iteratively in the real world*	"I think that it is appropriate to apply a trial and error mentality or a certain ease when developing a new business model." "[…] we actively approached several carmakers. We discussed our idea with them and incorporated their feedback." "The cable engineering and installation requirements were relatively small in this first project. [...] It can be seen as a test with customers. It determined the core service package of [the new business model]" "We actively insisted on a much earlier installation of the first line for experimentation and training purposes."	Code if it indicates a flexible and/or iterative approach to real-world testing of the new value proposition.	"[…] they promised a lot to the customer. They strongly emphasized the firm's existing skill set." "At some points [in the production] we even surpassed the quality requirements. If there was a quality problem, we were able to find out exactly if it had been caused by an operator, by the raw material or by a tool, and we could identify which other parts might have been affected by the source of error."	
5		*Sub-Phase:* Development *Block:* Value Constellation	Business unit managers should find those human and non-human resources, as well as external partners, which enable the delivery of the value proposition at a profit. If those resources are not available in the traditional business model, they must be built up. *Find the right resources*	"For the first time, when executing the [...] project, we hired new staff dedicated to the new business model." "In the [first] project, we deployed our internal 'blue collar team' for the first time ever directly at the customer's site. Meanwhile, all team members have been trained to become construction managers and supervisors." "They had to learn how to operate and program the robots for an optimized paint application. […] [The equipment manufacturer] strongly supported the training." "Today, we supply to the customer the entire system including cables, connectors, electronics, and fiber optic elements. In order to achieve this, we built up new competencies in electric design." "The operators from the established business model were not capable of operating the new machines."	Code if it indicates changes in the existing resources for delivering the new value proposition.	"An acquisition of engineering competencies never happened." "As for the product engineering, the management trusted the existing team. Additional product engineers for the new business were not hired." "If I had the chance to enter this business again, I would try to deliver specialized products instead of standard ones. Maybe, from this basis one could enter into the high volume/standard products business. Our company is strong at managing special orders."	Opposite to coding rule for successful cases
6			Business unit managers should let their (major) decisions on new resources be guided solely by the extent to which the new value proposition is realizable. *Be guided by the new offering's realization chances*	"For the purpose of planning and execution of the *[first smaller]* projects, we called in other internal resources from [our site], as well as external companies and consultants." "For the first time, when executing the [first larger] project, we hired new staff dedicated to the new business model." "In the beginning, it is not necessary to determine exactly which machinery is to be put up. It is dependent on identifying the most interesting directions and the most potential sales volume, and on the orders won." "We won the contract. We had to recruit a new team that would do the job."	Code if it indicates that building the value constellation depends on the value proposition's development state.		

(Continued)

7	Realization Phase	Sub-Phase: Integration	Business unit managers should integrate the new business model into the established organization once a clearly-outlined, tested and promising new value proposition can be delivered from a stable value constellation. *Integrate once the new BM is viable and stable*	"The trigger [for integration] was surely the size of this area and the reached capacity usage from high runners. This decision was driven by the will to not duplicate overhead functions, to guarantee somehow unified processes within the organization and to terminate the special project characterization […]" "Momentarily, there are two parallel business models existing in our unit: the product- and the solution-oriented one. […] The solution-oriented business model is financially very successful […]." "[After integration, other carmakers] very quickly also adopted the new offering."	Code if it indicates the integration of a new business model that is successful.	"The old management believed that it would eventually make a profit." "I assume that the business plan, which was the basis of decision to enter into the framework contract, did not contain all of our costs."	Opposite to coding rule for successful cases
8			Business unit managers should assess which resources from the established organization can rationally be shared with the new business model while integrating. *Share where it is operable*	"The manufacturing planning and control functions were put together." "[…] many investors value that the business unit belongs to a solvent corporation; especially when awarding a general contract." "Within global key accounts, we run both 'business models'."	Code if it indicates that resources are rationally shared while integrating.		
9		n/a	Business unit managers should engage into BMI when profits from the traditional business model are (still) within corporate's expectations. *Act while the traditional BM is (still) profitable*	"The company has been doing financially well over a longer period." "Our typical product business is close to becoming commoditized." "I presented to the top management that due to [various reasons] the pressure on profit margins in our traditional business model would increase." "The business went well back then."	Code if it indicates proactive action.	"Because of the ongoing poor financial performance the former plant director was replaced […]." "The trigger event for the request of a second controller was the business unit's ongoing bad sales and profit situation."	
10			Business unit managers should lead and be closely involved in the realization of the new business model. *Lead and be involved*	"I assigned two more of my best employees […] to this task. The team was taken out of the line organization and reported directly to me." "We went into this first project [in which a new value proposition was tested] with such enthusiasm." "The new business unit manager was as strongly motivated as [her] predecessor."	Code if it indicates leadership by the business unit manager.		

(Continued)

11	Realization Phase	n/a	Business unit managers should overcome any form of unit-internal resistance against the realization the new business model. *Overcome internal resistance*	"The head of production objected to transfer his best people to the new machines. Only after the [business unit manager's] intervention did he do it." "[…] current processes were well defined and stable. Thus, the question arose: 'Why should we even engage in something so new?'" "When we integrated the new business model into the existing organization, we were confronted with resistance." "The internal resistance [against the development of the new business model] was clearly noticeable on all hierarchical levels." "Throughout the project, the internal resistance was immense."	Code if it indicates internal resistance that was to be overcome.		Opposite to coding rule for successful cases
12			Business unit managers should convincingly persuade corporate management of the new opportunity. *Convince corporate*	"The business plan was presented to [corporate management] with the aim of having the investments approved." "[Corporate management] was concerned about the legal risks inherent to the new business model." "[…] we had to regularly inform [corporate management] about our progress." "[Corporate management] initially rejected the project. […] Then, the second time, we were better prepared and convinced them."	Code if it indicates corporate approval of the new business model.	"[The firm] rather focuses on risk avoidance and cash protection." "I [new plant director] sensed that from the summer of 2010 [corporate management] did no longer want to be bothered with it." "[Corporate management] did not believe in the predicted growth in the […] market."	

References

Aaker, D. A., Kumar V., Day G. S. & Leone R. P. (2011). *Marketing research* (10th ed., international student version). Hoboken: Wiley.

Abdelkafi, N., Makhotin, S. & Posselt, T. (2013). Business Model Innovations for Electric Mobility — What Can Be Learned From Existing Business Model Patterns? *International Journal of Innovation Management*, *17*(1), 1340003. doi: 10.1142/S1363919613400033

Abraham, S. (2013). Will business model innovation replace strategic analysis? *Strategy & Leadership*, *41*(2), 31–38. doi: 10.1108/10878571311318222

Agarwal, R., & Helfat, C. E. (2009). Strategic Renewal of Organizations. *Organization Science*, Mar/Apr2009, *20*(2), pp. 281–293. doi: 10.1287/orsc.109 0.0423

Ahuja, G., & Lampert, C. M. (2001). Entrepreneurship in the large corporation: a longitudinal study of how established firms create breakthrough invention. *Strategic Management Journal*, *22*(6/7), 521–543. doi: 10.1002/smj.176

Amit, R., & Zott, C. (2001). Value creation in e-business. *Strategic Management Journal*, *22*(6/7), 493–520. doi: 10.1002/smj.187

Amit, R., & Zott, C. (2010). *Business model innovation: Creating value in times of change* (Working paper no. 870). Navarra: IESE Business School. Retrieved from http://papers.ssrn.com/sol3/papers.cfm?abstract_id=1701660

Amit, R., & Zott, C. (2012). Creating Value Through Business Model Innovation. *MIT Sloan Management Review*, *53*(3), 40–49. Retrieved from EBSCOhost research databases.

Aspara, J., Hietanen, J., & Tikkanen, H. (2010). Business model innovation vs replication: Financial performance implications of strategic emphases. *Journal of Strategic Marketing*, *18*(1), 39–56. doi: 10.1080/09652540903511290

Aspara, J., Lamberg, J.-A., Laukia, A., & Tikkanen, H. (2011). Strategic management of business model transformation: lessons from Nokia. *Management Decision*, *49*(4), 622–647. doi: 10.1108/00251741111126521

Axinn, W. G., & Pearce, L. D. (2006). *Mixed method data collection strategies.* Cambridge: Cambridge Univ. Press.

Baden-Fuller, C., & Morgan, M. S. (2010). Business Models as Models. *Long Range Planning*, *43*(2/3), 156–171. doi: 10.1016/j.lrp.2010.02.005

Barney, J. (1986). Strategic Factor Markets: Expectations, Luck, and Business Strategy. *Management Science*, *32*(10), 1231–1241. Retrieved from EBSCOhost research databases.

Berg, B. L. (2007). *Qualitative research methods for the social sciences* (6th ed.). Boston: Pearson.

Berghman, L. A. (2012). Strategic Innovation in Established Companies: an Empirical Study of Appropriate Ambidexterity Strategies. *International Journal of Innovation Management*, *16*(1), 1250007. doi:10.1142/S1363919611003520

Berglund, H., & Sandström, C. (2013). Business model innovation from an open systems perspective: structural challenges and managerial solutions. *International Journal of Product Development*, *18*(3), 274–285. doi: 10.1504/IJPD.2013.055011

Bieger, T., & Rüegg-Stürm, J. (2002). Net Economy – Die Bedeutung der Gestaltung von Beziehungskonfigurationen. In T. Bieger, N. Bickhoff, R. Caspers, D. Knyphausen-Aufseß & K. Reding (Eds.), *Zukünftige Geschäftsmodelle (*pp. 15-33). Berlin: Springer.

Bieger, T. , & Krys, C. (2011). Einleitung – Die Dynamik von Geschäftsmodellen. In T. Bieger, D. Knyphausen-Aufseß and C. Krys (Eds.), *Innovative Geschäftsmodelle* (pp. 1-10). Berlin: Springer.

Bieger, T., & Reinhold, S. (2011). Das wertbasierte Geschäftsmodell – Ein aktualisierter Strukturierungsansatz. In T. Bieger, D. Knyphausen-Aufseß and C. Krys (Eds.), *Innovative Geschäftsmodelle* (pp. 13-70). Berlin: Springer.

Björkdahl, J., & Holmén, M. (2013). Editorial: Business model innovation–the challenges ahead. *International Journal of Product Development*, *18*(3/4), 213–225. Retrieved from http://www.inderscience.com/info/inarticletoc.php?jcode=ijpd&year= 2013&vol=18&issue=3/4.

Bock, A. J., Opsahl, T., & George, G. (2010). *Business model innovation and strategic flexibility: a study of the effects of informal and formal organization* (Working paper no. SSRN 1533742). London: Imperial College. Retrieved October 10, 2011, from http://ssrn.com/abstract=1533742

Bock, A. J., Opsahl, T., George, G., & Gann, D. M. (2011): The effects of culture and structure on strategic flexibility during business model innovation. *Journal of Management Studies, 49*(2), 279–305. doi: 10.1111/j.1467-6486.2011.01030.x

Brette, O., Chappoz, Y., Dussuc, B., & Poivret, C. (2011). Management de l'innovation et business models des PMI. Le cas de l'industrie plasturgiste. *Management & Avenir*, *41*, 236–253. Retrieved from EBSCOhost research databases.

Brüderl, J., & Schüssler, R. (1990). Organizational mortality: The liabilities of newness and adolescence. *Administrative Science Quarterly*, *35*(3), 530–547. Retrieved from http://www.jstor.org/stable/10.2307/2393316

Bucherer, E. (2010). *Business model innovation – Guidelines for a structured approach*. Aachen: Shaker.

Bucherer, E., Eisert, U., & Gassmann, O. (2012). Towards Systematic Business Model Innovation: Lessons from Product Innovation Management. *Creativity and Innovation Management*, *21*(2), 183–198. doi: 10.1111/j.1467-8691.2012.00637.x

Buzzavo, L. (2012). *Strategy innovation as business model reconfiguration* (Working paper no. 2/2012). Venice: Ca'Foscari University of Venice. Retrieved from http://papers.ssrn.com/sol3/papers.cfm?abstract_id=2037408

Casadesus-Masanell, R., & Ricart, J. E. (2010). From strategy to business models and onto tactics. *Long Range Planning*, *43*(2/3), 195–215. doi: 10.101 6/j.lrp.2010.01.004

Casadesus-Masanell, R., & Ricart, J. E. (2011). How to design a winning business model. *Harvard Business Review*, *89*(1/2), 100–107. Retrieved from EBSCOhost research databases.

Cavalcante, S., Kesting, P., & Ulhøi, J. (2011). Business model dynamics and innovation: (re)establishing the missing linkages. *Management Decision*, *49*(8), 1327–1342. doi: 10.1108/00251741111163142

Cavalcante, S. A. (2012). Preparing for business model change: the "pre-stage" finding. *Journal of Management and Governance*. doi: 10.1007/s10997-012-9232-7.

Chandler, A. D. (1991). The functions of the HQ unit in the multibusiness firm. *Strategic Management Journal*, *12*(S2), 31–50. doi:10.1002/smj.4250121004

Chandrasekaran, A. (2009). *Multiple Levels of Ambidexterity in Managing the Innovation-Improvement Dilemma: Evidence from High Technology Organizations* (Doctoral dissertation, University of Minnessota). Retrieved from ProQuest.

Chatterjee, S. (2013). Simple Rules for Designing Business Models. *California Management Review*, *55*(2), 97–124. doi: 10.1525/cmr.2013.55.2.97

Chesbrough, H., & Rosenbloom, R. S. (2002). The role of the business model in capturing value from innovation: evidence from Xerox Corporation's technology spin-off companies. *Industrial and Corporate Change*, *11*(3), 529–555. doi:10.1093/icc/11.3.529

Chesbrough, H. (2007). Business model innovation: it's not just about technology anymore. *Strategy & Leadership*, 2007, *35*(6), 12–17. doi: 10.1108/10878570710833714

Chesbrough, H. (2010). Business model innovation: Opportunities and barriers. *Long Range Planning*, *43*(2/3), 354–363. doi:10.1016/j.lrp.2009.07.010

Christensen, C. M., & Raynor, M. E. (2003). *The innovator's solution.* Boston: Harvard Business Review Press.

Cliffe, S. (2011): When your business model is in trouble, in: *Harvard Business Review*, Jan/Feb2011, 89(1/2), pp. 96–98. Retrieved from EBSCOhost research databases.

Collis, D., Young, D., & Goold, M. (2007). The size, structure, and performance of corporate headquarters. *Strategic Management Journal*, *28*(4), 383–405. doi:10.1002/smj

Colvin, G. (2013, February 25). Your business model doesn't work anymore. *Fortune*, *167*(3), 42. Retrieved from EBSCOhost research databases.

Comes, S., & Berniker, L. (2008). Business Model Innovation. In: D. Pantaleo & N. Pal. (Eds.), *From strategy to execution* (pp. 65–86). Berlin: Springer.

Covin, J. G., & Kuratko, D. F. (2009). The Concept of Corporate Entrepreneurship. In V. K. Narayanan & G. C. O'Connor (Eds.), *Encyclopedia of Technology and Innovation Management* (pp. 207-213). Chichester: Wiley.

Crossland, C., & Hambrick, D. (2007). How national systems differ in their constraints on corporate executives: A study of CEO effects in three countries. *Strategic Management Journal*, *28*(8), 767–789. doi:10.1002/smj

Dahan, N. M., Doh, J. P., Oetzel, J., & Yaziji, M. (2010). Corporate-NGO Collaboration: Co-creating New Business Models for Developing Markets. *Long Range Planning*, *43*(2/3), 326–342. doi:10.1016/j.lrp.2009.11.003

Davidson, A., & Leavy, B. (2008). Interview with growth consultant Chris Zook: a less risky path to business model innovation. *Strategy & Leadership*, *36*(1), 27–32. doi: 10.1108/10878570810840661

Delong, D., Schlesinger, L. A., & Applegate, L. M. (2001). *Taco Bell Inc. (1983-1994)* [Case study]. Boston: Harvard Business School Publishing.

Demil, B., & Lecocq, X. (2010). Business Model Evolution: In Search of Dynamic Consistency. *Long Range Planning*, *43*(2/3), 227–246. doi: 10.1016/j.lrp.2010.02.004

De Reuver, M., Bouwman, H., & Haaker, T. (2013). Business Model Roadmapping: a Practical Approach To Come From an Existing To a Desired Business Model. *International Journal of Innovation Management*, *17*(1), 1340006. doi: 10.1142/S1363919613400069

Dess, G. G., Lumpkin, G. T., & Eisner, A. B. (2008). *Strategic Management: Creating Competitive Advantages* (4th ed.). New York: McGraw-Hill/Irwin.

De Vaus, D. A. (2002): *Surveys in social research* (5th ed.). London: Routledge.

Dimitriev, V., Truong, Y., Palmer, M., & Schneckenberg, D. (2013). *Generating ideas and organizing in business model development during the commercialization of technological innovations.* Paper presented at the EURAM 2013 conference, Istanbul.

Doz, Y. L., & Kosonen, M. (2010). Embedding Strategic AgilityA Leadership Agenda for Accelerating Business Model Renewal. *Long Range Planning*, *43*(2/3), 370–382. doi: 10.1016/j.lrp.2009.07.006

Dul, J., & Hak, T. (2008). *Case study methodology in business research*. Oxford: Butterworth-Heinemann.

Eisenhardt, K. M. (1989). Building Theories from Case Study Research. *Academy of Management Review*, *14*(4), 532–550. doi: 10.5465/AMR.1989.4308385

Eisenhardt, K. M., & Graebner, M. E. (2007). Theory Building From Cases: Opportunities and Challenges. *Academy of Management Journal*, *50*(1), 25–32. doi: 10.5465/AMJ.2007.24160888

EIU (2005). *Business 2010: Embracing the challenge of change*. Retrieved August 2, 2012, from http://graphics. eiu.com/files/ad_pdfs/Business%202010_Global _FINAL.pdf

Enkel, E., & Mezger, F. (2013). Imitation Processes and Their Application for Business Model Innovation: an Explorative Study. *International Journal of Innovation Management*, *17*(1), 1340005. doi: 10.1142/S1363919613400057

Eppler, M. J., Hoffmann, F., & Bresciani, S. (2011). New Business Models Through Collaborative Idea Generation. *International Journal of Innovation Management*, *15*(6), 1323-1341. doi: 10.1142/S1363919611003751

Fielt, E. (2012). *A "Service Logic" Rationale for Business Model Innovation*. Paper presented at the EURAM 2012 conference, Rotterdam.

Foss, N. J., & Knudsen, T. (2003). The Resource-Based Tangle: Towards a Sustainable Explanation of Competitive Advantage. *Managerial and Decision Economics*, *24*(4), 291-307. doi: 10.1002 mde.1122

Foss, N. J., & Lyngsie, J. (2011). *The Emerging Strategic Entrepreneurship Field: Origins, Key Tenets and Research Gaps* (SMG WP 7/2011). Retrieved June 2, 2012, from http://ssrn.com/ abstract=1747711.

Frankenberger, K., Weiblen, T., Csik, M., & Gassmann, O. (2013). The 4I–framework of business model innovation: a structured view on process phases and challenges. *International Journal of Product Development*, *18*(3/4), 249–273. doi: 10.1504/IJPD.2013.055012

Gambardella, A., & McGahan, A. M. (2010). Business-Model Innovation: General Purpose Technologies and their Implications for Industry Structure. *Long Range Planning*, *43*(2/3), 262–271. doi: 10.1016/j.lrp.2009.07.009

Gebauer, H., Worch, H., & Truffer, B. (2011). Absorptive capacity, learning processes and combinative capabilities as determinants of strategic innovation. *European Management Journal*, 57–73. doi: 10.1016/j.emj.2011.10.004

Ghezzi, A., Balocco, R., & Rangone, A. (2010). How to get strategic planning and business model design wrong: the case of a mobile technology provider. *Strategic Change*, *19*(5/6), 213–238. doi: 10.1002/jsc

Giesen, E., Berman, S. J., Bell, R., & Blitz, A. (2007). Three ways to successfully innovate your business model. *Strategy & Leadership*, *35*(6), 27–33. doi: 10.1108/10878570710833732

Gilbert, C. G. (2001). *A dilemma in response: Examining the newspaper industry's response to the internet* (Doctoral dissertation, Harvard University). Retrieved from ProQuest.

Glaser, B. G., & Strauss, A. L. (1967). *The Discovery of Grounded Theory: Strategies for Qualitative Research (*3rd paperback printing 2008). New Brunswick: Transaction Publishers.

Golden, B. (1992). Research notes. The past is the past--or is it? The use of retrospective accounts as indicators of past strategy. *Academy of Management Journal*, *35*(4), 848–860. doi: 10.2307/256318

Govindarajan, V., & Gupta, A. K. (2001). Strategic innovation: a conceptual road map. *Business Horizons*, *44*(4), 3–12. Retrieved from EBSCOhost research databases.

Govindarajan, V., & Trimble, C. (2011). The CEO's role in business model reinvention. *Harvard business review*, *89*(1/2), 108–114. Retrieved from EBSCOhost research databases.

Greve, H. R. (2003). Why are there So Many Multiunit Organizations? *Strategic Organization*, *1*(1), 109–115. doi: 10.1177/1476127003001001220

Griffin, A., & Page, A. L. (1993). An Interim Report on Measuring Product Development Success and Failure. *Journal of Product Innovation Management*, *10*(4), 291–308. doi: 10.1111/1540-5885.1040291

Gummesson, E. (2008). Case Study. In R. Thorpe & R. Holt (Eds.), *The Sage Dictionary of Qualitative Management Research* (pp. 38-40). London: Sage.

Günzel, F., & Holm, A. B. (2013). One Size Does Not Fit All — Understanding the Front-End and Back-End of Business Model Innovation. *International Journal of Innovation Management*, *17*(1), 1340002. doi: 10.1142/S1363919613400021

Hacklin, F., & Wallnöfer, M. (2012). The business model in the practice of strategic decision making: insights from a case study. *Management Decision*, *50*(2), 166–188. doi: 10.1108/00251741211203515

Hamel, G. (2012). *What matters now.* San Francisco: Jossey-Bass.

Harren, H. (2012). *Management of multiple business models* (Doctoral dissertation no. 2012/5052, Technische Universität Berlin).

Hauschildt, J., & Salomo, S. (2011). *Innovationsmanagement* (5th ed.). München: Vahlen.

Hitt, M. A., Ireland, R. D., Camp, S. M., & Sexton, D. L. (2001). Strategic entrepreneurship: entrepreneurial strategies for wealth creation. *Strategic Management Journal*, *22*(6/7), 479–491. doi: 10.1002/smj.196

Hoffmann, F., Bresciani, S., & Eppler, M. (2012). *Business Model Ideation: An Experimental Approach for the Evaluation of Team-based Methods*. Paper presented at the EURAM 2012 conference, Rotterdam.

Hofstede, G. (1993). Cultural constraints in management theories. *Academy of Management Perspectives*, *7*(1), 81–94. doi: 10.5465/AME.1993.9409142061

Holm, A., Günzel, F., & Ulhøi, J. (2013). Openness in innovation and business models: lessons from the newspaper industry. *International Journal of Technology Management*, *61*(3/4), 324–348. Retrieved from http://inder science.metapress.com/index/J257650558085634.pdf

Horn, C. & Brem, A. (2013). Strategic directions on innovation management – a conceptual framework. *Management Research Review, 36*(10), 939-954. doi: 10.1108/MRR-06-2012-0142.

Hull, J. C. (2006). *Options, Futures and Other Derivatives* (6th ed.). Upper Saddle River: Pearson Prentice Hall.

Hungenberg, H. (2006). *Strategisches Management in Unternehmen* (4th ed.). Wiesbaden: Gabler.

IBM (2006). *Expanding the Innovation Horizon: The Global CEO Study 2006*. Retrieved August 2, 2012, from http://www-.ibm.com/smb/includes/content/ industries/electronics/pdf/Global_CEO_ Study_-_Electronics.pdf

IBM (2008). *The Enterprise of the Future: Global CEO Study*. Retrieved August 2, 2012, from http://www-03.ibm.com/industries/ca/en/healthcare/files/2008_ibm _global_ceo_study.pdf, accessed 8/02/2013

IBM (2010). *Capitalizing on Complexity: Insights from the Global CEO Study*. Retrieved August 2, 2012, from http://public.dhe.ibm.com/common/ssi/ecm/ en/gbe03297usen/GBE03297USEN.PDF, accessed 8/02/2013

Jaeggi, M. (2010). *Business model innovation in wealth management* (Doctoral dissertation no. 3748, University of St. Gallen).

Jensen, A. B. (2012). *How business models are changed - bridging strategy and innovation*. Paper presented at the EURAM 2012 conference, Rotterdam.

Johnson, M. W., Christensen, C., & Kagermann, H. (2008). Reinventing your business model. *Harvard Business Review*, *86*(12), 50–58. Retrieved from EBSCOhost research databases.

Johnson, M. W. (2010). *Seizing the white space – Business model innovation for growth and renewal.* Boston: Harvard Business Press.

Kaplan, S. (2012). *The business model innovation factory.* Hoboken: Wiley.

Kashani, K., & Miller, J. (2003). *Innovation & Renovation: The Nespresso Story* [Case study]. IMD Lausanne.

Kashani, K., & Francis, I. (2011). *Xiameter: The Past and Future of a "Disruptive Innovation"* [Case study]. IMD Lausanne.

Katz, R., & Allen, T. (2007). Investigating the Not Invented Here (NIH) syndrome: A look at the performance, tenure, and communication patterns of 50 R & D Project Groups. *R&D Management*, *12*(1), 7–20. Retrieved from http://onlinelibrary.wiley.com/doi/10.1111/j.1467-9310.1982.tb00478.x/abstract

Kim, W. C., & Mauborgne, R. (1997). Value innovation: the strategic logic of high growth. *Harvard Business Review*, *75*(1), 103–112. Retrieved from EBSCOhost research databases.

Kim, W. C., & Mauborgne, R. (2004). Blue ocean strategy. *Harvard Business Review*, *82*(10), 76–84. Retrieved from EBSCOhost research databases.

Kim, W. C., & Mauborgne, R. (2005). Blue ocean strategy, from theory to practice. *California Management Review*, *47*(3), 105–121. Retrieved from EBSCOhost research databases.

Klang, D., & Hoffmann, F. (2012). *The Role of Top Level Leader Behavior in Business Model Innovation of Incumbent Firm.* Paper presented at the EURAM 2012 conference, Rotterdam.

Koen, P. A., Bertels, H., Elsum, I. R., Orroth, M., & Tollett, B. L. (2010). Breakthrough Innovation Dilemmas. *Research Technology Management*, *53*(6), 48–51. Retrieved from EBSCOhost research databases.

Koen, P. A., Bertels, H. M. J., & Elsum, I. R. (2011). The Three Faces of Business Model Innovation: Challenges for Established Firms. *Research-Technology Management*, *54*(3), 52–59. doi: 10.5437/08953608X5403009

König, A. (2009). *Cognitive Framing and Incumbent Inertia in Response to Technological Discontinuities.* Berlin: Verlag Pro Business.

Kuckartz, U. (2007). *Einführung in die computergestützte Analyse qualitativer Daten* (2nd ed.). Wiesbaden: Verlag für Sozialwiss.

Kuhn, J. S., & Marsick, V. J. (2005). Action learning for strategic innovation in mature organizations: key cognitive, design and contextual considerations. *Action Learning: Research and Practice*, *2*(1), 27–48. doi: 10.1080/14767330500041236

Lasinger, D. (2011). *Die Leistung vor der Innovation.* Wiesbaden: Gabler.

Leavy, B. (2010). A system for innovating business models for breakaway growth. *Strategy & Leadership*, *38*(6), 5–15. doi: 10.1108/10878571011088014

Lecocq, X., Demil, B., & Ventura, J. (2010). Business Models as a Research Program in Strategic Management: An Appraisal based on Lakatos. *Management*, *13*(4), 214–225. Retrieved from EBSCOhost research databases.

Liedtka, J. M., & Meyer, A. (2009). *Business model innovation: A process model* (Technical Note UVA-BP-0538, University of Virginia Darden School Foundation, Charlottesville, VA). Retrieved October 9, 2011.

Lindgardt, Z., Reeves, M., Stalk, G., & Deimler, M. S. (2009). *Business model innovation: When the game gets tough, change the game*. Retrieved October 10, 2011, from, http://www.bcg.com/documents/ file36456.pdf

Lindgardt, Z., Reeves, M., Stalk, G., & Deimler, M. S. (2013). Business Model Innovation: When the game gets tough, change the game. In M. S. Deimler (Ed.), *Own the future: 50 ways to win from the Boston Consulting Group* (pp. 291-298). Hoboken: Wiley.

Lindgren, P. (2012). Business Model Innovation Leadership: How Do SME's Strategically Lead Business Model Innovation? *International Journal of Business and Management*, *7*(14), 53–67. doi: 10.5539/ijbm.v7nl4p53

Lindgren, P., & Abdullah, M. (2013). Conceptualizing strategic business model innovation leadership for business survival and business model innovation excellence. *Journal of Multi Business Model Innovation and Technology*, *1*, 115–134. Retrieved from http://riverpublishers.com/journal/journal_articles/ download_file.php?file=RP_Journal_2245-456X_123.pdf

Löwer, C. (2011, October 27). Maschinenbauer ziehen Mietmodelle ins Kalkül. *Handelsblatt,* p. 59.

Markides, C., & Charitou, C. D. (2004). Competing with dual business models : A contingency approach. *Academy of Management Executive*, *18*(3), 22–36. doi: 10.5465/AME.2004.14776164

Markides C. (2006). Disruptive Innovation: In Need of Better Theory. *Journal of Product Innovation Management*, *23*(1), 19-25. doi: 10.1111/j.1540-5885.200 5.00177.x

Markides, C., & Oyon, D. (2010). What to Do Against Disruptive Business Models (When and How to Play Two Games at Once). *MIT Sloan Management Review*, *51*(4), 24–32. Retrieved from EBSCOhost research databases.

Mason, K., & Spring, M. (2011). The sites and practices of business models. *Industrial Marketing Management*, *40*(6), 1032–1041. doi: 10.1016/j.indmar man.2011.06.032

Matzler, K., Ballom, F., Eichen, S. F., & Kohler, T. (2013). Business model innovation: coffee Triumphs for Nespresso. *Journal of Business Strategy*, 2013, *34*(2), 30–37. doi: 10.1108/02756661311310431

Mayring, P. (2010). Qualitative Inhaltsanalyse. In G. Mey & K. Mruck (Eds.), *Handbuch Qualitative Forschung in der Psychologie* (pp. 601-613). Wiesbaden: Verlag für Sozialwiss.

McGrath, R. G. (2010). Business Models: A Discovery Driven Approach. *Long Range Planning*, *43*(2/3), 247–261. doi: 10.1016/j.lrp.2009.07.005

Mezger, F., & Enkel, E. (2012). *Disruptive Business Model Innovation: Exploring the Potential of Cross-Industry Adaptation.* Paper presented at the EURAM 2012 conference, Rotterdam.

Mezger, F., Enkel, E., & Bader, K. (2013). *Antecedents of business model innovation: examining the role of corporate culture and environmental turbulence.* Paper presented at the EURAM 2013 conference, Istanbul.

Miles, M. B., & Huberman, A. M. (1994). *Qualitative data analysis: an expanded sourcebook* (2nd ed.). Thousand Oaks: Sage.

Mitchell, D. W., & Coles, C. B. (2003). The ultimate competitive advantage of continuing business model innovation. *Journal of Business Strategy*, *24*(5), 15–21. doi: 10.1108/02756660310504924

Mitchell, D. W., & Coles, C. B. (2004). Business model innovation breakthrough moves. *Journal of Business Strategy*, *25*(1), 16–26. doi: 10.1108/02756660410515976

Moingeon, B., & Lehmann-Ortega, L. (2010). Creation and Implementation of a New Business Model: a Disarming Case Study, *13*(4), 266–297. Retrieved from EBSCOhost research databases.

Morris, M. H., Kuratko, D. F., & Covin, J. G. (2011). *Corporate Innovation and Entrepreneurship: Entrepreneurial Development within Organizations* (3rd ed.). Mason: South-Western Cengage Learning.

Nenonen, S. and K. Storbacka (2010): Business model design: conceptualizing networked value co-creation, in: *International Journal of Quality and Service Sciences*, 2010, 2(1), pp. 43-59.

Neubauer, R. M. (2011). *Business models in the area of logistics.* Wiesbaden: Gabler.

Nielsen, C. & Bukh, P. N. (2011). What constitutes a business model: the perception of financial analysts. *International Journal of Learning and Intellectual Capital, 8*(3), 256-271.

Nippa, M., Pidun, U., & Rubner, H. (2011). Corporate Portfolio Management: Appraising Four Decades of Academic Research, in: *Academy of Management Perspectives*, *25*(4), 50-66. doi: org/10.5465/amp.2010.0164

Nonaka, I., Toyama, R., & Konno, N. (2001). SECI, Ba and Leadership: a Unified Model of Dynamic Knowledge Creation. In I. Nonaka & D. J. Teece (Eds.), *Managing Industrial Knowledge: Creation, Transfer and Utilization* (pp. 13-43). London: Sage.

Nunes, P., & Breene, T. (2011). Reinvent Your Business Before It's Too Late. *Harvard Business Review*, *89*(1/2), 80–87. Retrieved from EBSCOhost research databases.

Osterwalder, A., & Pigneur, Y. (2010). *Business Model Generation*. Hoboken: Wiley.

Pacheco-de-Almeida, G. (2010). Erosion, time compression, and self-displacement of leaders in hypercompetitive environments. *Strategic Management Journal*, *31*(13), 1498–1526. doi: 10.1002/smj

Pohle, G., & Chapman, M. (2006). IBM's global CEO report 2006: business model innovation matters. *Strategy & Leadership*, *34*(5), 34–40. doi: 10.1108/ 10878570610701531

Prahalad, C., & Bettis, R. (1986). The dominant logic: A new linkage between diversity and performance. *Strategic Management Journal*, *7*(6), 485–501. Retrieved from EBSCOhost research databases.

Rauter, R., Müller, C., Vorbach S., & Marko, W. A. (2012). *Business Model Innovation and Knowledge Transfer*. Paper presented at the EURAM 2012 conference, Rotterdam.

Reinhold, S., Reuter, E., & Bieger T. (2011). Innovative Geschäftsmodelle – Die Sicht des Managements. In T. Bieger, D. Knyphausen-Aufseß and C. Krys (Eds.), *Innovative Geschäftsmodell* (pp. 71-91). Berlin: Springer.

Ricard, J. E. (2012). *Business Models: A New Language in Strategic Management*. Paper presented at the EURAM 2012 conference, Rotterdam.

Roland Berger Strategy Consultants (2011). *think: act BUSINESS - COO Insights December 2011*. Retrieved September 10, 2012, from https://www.rolandberger.com/services/form/rbcom_rb_2280467317

Sahut, J. M., Hikkerova, L., & Khalfallah, M. (2013). Business Model and Performance of Firms. *International Business Research*, *6*(2), 64–76. doi: 10.5539/ibr.v6n2p64

Santos, J., Spector, B., & Van der Heyden, L. (2009). *Toward a theory of business model innovation within incumbent firms* (Working paper no. 2009/16/EFE/ST/TOM, INSEAD Fontainebleau). Retrieved October 9, 2011, from http://www.insead.edu/faculty research/research/doc.cfm?did=41374

Schallmo, D. (2013). *Geschäftsmodell-Innovation.* Wiesbaden: Springer Gabler.

Schlegelmilch, B., Diamantopoulos, A., & Kreuz, P. (2003). Strategic innovation: the construct, its drivers and its strategic outcomes. *Journal of Strategic Marketing*, *11*(2), 117–132. doi: 10.1080/0965254032000102948

Schneider, S., & Spieth, P. (2012). *Business Model Innovation: Towards an Integrated Future Research Agenda.* Paper presented at the EURAM 2012 conference, Rotterdam.

Schneider, S., & Spieth, P. (2013a). Business Model Innovation: Towards an Integrated Future Research Agenda. *International Journal of Innovation Management*, *17*(1), 34 pages. doi: 10.1142/S136391961340001X

Schneider, S., & Spieth, P. (2013b): *Business model innovation – an entrepreneurial response to environmental dynamism.* Paper presented at the EURAM 2013 conference, Istanbul.

Schnell, R., Hill, P. B., & Esser, E. (2005). *Methoden der empirischen Sozialforschung* (7th ed.). München: Oldenbourg.

Schöberl, M. (2008). *Responses of incumbent firms in the face of disruptive strategic innovations.* Berlin: Verlag Pro Business.

Shafer, S., Smith, H., & Linder, J. (2005). The power of business models. *Business Horizons*, *48*(3), 199–207. doi: 10.1016/j.bushor.2004.10.014

Sharma, P., & Chrisman, J. J. (1999). Toward a reconciliation of the definitional issues in the field of corporate entrepreneurship. *Entrepreneurship: Theory and Practice*, *23*(1), 11-27. Retrieved from EBSCOhost research databases.

Sims, D. (2008). Interviewing. In R. Thorpe & R. Holt (Eds.), *The Sage Dictionary of Qualitative Management Research* (pp. 116-118). London: Sage.

Sinfield, J. V., Calder, E., McConnell, B., & Colson, S. (2012). How to Identify New Business Models. *MIT Sloan Management Review*, *53*(2), 85-90. Retrieved from EBSCOhost research databases.

Skarzynski, P., & Gibson, R. (2008). *Innovation to the Core.* Boston: Harvard Business Press.

Sorescu, A., Frambach, R. T., Singh, J., Rangaswamy, A., & Bridges, C. (2011). Innovations in Retail Business Models. *Journal of Retailing*, *87*, S3–S16. doi: 10.1016/j.jretai.2011.04.005

Sosna, M., Trevinyo-Rodríguez, R. N., & Velamuri, S. R. (2010). Business Model Innovation through Trial-and-Error LearningThe Naturhouse Case. *Long Range Planning*, *43*(2/3), 383–407. doi: 10.1016/j.lrp.2010.02.003

Spieth, P., Tidd, J., Matzler, K., Schneckenberg, D., & Vanhaverbeke, W. (2013). Special Issue on Business Model Innovation — Editorial Note. *International*

Journal of Innovation Management, *17*(1), 1302001. doi: 10.1142/S1363919613020015

Storbacka, K. (2011). A solution business model: Capabilities and management practices for integrated solutions. *Industrial Marketing Management*, *40*(5), 699–711. doi: 10.1016/j.indmarman.2011.05.003

Strauss, A., & Corbin, J. (1990). *Basics of qualitative research: grounded theory procedures and techniques*. Newbury Park: Sage.

Sutton, R. I. (1997). The virtues of closet qualitative research. *Organization Science*, *8*(1), 97–106. Retrieved from http://www.jstor.org/stable/10.2307/ 2635232

Szulanski, G., & Winter, S. (2002). Getting it right the second time. *Harvard Business Review*, *80*(1), 62–69. Retrieved from EBSCOhost research databases.

Taran, Y., Boer, H., & Lindgren, P. (2009). *Theory building towards an understanding of business model innovation processes*. Paper presented at the DRUID-DIME Academy Winter 2009 PhD Conference, Aalborg. Retrieved September 15, 2012, from http://www2.druid.dk/conferences/viewpaper.php?id=4451&cf=33

Taran, Y. (2012). *RETHINKING IT ALL: Overcoming Obstacles to Business Model Innovation* (Doctoral dissertation, Aalborg University). Retrieved January 8, 2013, from http://www.businessmodelcommunity.com/#Other_Resources.E

Teece, D. J. (2010). Business Models, Business Strategy and Innovation. *Long Range Planning*, *43*(2/3), 172–194. doi: 10.1016/j.lrp.2009.07.003

Tidd, J., & Bessant, J. (2009). *Managing innovation: integrating technological, market, and organizational change* (4th ed.). Chichester: Wiley.

Tuff, G., & Wunker, S. (2010). *Beacons for business model innovation* (Monitor Perspectives). Retrieved October 13, 2011, from http://news.doblin.com/post/18076830392/beacons-for-business-model-innovation

Velamuri, V. K., Bansemir, B., Neyer, A.-K., & Möslein, K. M. (2013). Product Service Systems As a Driver for Business Model Innovation: Lessons Learned From the Manufacturing Industry. *International Journal of Innovation Management*, *17*(1), 1340004. doi: 10.1142/S1363919613400045

Venkatraman, N., & Henderson, J. C. (2008). Four vectors of business model innovation: Value capture in a network era. In D. Pantaleo & N. Pal (Eds.), *From strategy to execution* (pp. 259-280). Berlin: Springer.

Webster, J., & Watson, R. T. (2002). Analyzing the Past to Prepare for the Future: Writing a Literature Review. *MIS Quarterly*, *26*(2), xiii–xxiii. Retrieved from EBSCOhost research databases.

Whittington, R. (2006). Completing the Practice Turn in Strategy Research. *Organization Studies*, *27*(5), 613–634. doi: 10.1177/0170840606064101

Winter, S. G., & Szulanski, G. (2001). Replication as Strategy. *Organization Science*, *12*(6), 730–743. doi: 10.1287/orsc.12.6.730.10084

Wirtz, B. W., Schilke, O., & Ullrich, S. (2010). Strategic Development of Business Models: Implications of the Web 2.0 for Creating Value on the Internet. *Long Range Planning*, *43*(2/3), 272–290. doi: 10.1016/j.lrp.2010.01.005

Wirtz, B. W. (2011). *Business Model Management: Design, Instrumente, Erfolgsfaktoren von Geschäftsmodellen.* (2nd ed.). Wiesbaden: Gabler.

Woodside, A. G. (2010): *Case Study Research: Theory, Methods, Practice.* Bingley: Emerald.

Yin, R. K. (2009): *Case study research: Design and methods (*4th ed.). Thousand Oaks: Sage.

Yunus, M., Moingeon, B., & Lehmann-Ortega, L. (2010). Building Social Business Models: Lessons from the Grameen Experience. *Long Range Planning*, *43*(2/3), 308–325. doi: 10.1016/j.lrp.2009.12.005

Zeschky, M. (2010). *Exploration for Innovation: Capability-based Search Approaches in Established Firms.* Lichtenberg: Harland Media.

Zimmermann, N. (2011). *Dynamics of Drivers of Organizational Change.* Wiesbaden: Gabler.

Zollenkop, M. (2006): *Geschäftsmodellinnovation.* Wiesbaden: Gabler.

Zollenkop, M. (2011). Geschäftsmodellinnovation im Spannungsfeld zwischen Unternehmensgründung und Konzernumbau. In T. Bieger, D. Knyphausen-Aufseß & C. Krys, (Eds.), *Innovative Geschäftsmodelle* (pp. 201-211). Berlin: Springer.

Zott, C., & Amit, R. (2010). Business Model Design: An Activity System Perspective. *Long Range Planning*, *43*(2/3), 216–226. doi: 10.1016/j.lrp.2009.0 7.004

Zott, C., Amit, R., & Massa, L. (2011). The business model: Recent developments and future research. *Journal of Management*, *37*(4), 1019-1042. Retrieved from http://jom.sagepub.com/content/37/4/1019.short

MIX
Papier aus verantwortungsvollen Quellen
Paper from responsible sources
FSC® C105338

If you have any concerns about our products,
you can contact us on
ProductSafety@springernature.com

In case Publisher is established outside the EU,
the EU authorized representative is:
Springer Nature Customer Service Center GmbH
Europaplatz 3, 69115 Heidelberg, Germany

Printed by Libri Plureos GmbH
in Hamburg, Germany